T0325526

At the Speed
of Irrelevance

At the Speed of Irrelevance

How America Blew Its AI Leadership Position and How to Regain It

AL NAQVI
MANI JANAKIRAM

WILEY

Library of Congress Cataloging-in-Publication Data is Available:

ISBN 9781119861270 (Hardback)
ISBN 9781119861294 (ePDF)
ISBN 9781119861287 (ePub)

COVER DESIGN & ILLUSTRATION: PAUL McCARTHY

SKY10034741_071222

For Nur, Mahek, and Marya

Dr. Al (Ali) Naqvi

Dedicated to my wife, my son, and my parents

Dr. Mani Janakiram

Contents

Preface

A S THE REVERBERATIONS ABOUT China's ascendency over the United States in artificial intelligence are coagulating, America must consider the root causes of falling behind. The popular narrative is about China doing something magical to close the technological gaps. This book argues that America is losing the AI competition not because China is doing something extraordinary but because the American national strategy for AI is flawed.

There are many books on AI. There are many books on China's rise. But there is no book that explains why America is lagging in AI. Developing that perspective requires taking a bold stand and applying critical thinking.

We observed an overwhelming concern about China's rise in AI. From Congress to various government agencies, the threat of China's advancement in AI has led to rapid and hasty reactions and policies. But none of those reactions have taken a critical approach to uncover what are the root causes of falling behind.

The American Institute of Artificial Intelligence captures the adoption of AI across economies, industries, governments, companies, and agencies. Professor Naqvi is the CEO of AIAI and has authored several books on industrialization of AI. He is an AI industrialization expert. Dr. Janakiram offers a unique understanding of the semiconductor value chain. Bringing both ends of the spectrum—the AI software and the AI hardware—the authors take a critical approach to analyze the descent of American AI.

In our discussions with many Americans knowledgeable about the AI competitive dynamics, we observed tremendous unease about the Chinese AI advantage and the damage it will cause to American competitiveness in the long run.

We do not believe that ignoring what has transpired in the past will restore the future. Unless corrected, the mistakes of the past will shape the future. America will struggle to rise back up to the leadership position and that will impact every other aspect of nation building. From political turmoil to economic decline and from social meltdown to national security collapse, AI has the power to impact all aspects of human life and institutions. Loss of leadership in AI implies a loss in everything else. Despite the importance of this technology, little planning went into how AI should be launched and socialized in America at a national level.

In America, the AI technology was launched with a narrative that repels rather than attracts interest, an R&D plan that constrains national adoption rather than encourage it, a national strategy that destroys value instead of increasing it. The result is a technology development model that favors monopolies and elite universities at the expense of American innovation and the American public. This creates social and economic inequality, wealth disparity, poverty, and plutocracy—and it weakens democracy.

The plan to restrict access to AI and to limit its nationwide growth has fallen on its face. Adversaries who may not have been liberal democracies have both liberated and democratized AI and solidified the future of their countries. America remains mired in its problems, uninterested, and uninspired about the greatest change ever in human civilization.

We also argue that the fundamental R&D system is due for a change in America. America has already experienced three R&D systems in the twentieth century. The R&D system includes both its processes and the funding model, and AI is changing both. Despite that, the investment model and approach of the Office of Science and Technology Policy (OSTP) remain antiquated. The OSTP appears as the greatest barrier to success in American AI. The office has overstepped its responsibility and has trodden into areas where it does not have any expertise: strategy development. In the end, the failed policies of OSTP are harming American national interests and giving China an easy victory.

We conclude the book by recommending an alternative path. Our tone in this book is critical and at times harsh. But that is intentional. We want the audience to recognize the importance of getting this right. America must move at the superspeed of relevance. Time is running out.

Acknowledgments

W E WOULD LIKE TO thank the Wiley team, our publisher, for being extremely helpful, understanding, and efficient with our project. Specifically, we would like to thank Sheck Cho and Susan Cerra. For topics like AI, there are many choices to partner with reputable publishers. We partnered with Wiley because of the excellent support we receive in all steps of the publishing process. One of the authors has published two other books on AI with Wiley and his experience has been excellent.

We would like to thank many of our colleagues for their valuable inputs and comments related to the American AI: Dale Rogers, Arizona State University, Bob Bruck, Applied Materials, Tom Maher, Dell, Jamie Butcher, Chemonics, Tom Derry, Institute of Supply Management, Paul Dillahay (CEO of NCI), Bridget Medeiros, (Bubba) Carlton Fox, Dr. Allen Badeau, Major General (Retired) Dale Meyerrose, Tom Albert, Dr. Hassan Abbas, Terry Wolff, Ron Raczkowski, Russ Malz, TK Gonsalves, Kirit Amin, Neil Callahan, Tiffany Parker, Aaron Morales (Senator Heinrich's office), Senator Martin Heinrich, and Dr. Mark Munoz. Many thanks to the American Institute of Artificial Intelligence team for assisting with the research.

In addition, many thanks to all those authors whose work we have quoted.

Dr. Al Naqvi and Dr. Mani Janakiram

About the Authors

 ## DR. AL (ALI) NAQVI

Dr. Naqvi is the founder and CEO of the American Institute of Artificial Intelligence. His work in artificial intelligence industrialization is globally recognized by scientific and professional societies, companies, agencies, and governments. He is the author of several books on artificial intelligence industrialization. With hands-on experience in machine learning product development and AI research, Dr. Naqvi leads a team of researchers who monitor and analyze the AI absorption and adoption across companies, industries, agencies, and countries. Dr. Naqvi sits on the boards of several AI companies, and he advises C-level executives, agency heads, and senior government executives on AI strategic industrialization planning. His doctorate research was on Discovering the Process for New Product Development (NPD) in Machine Learning Software. Dr. Naqvi presents at leading global conferences. He teaches at the American Institute of Artificial Intelligence.

 ## DR. MANI JANAKIRAM

Dr. Janakiram is a Mfg. Supply Chain and Analytics executive and also an academician. His 25+ years of professional experience includes semiconductor/hitech, automotive and aerospace industries at Intel, Honeywell, and Motorola in supply chain, strategy, systems, analytics, manufacturing, and research, planning. He is on the adjunct faculty at Arizona State University and also taught at various schools, including MIT, and Thunderbird School of Global Management. Mani has two patents and has published over 100 papers on supply chain, statistical modeling, capacity modeling, data mining, Lean Six Sigma, factory operations research and process control. He is an accomplished speaker and serves on several committees to advance practical application of AI and analytics in manufacturing and supply chain. Mani holds a PhD in Industrial and Systems Engineering from Arizona State University and an MBA from Thunderbird School of Global Management. He is a recognized Six Sigma Master Black Belt and an APICS certified supply chain professional. He was recognized by Drexel University and CIO.com as one of the Top 50 Analytics Executives and is also an ASCM Fellow.

The views and opinions expressed in this publication are solely those of the authors. They do not purport to reflect the opinions or views of any current or former employer of either author.

CHAPTER ONE

The Dawn of Irrelevance

F OR THE OUTSIDERS IT was an uneventful cloudy October Sunday in Washington, DC. Over the weekend, the Washington football team had lost to the New Orleans Saints. Baltimore, another local team from the DMV area, was supposed to play on Monday. No earth-shattering news was making the headlines. Ten months after what some media outlets termed the "insurrection," American media was still obsessed with the domestic ideological wars. Sound bites from politicians were making rounds. Fights over *to mask* or *not to mask* were erupting all over the country. Despite a new wave of Covid claiming thousands of lives daily, traffic in restaurants and shopping areas was increasing. Amazon had started its Black Friday sales early. America had adjusted to a new normal. But unknown to most Americans, a fateful event had transpired that weekend. In contrast with the obliviousness of the American media, foreign media had a field day with the news about that story. As the history of this event will be written half a century from now, it would go down as probably the most solemn and depressing weekend for America. That was when Nicolas Chaillan, former chief software officer for the US Air Force and who oversaw the Pentagon's cybersecurity efforts, announced, in no uncertain words, the surrender of the United States in the artificial intelligence (AI) war against China. He gave an interview to the *Financial Times*—his first after his sudden resignation in September of 2021—and stated, "We have no competing fighting chance against China in 15 to 20 years. Right now, it's already a done deal; it is already over in my opinion" (Manson 2021). Chaillan's statement did not appear as a warning, or a battle cry, or some inspirational slogan to rise and claim back America's AI leadership. It was a cold, matter-of-fact, and outright acknowledgment that it was already too late to have any hope for sustained American leadership in AI.

Chaillan's capitulating comment came after he had expressed his frustration about the inertia in the government and had resigned by submitting a fierce resignation letter. His tenure with the government had lasted barely three years. Chaillan is a naturalized citizen and had become a US citizen in 2016. That didn't stop him from getting a top position with the government. Upon joining, Chaillan was shocked over the state of technology and saw that as an opportunity to bring about a cultural change. Strong-willed and inspired by a vision of transformation, he began acting as a change agent. But he recognized that the problems were far deeper than what he had thought. AI was being approached as any regular technology. Chaillan gave an account of what was transpiring. The organizational dynamics represented a bureaucratic nightmare. Unskilled people were made in charge, and while money was being spent, the procurement costs were high and funds were being allocated in the wrong areas. Most importantly, AI was not being viewed as a national priority. Before resigning from his position with the government and during a CyberSatGov conference, he had claimed that American national security satellite providers were unable to develop "at the speed of relevance" as they were stuck in the Pentagon's ecosystem. In other words, getting unstuck from the Pentagon's ecosystem implied achieving the speed of relevance.

On Monday morning after the Chaillan news hit the international press, Tom Albert, a friend of the American Institute of Artificial Intelligence and an AI entrepreneur (founder and CEO of MeasuredRisk), video called Al Naqvi (one of the authors), and expressed his frustration. Tom is passionate about creating and mobilizing American intellects to rise and fight back against the Chinese dominance in AI. He is putting together a major initiative to inspire American investors and entrepreneurs to develop more advanced AI capabilities. Tom carries a genuine smile and has a great sense of humor. He jokes frequently and laughs loudly. But his voice changes and his face turns red when he starts talking about the lack of visionary leadership for AI at the helms in America. With his fists clenched and teeth gritting, he complains about how America is self-inflicting this catastrophe upon itself. Several minutes into the conversation, he asked Al Naqvi the name of the book that Naqvi was coauthoring. Al Naqvi responded that the name of the book was *At the Speed of Irrelevance*, and that made Tom smile and he said, "It would have been immensely funny if it wasn't so tragic." Tom and Al talked for over an hour, and Tom felt this book will be critical to drive hope and to inspire the nation. Tom is among a small number of Americans who understood what the term "speed of relevance" meant and its profound significance for AI and for the United States of America. America's last hope to maintain its global leadership position—the American AI—was in jeopardy. The great experiment was at risk.

 ## AT THE SPEED OF RELEVANCE

Four years before Chaillan threw in the towel, then secretary of defense General James Norman Mattis issued a document in January 2018. This document was the first open and clear expression of a strategy to confront China's growing power. Titled "The National Defense Strategy" (NDS), it refers to the delivery of performance at the *speed of relevance*. That was the time when General Mattis and President Trump were still on good terms and President Trump bragged about his secretary of defense. The honeymoon didn't last, as a year later General Mattis resigned and gave a two-month notice. Feeling rejected and ignoring the notice, President Trump ended General Mattis's tenure immediately. Shortly after that, President Trump said that he "essentially fired him" and then in June of 2019 went after General Mattis again and said that he felt great about asking General Mattis to resign and that he didn't like General Mattis's leadership style and was happy that General Mattis was gone (Shane III 2019).

Regardless of President Trump's view about him, what is generally acknowledged about General Mattis is that he was trying to change the culture of DoD. The report signed by him said:

> **Deliver performance at the speed of relevance.** Success no longer goes to the country that develops a new technology first, but rather to the one that better integrates it and adapts its way of fighting. Current processes are not responsive to need; the Department is over-optimized for exceptional performance at the expense of providing timely decisions, policies, and capabilities to the warfighter. Our response will be to prioritize speed of delivery, continuous adaptation, and frequent modular upgrades. We must not accept cumbersome approval chains, wasteful applications of resources in uncompetitive space, or overly risk-averse thinking that impedes change. Delivering performance means we will shed outdated management practices and structures while integrating insights from business innovation. (Mattis 2018)

While work on the American AI had begun before 2016, it was General Mattis's recognition that developing a technology first is not what will lead to America's victory; rather, what is critical is adapting and integrating new technologies. General Mattis was trying to evangelize the term "speed of relevance" to imply a more responsive way of delivering results and eliminating red tape and the typical government inefficiencies. Joe Dransfield analyzed the use of the term in an article that appeared on "The Bridge," an online publication of The Strategy Bridge, a nonprofit organization focused on the development of people in strategy, national security, and military affairs. Dransfield pointed out that Mattis had also used the term in his written statement to the House Armed Services Committee on February 6, 2018, and described it as his aspiration to move the Department of Defense to a "culture of performance and affordability that operates at the speed of relevance." In another document, Dransfield explains, Joint Chiefs of Staff General Joseph Dunford also used the term, but his usage seemed to imply improving the decision cycle, prioritizing and allocating optimal resources, and enabling better decision-making. Both Mattis and Dunford, Dransfield contends, used the term "as being an adaptation and an aspiration that is fundamental to gaining competitive advantage" (Dransfield 2020).

The term was instantaneously picked up by other agencies, the DC analysts, and supplier communities and quickly became a buzzword. Dransfield (and Chaillan's later statement) clarified that the US Air Force used it to signify technological transformation. The US Army interpreted it as human aspects of the speed of relevance. "The US Navy," Dransfield claimed, "tended to use former Chief of Naval Operations Admiral John Richardson's preferred nomenclature of 'high-velocity outcomes' to cover similar aspirations regarding the speed of relevance" (Dransfield 2020). The Department of Defense referred to their cloud-based computing as an example of speed of relevance. Raytheon placed it in an ad. Government contractors included it in their RFPs. And as often happens with buzzwords, they get talked about so much that they lose their higher meaning.

General Mattis is not an AI expert. Neither is General Dunford. But what was profound in their vision is the power of mission relevant and integrated automation, higher prediction power, faster and more effective decision-making, and highly efficient execution speed—all of these improvements are made possible by AI, and all are necessary to advance AI. They were defining and describing what the American AI needed to be. They were setting a challenge for the nation.

The American AI Initiative Was Born

The "American AI Initiative" is America's strategy and plan to maintain and expand America's lead in AI. It was supposed to be the game changer. It was America's response to a rising threat from adversaries and competitors. It was the need of the hour. It could have been a vision truly based on an unpoliticized *America First* thinking.

But speed of relevance cannot result from pursuing sporadic AI projects and pushing buzzwords in one or two organizations (for example, the DoD). It cannot materialize by fanning out mindless R&D and blindly pumping money into research without having a corresponding industrialization and economic strategy. In addition to focusing on science and technology, it requires approaching the transformation from an industrialization mindset. It needs building an ecosystem of interdependent technologies and capabilities, a meticulously developed national strategy that is articulated to inspire and mobilize the nation, a favorable economic structure, and an entire economy based on AI. It needs an economy-wide change in all areas of commerce and industry. It requires AI to emerge as a social force that gives energy to the nation.

Three and a half years after General Mattis presented his strategy, a new US secretary of defense under a new administration, General Lloyd Austin, proudly claimed that 600 AI efforts were already underway in the Pentagon and that would accelerate the Pentagon's adoption of AI. General Austin saw AI as somehow related to projects, initiatives, and use cases. And this is where America is continuing to fail in architecting its national AI strategy. America is not thinking big enough. AI is not just a technology—it is paradigm change in the economy, science, society, politics, and human civilization. A change of that magnitude cannot be managed by pushing "projects" and "initiatives." As any other revolutionary technology, AI also requires developing industrialization plans, supporting infrastructure, processes for social and business acceptance, maps of value creation across sectors and industries, social sensemaking and meaning construction, leadership that inspires the nation, and designs that help with diffusing the technology. But the American AI Initiative had none of that. It was growing up in an orphaned state—and even worse, as a hated and undesirable technology.

Chaillan is right. Retired military professionals with no background or experience may not be able to do it. But neither can software experts, Big Tech firms, opportunistic professors, or leading AI technology experts from top universities. AI planning requires a strategic perspective, and that in turn needs a national-level all-inclusive, sector-by-sector industrialization planning with the singular focus on building American capabilities. Above all, it requires a patriotic positioning.

General Mattis's dream of moving American technology forward at the *speed of relevance* will stay as an unaccomplished goal until an America-focused comprehensive and integrated AI national industrialization strategy is outlined and deployed. Even if General Mattis had been able to fix the culture of his organization and create efficiencies within the DoD, what about the legacy technology cultures of the government suppliers? What about the influence of Big Tech over policy? What about the inability of the political leadership to inspire the nation and mobilize resources? What about the ongoing meltdown of civility and the rise of the ideological wars in America? What about the daily bot and cyber-attacks where enemies and adversaries are constantly bombarding the US to further divide and weaken the nation? What about the opportunistic and commercialized academia where professors place their own selfish interests above national interests? What about the consulting firms whose bread and butter are long, slow-moving, use case–focused, systems (dis)integration projects? What about the rampant influx of foreign money and influence to distract American attention? And what about the troubled supply chains and an old rotten infrastructure in dire need of replacement? The American AI Initiative needed the right breathing space and a healthy environment to grow—but the nation's ecosystem was not conducive for the spark to happen.

In the absence of becoming a national force and a social phenomenon, the entire focus of the American AI Initiative strategy remained on two things—research and investment in research. As General Mattis said in his report, developing the technology first is not an advantage. America needed to build the industrial capacity, social and business adoption, diffusion, and absorption of the technological revolution at a social sensemaking level. But none of that happened.

If *speed of relevance* implied competitive advantage, then Chaillan had declared that China has already acquired that over the United States. In 2019, ITIF (Information Technology and Innovation Foundation) conducted a study that concluded that China has already surpassed the U.S. in AI adoption and data, and that China's trend of steady progress could eventually destroy the U.S. lead (Castro and McLaughlin 2021). If the term meant overcoming bureaucratic inertia, Chaillan enlightened us with the incompetence and bureaucracy that still exists in the government. If the term signified capabilities, Chaillan called the cyber defenses of several government agencies being at a "kindergarten level." So much for the speed of relevance!

The fact is that four years after General Mattis evangelized the term, Chaillan acknowledged that the reality was much different. Clearly, America was working at the speed of irrelevance—and that was nothing short of suicidal. In the age of AI, comparative and competitive advantages of countries will be determined by their AI technologies. America was already at a disadvantage. The American AI Initiative was already in trouble.

 ## OUR JOURNEY IN THIS BOOK

This book captures the tragic story of American slide to irrelevance. It shows the disaster that engulfed and continues to haunt America today. It is a story of failure of leadership at all levels—and of the flawed execution that came with it. This story is being told with the recognition that America can still bounce back from the clutches of defeat, that America performs best when the nation finds its motivation, and that this will not be the first time that America has risen after being cornered and pinned down. Although we do claim that this will be America's toughest and greatest fight ever, we believe (with Churchill's spirit) this could be America's finest moment ever. With that in mind, we begin the story of how America ended up in this dilemma. We have made two simple arguments in this book.

First, we argue that many problems in America are worsening due to one and one reason only: the failure to adopt AI strategically. Ironically, both the identification of and the solutions to such problems are dependent on AI. Consider the following:

Supply chains: There are now cracks emerging in the American supply chains. The infusion of automation technology at some levels in the value chain and not at others is creating problems. These problems will likely become out of control. Haphazard deployment of AI is not strategic. The problems are exacerbated by the technological rivalry with China— another problem rooted in the lack of strategic adoption of AI.

AI deployment is not real: We observe a stark difference in how China is adopting AI and how many US companies, agencies, and industries are approaching AI. What many companies, agencies, and industries are calling AI is neither intelligent automation nor what AI means today. It is very basic automation, and calling it AI is a stretch. This misconception of what AI capabilities are will lead to a decline in competitive advantage and performance potential of US companies and agencies.

The competitive structure is not favorable: The economic structure and environment should be favorable for strategic adoption of AI. But the American economic structure—which is dominated by a small number of very large firms and individuals with tremendous concentration of power and wealth—is not ripe for strategic diffusion of technology. The dominant investment style in AI is creating a negative innovation environment, waste, and increasing the cost of capital. Ironically, AI is contributing to further concentration of power and wealth.

The national narrative: Nation-inspiring narratives are the harbingers of fantastic news. They mobilize and inspire nations to do great things. The American AI Initiative is suffering from anemic and conflicting messaging. The social construct and narrative behind the technology are weak. On the other hand, AI ideology–centric narratives are dividing the nation and creating domestic conflict.

External force: Unlike during the Internet revolution, where America stood as the clear and uncontested leader in the world, today's geopolitical situation is different. The technological leadership is being redefined by global players such as China. With AI, the power of such rivals will increase exponentially.

The productivity growth: Despite significant investment in AI and years of so-called planning and execution, the productivity growth in America has stayed low. The capital being poured into the technology is not showing results—indicating it is misdirected and misallocated. AI must lead to productivity growth, but that is not happening.

Knowledge economy: As explained later in the book, AI is not just any technology. It is a technology that creates new knowledge, new science, and new technology. It finds scientific breakthroughs for which theory does not exist. It releases science from the linear model of hypothesis-test-results-theory to the paradigm of test-results-hypothesis-theory. Without strategic AI, the industries will remain malnourished to produce new knowledge and discoveries.

The risks for the entire economy and for the country are increasing. So much so that now it is recognized that China has surpassed America in AI. This means America has failed to strategically embrace the AI paradigm. AI is the key to unlock the potential of the national economy. It is the elixir to understand, solve, and identify almost all types of problems.

The AI magic has already begun. Some economies are performing great, while others are struggling. Schumpeter's creative destruction and the related disruption have already started. The loss of AI leadership to China is now becoming far more visible, and it is showing up in numerous ways.

Our second argument is that we hold the White House's Office of Science and Technology Policy (OSTP) as primarily responsible for America's decline and fall in AI. Throughout this book we cover the story of OSTP's continued failure to provide the true leadership that America needed. The problem was not that the OSTP did not do what it was supposed to do. The OSTP did give America a powerful R&D and federal investment plan. The real problem—which led to America's failure on the AI front—was that the OSTP could not distinguish between a national strategy of AI and the R&D-centric federal investment strategy of AI. The OSTP overplayed its hand, assumed the role of a strategic economic advisor, acted in the capacity of an industrialization expert, created a massive deception about its role and plans, intentionally or intentionally (we do not know) covered up hugely relevant information, and completely ignored the process of how strategy (national or business) is developed. In doing so the OSTP forgot its core mission: first, to provide the president and his [her] senior staff with accurate, relevant, and timely scientific and technical advice on all matters of consequence; second, to ensure that the policies of the executive branch are informed by sound science; and third, to ensure that the scientific and technical work of the executive branch is properly coordinated so as to provide the greatest benefit to society. Overstepping its mission, report after report, the OSTP made the national investment plan in R&D appear like a national strategic plan. They are not the same.

A legitimate national AI strategy cannot materialize without following a proper strategy development process. It is not a product of one or two brainstorming sessions by a group of scientists, academics, agency heads, and Big Tech VPs. It requires an elaborate process to understand the economic and business environment, study national priorities and understand national goals, analyze relative strengths and weaknesses, identify the stakeholders, assess the mood of the nation, develop narratives and communications strategy, and many other such process steps. Strategy development process, whether for a business or a country, requires following a methodical approach. Strategy and plan development are, of course, well-developed specialty areas with hundreds of years of research, history, practices, and well-established knowledge domains. But the OSTP engaged in none of that. With the groupthink that led to seven (eight, as one was added later) strategies, the OSTP somehow turned what was the R&D plan into a national strategy. This would be analogous to an aeronautical engineer who knows about planes but is not a pilot, trying to fly a commercial flight full of passengers. Three presidents and Congress relied on the strategy and the positioning coming from the OSTP. Legislation was thrusted based on those priorities. Money was allocated. Executive orders were signed. Agendas were pushed. And America was led through a national strategy for AI that was nothing more than an R&D plan. Imagine if a company confused its R&D plan with its overall strategy and ignored all other aspects of strategic planning. As expected, year after year America continued to miss the mark on the greatest opportunity presented to the nation.

Many did not realize what was going on. They confused the R&D plan with a national strategy. Others understood the great error but stayed quiet because speaking out would have meant loss of funds. So great was this self-deception that the raw potential of AI was somehow caged in a meaningless shell of ethics, values, and governance. All those things are critical for AI—please do not get us wrong here. But they have a place, context, and a position in the industrialization and social construction narratives of AI. However, the way it was shoved down the national throat was such that every time someone talked about AI, they felt compelled to discuss ethics and governance as if they were about to do something wrong, evil, sinister, or illegal. It became a guilt trip, almost an aversion to embrace technology. Interestingly, most of the ethical problems were coming from the big technology firms—the same firms on whom OSTP was relying for advice and who were sponsoring the OSTP conferences. Professors with commercial interests (or their institutions), who received grants from big technology firms or had personal interests in AI tech firms and who rarely disclosed their conflicts of interest, were the other set of advisors for the OSTP. So, while governance, values, and ethics are essential for AI, it seems very hypocritical that the OSTP was in bed with the same exact firms who were not able to keep their own ethics boards intact, much less to come up with a proper AI governance and ethics strategy. Immersed in the rockstar-like power that comes with being in the limelight, the OSTP czars did not care.

The on-the-ground reality of what was transpiring on the industrial side was laughable. At an industry level American firms continued to lose their competitive advantage. Many companies could not even differentiate between what intelligent automation was vs. just plain old automation. Many couldn't tell the difference between robotic process automation (RPA) and machine learning. For many, chatbots represented their total AI plans. From a military angle, China, Russia, and even North Korea perfected their hypersonic weapons while the American program seemed to have run into problems. Even in areas such as social media, where America always maintained a core advantage, Chinese firms surpassed the American firms. Most importantly, despite all the hype about AI, the American productivity growth did not change.

The OSTP's miscalculation—to turn a national R&D plan for federal investment into some type of national AI strategy—was a blunder and an extreme disservice to America. It also had a cascading effect on other initiatives that came from Congress and government agencies, which further derailed the American AI Initiative. It created a national-level mess that will take years to clean up.

We share the story of the chaos that this blunder has created. Today, America is continuing to feel the aftershocks.

On the domestic front, the so-called American AI strategy was too slow and too flawed. Developed by technologists and professors, it failed to apply the basic strategy development process. To be completely frank, it was never a strategy. It was simply a research funding plan—a way to pump lots of money into top universities—universities from which the developers of those so-called strategies came. Led by researchers and academics, the focus of the American AI strategy has been on research and on funding the research. That created a massive confusion. The research strategy was viewed as a national strategy, and America was misled. The "If you build it, they will come" mindset of American policymakers and the czars of White House AI programs was detrimental to the national interests.

The burden on American AI became overwhelming. The anemic start of the American AI Initiative was now being crushed under the weight of a pandemic, rising domestic tensions, a supply chain meltdown, and escalating geopolitical tensions. There is every sign that the dream will be lost, the promise broken, and the great experiment will come to an end. But there is hope. We explain in the book how the mistakes of the past can be fixed and how a new plan can be architected. We remind business leaders and government leaders of their responsibility. It will not be easy. In fact, this will be the hardest battle that America will ever fight. This will be the defining moment for the country. But it all begins by understanding how and where things fell apart. It begins with self-reflection about what led us to this point.

We then show what steps need to be taken to turn around the future of American AI. We conclude that there is still hope but time is running out quickly.

We have three goals:

Goal 1: We want Americans, at all levels, to understand how powerful and disruptive a force AI is. Our main argument is that the reason China has suddenly become a hot issue for us is because of AI. The proof of that is our focus on banning their AI firms. Notice that we are not banning their coal producers or power companies, despite President Biden's environmental commitments. In fact, we are not even sanctioning their defense firms that manufacture combat weapons. The focus is only on AI firms. That tells you something.

Goal 2: We want Americans to view AI as a necessary national capability and not some globalized science movement. We point out that Google employees' walkout is analogous to Alan Turing and his team walking out while working on Enigma (WWII) by claiming that decrypting Enigma would be an invasion of Germany's priority. In other words, in AI, we are no longer part of a global kumbaya – but instead we must view it as a necessary American capability. That sentiment should not be limited to NSA or DOD, but it should become a larger, more grassroots American sentiment. Americans don't view AI as such. We believe the national mood needs to change from "AI is a global science movement" to a serious "we must break-the-enigma-like national priority".

Goal 3: We want to communicate that to make progress in AI we need a national strategy and not a haphazard shotgun approach. Additionally, inspiring the nation and minimizing national ideological conflict will be necessary to make progress. Scientific revolutions are also social revolutions.

 ## WE ARE NOT ALONE

In the fall of 2018 Chinese Premier Le Keqiang made an unassuming statement at the World Economic Forum: "We are aware that China remains a developing country. We still rank at the lower end of the world in terms of per capita GDP" (Hu 2018). Perhaps this self-deprecating humbleness was a statement of fact, or perhaps it was one of those tactics where countries quietly acquire power without being in the limelight or getting noticed. Whatever it was, it was short-lived. To be fair, President Trump drew first blood by responding to Premier Keqiang by tweeting that China is "a great economic power," followed by Larry Kudlow, his economic advisor, complaining that "China is a first-world economy, behaving like a third-world economy" (Hu 2018). These calls did not come as a surprise for China. Most likely, these claims also did not cause a sudden surge in self-awareness of China about its own power. But apparently, they did compel China to lift the veil of humility and modesty. The giant was not awakened as much as it was forced to come out of the shadows. Lifting that veil did two things. First, it forced China's hand to close the gap between *playing big* and *acting big*. Second, like a shock to the system, it created an intense need for self-reflection for America. America could no longer feel as the single all-powerful, dominant nation in the world. A challenger had jumped into the ring. The game was on. The competition had begun. And the years that follow will change the future of the world.

THE WOLF IN PANDA'S SKIN

They call them the wolves of China, and their tactics are labeled as "the wolf warrior diplomacy." Their wolf fame emerged from their readiness to respond to US claims and policies with assertiveness and aggressiveness not seen in previous Chinese diplomats. Apparently, among a billion-plus Chinese, the wolf warriors have acquired a position of admiration and awe. What was surprising, however, and what demonstrated the internal calculus of China was that even with the US placing some pressure on the Asian country, it had the choice to acquire the David position and frame the narrative as the legendary biblical David vs. Goliath battle. But instead, China decided to emerge from the shadows of obscurity and in a matter of a few months entered the world stage as the Goliath. This upsurge was so strong that it made President Biden's Director of National Intelligence Avril Haines classify Beijing as "a near-peer competitor challenging the United States in multiple arenas, while pushing to revise global norms in ways that favor the authoritarian Chinese system" (Neuman 2021).

The term *Warrior Wolf* was not without context. A 2015 movie released in China with that title acquired a similar iconic position there as some of the American legendary movies had done in America. Patterned after a mix of *Rambo* and *Red Dawn*, the movie depicted Chinese military successfully defending a takeover attempt by foreign forces. The foreign forces shown in the movie were composed of mercenaries who appeared to be Europeans or Americans and spoke English. The Wolf Warrior represented a nation finding its voice. It was as if the country had finally come to terms with its might.

This playbook of specifying a foreign enemy to build nationalism has been played and perfected by many other countries, and China's use of it comes as no surprise. The underlying force that was moving the tectonic plates of Chinese emergence were more than a military movie.

Dr. Christopher Ford, Trump-era assistant secretary for nuclear proliferation, shed light on this issue by pointing to something he terms a "grievance state." From his perspective, countries can often inspire their populace by giving them an account that is based on historical grievance. He identifies four characteristics (Ford 2019):

> Grievance polities share four basic characteristics: (1) a sense of self-identity powerfully rooted in affronted grandeur; (2) oppositional postures to what is said to be malevolent foreign influences; (3) a need for foreign enemies to justify domestic authoritarianism; and (4) a revisionist sense of geopolitical mission in the world.

Dr. Ford's analysis opens the door for further inquiry. Is it not true that almost all countries that find and pursue power do possess some type of grievance against some external force—or at the very least have some type of a populace-motivating narrative? America, Japan, England, Germany, France, Italy—had all experienced some form of narratives that may have met the above conditions at some time in their history. Therefore, what makes China's rise different?

In fact, one can ask that if neither financial power nor military strength are fueling the Wolf Warrior mindset, then what is?

Chinese economic power was not unknown to America. Neither was its military strength. After all, it was not too long ago when America's top consulting firms were beating the "move operations to China" drums. For the past two decades, American executives were hammered to link both sides of their supply chains to China. They were told that the cure for anemic stock prices and sluggish economy was "made in China" and "sold in the US." Government after government praised the merits of globalization. For American companies, China strategy became the wherewithal to respond to never-ending market expectations for short-term revenue and profit increases. And then came the sudden halt.

Interestingly, other than some relatively minor grumbles, the "made in China" movement did not cause major upheaval in America. America not only enthusiastically embraced the move to the China paradigm, but the nation also convinced itself about the merits of that structure. The country adapted to the service economy, and life moved on for many Americans. As always, those who were left behind from the gigantic shift were forgotten as the collateral damage of the new and exciting global economy.

Almost all the relevant charts produced during that era depicted sharply rising trajectories of Chinese growth as an economy, market, producer, and military power. But none of that caused any alarms. The grievance, whether overt or covert, did not translate into Wolf Warrior-ism by China or lead to defensive maneuvering by America.

 ## THE EMERGENCE OF STRATEGIC CONFUSION

At the dawn of the third decade of the twenty-first century, America found itself in a completely different position. This position was one of confusion about the nature of strategic confrontation with China. Policymakers and analysts seemed baffled as to whether China is an adversary, enemy, competitor, coopetitor, or partner (all these terms have been used by various government officials to describe China). In fact, the state of strategic confusion is so awful that one week China is viewed as a trading partner and an economic competitor and the next week as a potent adversary requiring an allied military response. One week decoupling is pushed, only to be followed by next week's recoupling.

If it was not military or economic power—then what inspired a sudden reaction from America? The answer can be found in an analogy from ancient Rome. Rome built the roads that were eventually used to conquer it. In some ways, as America built the Internet, the roads to conquer the American super-power status suddenly became visible to the adversaries or challengers. They were the digital highways. Traveling on them was encouraged and applauded. And they will lead to something that even the designers of the Internet may not have anticipated.

AI RISES

Perhaps unknown to the policymakers who promoted China-based supply chains, a silent revolution was brewing in the academic and research circles. This revolution was not like any other revolutions known to humankind. It was also not an extension of the digital revolution or the Internet. It was as powerful as evolution itself. It carried a power of disruption never experienced before. And despite its immense capacity to alter the direction and structure of human civilization, its initial goals were set as relatively humble task automations. As soon as deep learning (an innovative AI technology based on neural networks) came to the forefront, it became obvious that the world would never be the same again.

Our fascination about aliens invading our planet is typically premised on some intelligent alien species passing through the colossal enormity of space to find their way to planet Earth. What captivates us is not so much having an adversary that invades us but instead the thrill of discovering that another intelligent species exists besides us. The enjoyment of a sci-fi flix comes from simulating a low-probability event, all while being certain of our safety. As we create intelligence with AI, the intelligent species is not emerging from space. It is being synthetically crafted in our labs. The rise of AI is now certain.

THE UNEXPECTED EMERGENCE

What was perhaps unanticipated was China's sudden rise in technologies that mattered. Apparently, three factors came along as major surprises for analysts.

First, by 2015 it became clear that the next few decades will belong to AI technology. The advent of AI will change the course of human civilization. But despite the evident power of the technology, analysts did not anticipate a major upheaval. People went to work thinking that another new app for their smartphones or another social media website would be the future of technology. Offices churned proposals for legacy software. Tech departments worried about upgrades for CRM or ERP applications. More advanced IT shops fretted about adopting microservices and shared services models. Cloud replaced legacy data centers. Business analytics, data visualization, and business intelligence were considered as state of the art. Defense and business analysts went about their daily business. Government contractors pulsated with winnings and losses of bids for legacy technology. Mesmerized with its own indolence, America was experiencing a calm equilibrium. But this was about to change. Like an unexpected perfect storm, AI emerged on the horizon and held the power to change all sectors and all industries. Everything done before AI seemed like child's play. In the words of Senator Ted Cruz, "Internet will only be remembered as the precursor to Artificial Intelligence," and "Today we are on the verge of a new technological revolution—that there may not be a single technology that will shape our world more in the next 50 years than artificial intelligence" (Moore 2016). AI is expected to change everything: manufacturing, services, professionals, education, sports, entertainment, industry, government, research, and even science. All of a sudden, the technology whose repeated failure to launch had been a far more notable story than its triumph would abruptly rise as the master of all technologies. Like the power unleashed by a lightning bolt from a surprise storm, no one thought that AI could so easily surge and outflank the established molds of technological structures.

Along with the unanticipated rise of AI came the second factor that analysts did not anticipate. AI would not be the typical US-led innovation that spills over to other countries based on a predetermined and controlled filtering and distribution process. It was quickly recognized that the leadership in technology was coming from other countries as well. Specifically, China, and Russia also became prominent pioneers in the field of AI. With determined leadership to position China as a leading player in this field, Chinese government instituted a long-term strategy. America was no longer the uncontested leader at the helm of this revolution.

Third, the productivity potential of AI was not limited to a single sector—it uplifts the entire economy and creates a productivity multiplier effect that no one could have anticipated. It was productivity on steroids. Not just digital, the digitonomous (digital + autonomous systems) transformation was on the horizon. China, if successful, can now accelerate its path to glory and unseat the United States as the global leader.

President Xi noticed that a strategic gap had opened up. He had two choices—to play the conventional strategic patience game or to openly challenge the American leadership—and he chose the latter. His gamble proved to be pivotal for the future of world. In a reactionary state, America found itself unprepared and shocked at best and beaten and overpowered at worst.

The combination of the three surprises led to a new China on the global stage. The traditional analytical frameworks of the analysts did not see this coming. The counterterrorism agendas and Russian ships in the Arctic Ocean dominated the traditional analyst narratives. Mired by the cognitive dissonance and still recovering from decades of "think global, act local" narrative, America was about to get a wake-up call.

 ## AI AND THE AMERICAN PERCEPTION

Since the Clinton/Gore era, the American psyche was shaped by hammering a perpetual state of excitement about information technology (IT) in our collective consciousness. IT was the field that created international legends and influencers who were worshipped by their global fan bases. The tech leaders enjoyed celebrity status that rivaled that of rock stars, movie actors and actresses, and sports personalities. Ma was seen as much a stateless celebrity as Zuckerberg, Musk, or Bezos. IT was viewed as the innocuous technology to make the world a better place, a unifier, an equalizer, a liberator. From burgeoning middle classes all over the world to democracy movements such as the Arab Spring were all attributed to the Internet. It was meant to be transnational and was supposed to collapse the artificially built national boundaries and walls and to bring people together. It was supposed to create a collective global consciousness independent of national interests. It was expected to be the final nail in the coffin of the Cold War–era nationalism and ideological rivalry. But all that optimism was about to change in a dramatic and abrupt manner.

The concept of AI as a national force to compete with other nations was originally proposed by President Putin, who in 2017 said that whoever reaches a breakthrough in developing artificial intelligence will come to dominate the world (CNBC 2017).

While most people pay attention to the domination part, we think the most important insight from President Putin's statement was the reference to "whoever." This implied that President Putin was not viewing America as a natural leader in AI—something he should have done given that America was truly a pioneer and leader in AI at that time. But Putin's statement was architected to signify that America will not be the unconditional crowned king of the AI dominion. America, like others, will have to fight for the first place. It signaled the beginning of the competition.

When Google's employees walked out to protest the firm working with the government, they were not thinking in nationalism terms; they were being responsible global citizens, patriots of a globalized world, in service of the collective humanity. Americans, especially the technology professionals, did not see AI as a national force or a country-specific capability. It was supposed to be for the world.

From the inception, the American AI Initiative was facing an uphill battle. The American public was under the spell of the IT's globalization narrative. Despite AI clearly becoming core to national security and national capability, it is not being viewed as such at the masses level. Americans remain oblivious to the link between their security and AI. They fail to understand the connection between their prosperity, livelihood, well-being, way of life—and AI. This relationship has not been explained to America.

This makes developing an AI strategy harder. Not only one has to shift the national attention away from viewing technology as some type of global kumbaya bandwagon but also hammer in the idea that it is okay for America to embrace this dual-purpose technology with applications in both civilian and military areas.

 ## THE AMERICAN AI DISASTER

The failure to build a comprehensive American AI strategy has left America in shambles. From a supply chain that has imploded to a nation at war with itself and rampant inflation leading to economic hardships, all can be attributed to America's failure to emerge as an AI leader. From a distance these factors seem unrelated, and AI simply looks like any other technology that will eventually find its way in America. But from up close they all look like part of the same problem: the failure of the nation to embrace AI at the speed of relevance.

Consider the following problems (see Figure 1.1):

Supply chain problems: They arose out of rapid changes in demand patterns as well as lack of flexibility and resiliency of the supply chain. The rise of AI-centric e-commerce has shifted the demand patterns. Failure of the existing models to identify the demand patterns and understand the disruptive nature of explosive demand implied that new and powerful AI-based demand forecasting models were needed. This could have been achieved by deploying AI. The supply shocks are also related to the policy

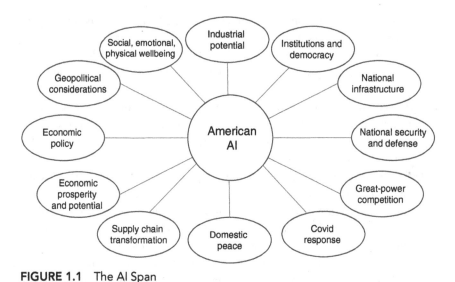

FIGURE 1.1   The AI Span

of decoupling from a China-dependent supply chain and the Chinese advances in technology where they are successfully exploiting the AI to revolutionize manufacturing and industrialization. This too is a direct consequence of AI competition. By becoming uncompetitive, America had no choice but to retreat and rebuild supply chains independent of China. If America had stayed as a leader in AI, there may have been less need for such a major alteration.

Inflation: The inability to apply AI to study the effects of monetary and fiscal policies on the American economy led to policy development that eventually triggered uncontrollable inflation. When combined with the inability to predict demand patterns, the government was unable to deploy an effective policy to manage the economy.

Productivity: The rising inflation and supply chain disruption can only be countered by a significant and material increase in productivity. But despite being the engine of productivity increase, American AI failed to provide the corresponding increase in productivity growth.

Military capacity: The ability to build new weapon systems and accelerate defense-related innovation are now greatly dependent on AI. China has reported great success in embedding AI in hypersonic weapon systems and in using AI to accelerate the design of new systems. Whether America achieves the next level of national security and defense capability will depend on American advances in AI technology.

Domestic conflict: Domestic conflict in America was fueled by the targeted deployment of cognitive bots that shaped the narrative and increased hatred, intolerance, and conflict in America. The inability to protect America against such attacks is largely based on the lack of development of American AI.

Cybersecurity: With thousands—and by some standards millions—of attacks daily, American cybersecurity infrastructure can only be safeguarded effectively with AI. Only AI gives the power to defend the nation against such attacks.

Infrastructure: The inability to build and modernize the infrastructure are twofold problems. First is the problem of communications and managing the social narrative for America to understand and support the infrastructure modernization—and to conduct such actions in the best interest of the nation. The hatred, misunderstanding, intolerance, and political bickering spewed by foreign bots has left America in a state of a never-ending internal conflict. Second, rebuilding the infrastructure by using, integrating, and understanding AI is the best way to move forward. Thus infrastructure, smart city designs, highways, buildings—everything can be done more efficiently by using AI, and all such planning must take into account the changes happening due to AI. In the future, when AI is used for such planning, it is possible that the infrastructure investment may turn out to be half of what it was expected. Therefore, AI funding in the infrastructure bill should not be viewed as one of the investment areas, it should be seen as a lens through which all other investments should be determined.

Covid: The American fight against Covid is based on three drivers: (1) vaccine discovery, (2) protecting populations, and (3) managing the social perception of Covid to increase vaccination and encouraging people to take proper precautions—and AI is at the center of all three. As Lv et al. (2021) reported, the AI played a major role in vaccine development. Managing the disease spread could have employed AI. It was successfully done in China but not in the US. How the social perception and meaning of Covid precaution and vaccination developed were also greatly related to AI. For instance, AI algorithms play a major role in social media where debates about masks and other Covid-related restrictions take place.

Those were some of the examples that show that the American AI strategy cannot be just about research and research funding—it must a broader spectrum of concerns. Most importantly, it needs a strategy development process.

BUILDING AI NATION IN A COMPETITIVE WORLD

Once it was settled that AI is the path to the future and that the competitive advantage of nations will be based on their AI capabilities, America needed a plan to maintain its leadership position: the American AI plan. It was now acknowledged at the highest levels in the government and the private sector that AI capabilities are at the center of progress and those capabilities need focused nurturing and support. It was also recognized that the AI capabilities define the dynamics of the competition with China and that it was not a competitor-less pursuit. The basis of the competition with China was not manufacturing. It was not trade. It was not intellectual property. It was not even military. It was AI and only AI because AI had the potential to change every other factor (manufacturing, services, scientific discovery, and military) in China's favor. In the terminology of *The Lord of the Rings*, AI was the one ring to rule them all.

America's plan A would have been simply to stay ahead in the AI technology and maintain a large competitive distance with the nearest rival. Had America moved at the speed of relevance, there would have been no need for a plan B.

But as America began to recognize China's swift rise, a plan B needed to be put in place. Plan B would also include countering China's rise. As America scrambled to develop a strategy to counter China's rapid advances in AI, the span of the counterstrategy would not be limited to just technology. It would require deploying the entire power structure of America. Since AI will affect every other aspect of nation building and national capital, both advancement and containment strategies will be needed to counter China's growing influence and capabilities.

The current American AI plan (plan B) seems to be divided into two main strategies:

- 1: Contain the Chinese technological prowess and expansion;
- 2: Strengthen the domestic American AI capacity (roughly the OSTP's co-called national AI strategy).

Strategy 1 would be played at the international stage, and there are indications that it was designed to create the following advantages:

- Increase the cost of business for China;
- Create strategic diversion and confusion;
- Slow down or retard Chinese technological expansion.

The goal of the policy appears to be to rein in and reduce Chinese power and not necessarily to start a new cold or hot war. The American policy related to strategy 1 was clearly articulated and defined.

Strategy 2 was domestically focused to develop an AI strategy for the nation, making investments, driving research and development, and building the industrial base.

Note that strategy 1 only became relevant due to the notable failure of strategy 2 in America. Strategy 1 belongs to plan B, and that, it appears, would have been invoked only if the competitive distance between America and the nearest competitor became alarmingly short. Otherwise, there was no need to shift the geopolitical agenda from a state of equilibrium to a chaotic realignment, which carries significant political and other risks. But by that time the American hands were tied. There was no other way to confront a rising competitive threat. The complacency and reckless negligence on the domestic front had cost America its leadership position. Plan A had failed. And that would lead to unpredictable and consequential geopolitical ripple effects.

While we will lightly touch on strategy 1 in this book, our primary focus is on the domestic strategy. We believe that while China's technology containment strategy is at least meeting the expectations set by the policymakers and belongs to an area where America has considerable experience, the domestic strategy is where America is failing terribly. Our focus will largely stay on that.

 ## JOIN US IN THE JOURNEY

Our narrative has several sides to it. We tell the story of how America dropped the ball on the most critical and consequential change that has ever taken place in the world. Through that reflection we show the gaps that must be closed. Our tone is critical, and at times readers will experience our frustration. But we firmly believe that this is what America needs: a dose of reality and truth. With that goal in mind, we take you on a powerful journey of transformation. In this journey you will experience, see, and hear the stories about the decisions, ideas, strategies, and policies that shook America to its core and that led to American disappointment in AI. You will feel pain, anger, and frustration. You will learn what factors contributed to it, and you will also experience a bit of disillusionment. Through this experience, we hope to inject a sense of urgency, reality, and confidence in America. We hope that our leaders will pay attention to our advice.

Every American has a role to play in rebuilding the national capacity. This could be the most patriotic book you will ever read because it is not driven by political ideology.

REFERENCES

Castro, Daniel and McLaughlin, Michael. 2021. "Who Is Winning the AI Race: China, the EU, or the United States?" [Online]. Available at: https://itif.org/publications/2021/01/25/who-winning-ai-race-china-eu-or-united-states-2021-update.

CNBC. 2017. "Putin: Leader in Artificial Intelligence Will Rule World." September 4, 2017. [Online]. Available from: https://www.cnbc.com/2017/09/04/putin-leader-in-artificial-intelligence-will-rule-world.html.

Dransfield, Joe. 2020. "How Relevant Is the Speed of Relevance?: Unity of Effort Towards Decision Superiority Is Critical to Future U.S. Military Dominance." The Strategy Bridge. [Online]. Available at: https://thestrategybridge.org/the-bridge/2020/1/13/how-relevant-is-the-speed-of-relevance-unity-of-effort-towards-decision-superiority-is-critical-to-future-us-military-dominance.

Ford, Christopher. 2019. "Ideological 'Grievance States' and Nonproliferation: China, Russia, and Iran." US Department of State. [Online]. Available at: https://2017-2021.state.gov/ideological-grievance-states-and-nonproliferation-china-russia-and-iran/index.html.

Hu, Krystal. 2018. "China's Premier Reminds the World: 'China Remains a Developing Country.'" Yahoo Finance. [Online]. Available at: https://www.yahoo.com/news/chinas-premier-reminds-world-china-remains-developing-country-145413881.html.

Lv, H., Shi, L., Berkenpas, J. W., Dao, F. Y., Zulfiqar, H., Ding, H., Zhang, Y., Yang, L., and Cao, R. 2021. "Application of Artificial Intelligence and Machine Learning for COVID-19 Drug Discovery and Vaccine Design." *Briefings in Bioinformatics*, 22(6). Available at: https://doi.org/10.1093/bib/bbab320.

Manson, Katrina. 2021. "US Has Already Lost AI Fight to China, Says Ex-Pentagon Software Chief in Washington." *Financial Times*. October 10, 2021.

Mattis, James. 2018. "The National Defense Strategy." Department of Defense. [Online]. Available at: https://dod.defense.gov/Portals/1/Documents/pubs/2018-National-Defense-Strategy-Summary.pdf.

Moore, Andrew W. 2016. "Subcommittee on Space, Science, and Competitiveness Committee on Commerce, Science, and Transportation United States Senate Hearing on 'The Dawn of Artificial Intelligence.'" [Online]. Available at: https://www.commerce.senate.gov/public/_cache/files/12eb9bc7-f5d5-4602-b206-113d6bf25880/B3C3D677FA18E98D85C616AF8326CEE0.dr.-andrew-moore-testimony.pdf.

Neuman, Scott. 2021. "Intelligence Chiefs Say China, Russia Are Biggest Threats to US." NPR [Online]. Available at: https://www.npr.org/2021/04/14/987132385/intelligence-chiefs-say-china-russia-are-biggest-threats-to-u-s.

Shane III, Leo. 2019. "Trump insists he fired Mattis, says former defense secretary was 'not too good' at the job." Military Times [Online]. Available at: https://www.militarytimes.com/news/pentagon-congress/2019/01/02/trump-insists-he-fired-mattis-says-former-defense-secretary-was-not-too-good-at-the-job/.

CHAPTER TWO

The Painful Effects of Losing the AI Battle

T WAS THE CHRISTMAS Day. An 18½ feet tall noble fir from Oregon rose in the Blue Room of the White House. On it hung 1200 needlepoint ornaments, meticulously created and decorated with pride and care. Over 500 volunteers had worked to decorate the White House. There was the normal hustle and bustle of Christmas, and the mood was festive. In the next few weeks over 100,000 guests would be entertained by the White House. But there was something dramatically different about this Christmas. Never before in the history of the United States had a Christmas Day looked so special. Those who experienced it knew that the joy on this day far exceeded the normal delight and enjoyment that Christmas brings.

Nearly 5000 miles away from Washington, DC, as the sun set on Christmas in Moscow, the mood was anything but pleasant. Against a darkening sky in the background, the flag of the Soviet Union was brought down for the very last time. It would never see daylight again. As the sun rose next morning, the Soviet Union was no longer. Millions of Soviet citizens watched in disbelief as their country was shattered into pieces, melting away the national pride and identity. The unthinkable had happened. A country along with its ideology had come to an end. The world had changed. In the words of President George H.W. Bush, "That confrontation is now over. The nuclear threat—while far from gone—is receding. Eastern Europe is free. The Soviet Union itself is no more. This is a victory for democracy and freedom. It's a victory for the moral force of our values. Every American can take pride in this victory, from the millions of men and women who have served our country in uniform, to millions of Americans who supported their country and a strong defense under nine presidents" (Bush 1991).

Christmas Day 1991 would go down in history as the day when after several decades of intense struggles and battles, America finally came out victorious in the Cold War. The war was over. On that Christmas Day, America had won. And no one thought there would be a day when another Soviet Union–type rivalry would emerge and would set the stage for a new type of competition.

THE NEW AMERICA: FUCK CHRISTMAS

The tree laden with Barbara Bush's needlepoint ornaments was surrounded by a rich collection of eighty houses. Under the shadow of the 1200 ornaments, and across the beautifully crafted houses and the grandeur of the decorations, a joyful toy train ran around the tree. The First Lady took great pride in showing off her Christmas decorations.

Thirty years later another first lady, Melania Trump, also revealed her Christmas decorations in 2020. Unlike the magnificence and splendor of the past, there was nothing except a desolate toy train placed on a depressing dark oval table. The sides of the track were laden with uninteresting shrubs that exhibited a dismal state of desolation. There was no excitement or fervor. There was no pride or showing off. Like a scene from some horror movie depicting a haunted train on an icy cold dark night, Mrs. Trump's gloomy train symbolized the American state of affairs. The mood of the nation had changed.

In a related unprecedented development, media reported that the First Lady was heard degrading and slurring Christmas. *New York Magazine* narrated it as:

> In the recording, Trump says she doesn't care for having to put together the holiday displays: "Who gives a fuck about Christmas stuff?" Discussing her frustration with critics who wanted her to do more about the administration's family separation policy, the First Lady said, "Oh, what about the children that were separated? Give me a fucking break." (Stieb 2020)

Mrs. Trump's crude comment, if true, can also be interpreted as *who cares about Christmas when we have much more to worry about*—and that interpretation wouldn't have been a stretch. Because, in an ironic twist of fate, while America was absorbing the gloomy toy train Christmas display and debating over the First Lady's comments, China was preparing to launch one of the world's fastest bullet trains. CNN reported that (Cripps and Deng 2021/Cable News Network):

> The CR400AF-G train, which can operate at speeds of up to 350 kilometers per hour (217 mph) in temperatures as low as −40 degrees Celsius (−40 degrees Fahrenheit), is part of the Fuxing series of high-speed electric multiple-unit (EMU) trains developed and operated by the state-owned China State Railway Group.

The train, rolled out in Beijing on January 6, 2021, will run on a new high-speed line connecting the Chinese capital with northeastern destinations including cities of Shenyang and Harbin—the latter of which is famed for its annual snow and ice festival.

Who would have thought that as China would be rolling out that train on January 6, 2021, America would be seeing an unprecedented attack on Capitol Hill? Thirty years later, the world had changed. Reminiscences of the American Christmas of 1991 now seemed like the relics of a departed era—a long forgone distant memory of an elderly person sitting in a nursing home and rekindling good old days of his youthful years without deeply reflecting on them. Christmas Day 2020 was very different from Christmas Day 1991. The effects of losing the AI battle to China were now fully evident and they were showing up in unexpected areas.

THE COGNITIVE WMD

The unimaginative simplicity of the joyless toy train was the least of the problems facing America. The past three decades had not been too forgiving for the country.

The country had gone through some tough times. The loss of manufacturing jobs to automation and foreign countries had devastated the rust belt. Promises of rebuilding the American economy for those areas had fallen flat on their faces. Wall Street scandals had shattered institutional confidence. Two long drawn wars—started on untruthful premises and with unclear goals—had created fatigue and frustration. The Great Recession had hit deep and devastated millions of families—all while enriching a small segment of society. Social conflict had increased, and political discourse had become both shallow and disrespectful. There were no lofty goals, no inspirational speeches, no motivational discourse. It was as if the energy had been sucked out of the country. The grandeur had been replaced with winner's complacency. Everything seemed politically charged and puny. The frustration among the populace was mounting. This was the perfect ground to sow the seeds of national discord, to turn national frustrations into national pains and anger, to conduct a precision strike on the scars that were once considered healed, and—like helping the ghosts escape in the movie *Ghostbusters*—to reopen the old wounds. This was the time for the adversaries to deploy the armies of bots that would control how America thinks. The social, political, and economic deployment of AI weapons had begun.

Lurking in the background were the ideology bots—engineered to attack the cognitive structures by diminishing the cognitive immunity of the mind. This process works as follows. First, the scouting bots are sent out to create personas and profiles of people. Then, like in the movie *Inception*, the second round of artillery bots are sent to breach the cognitive immunity. Once the defensive firewalls are brought down, the attack is followed by the delivery bots—the cavalry and the infantry—which delicately implant new ideas in people's minds. In the fourth layer of assault, the post-implant action bots are deployed to invite action from the targets. The actions undertaken by the targets become the feedback mechanism to gauge the success of the campaign. Finally, the neo-dominion bots are deployed to ensure that the cognitive firewalls remain breached and the controlled targets continue to think and act in predictable ways.

Once the adversaries engaged in a successful campaign in America, the rest was easy. America was being prepared to be at war with itself. A new civil war was brewing. The AI cognitive bomb, the ultimate cognitive weapon of mass destruction, was dropped on America, and no one felt a thing. Like colonialism, the craziest thing about cognitive bombs is that the victims welcome and happily embrace the suffering they bring.

 ## WAR UNLEASHED ON AMERICA

The AI era had just unleashed its first warfare. The bots that started the cognitive warfare had created the shockwaves that would reverberate through America in the years to come. A new reality was taking shape. The country would never be the same again.

Less than a month after Christmas 2020, the world watched in disbelief as thousands of protestors crashed into the Congress building as US congressmembers ran for their lives and had to escape through backdoors and alleys. The media and many politicians termed the act an "insurrection." What was also revealed was that the political, social, and economic instability were evident.

Everything that followed—all domestic issues and foreign policy positions—would be viewed through the lens of the new reality. The cultural war had commenced. America stood divided. Battles erupted in streets, in stadiums, in flights, in schools, in shops—and people were killed or critically wounded over their skin color, over their preference for wearing a Covid-related mask, their ethnicity, their political orientation, their dining preferences, and their school board orientations. Militias trained to prepare for some imaginary upcoming war—forcing President Biden to declare in his United Nations address his concerns about domestic terrorism in America.

The chaos had set in. The 2016 election campaigns became the Pearl Harbor of cognitive attacks. But unlike in World War II, five years later, in this new war America stood far from being victorious. The adversaries had conducted a skillful and precise operation. America was now in a reactionary mode.

Please note that it is not our view that the 2016 (or 2020) election outcome was not legitimate. The point we are trying to make is that the level of intolerance, anger, division, and hatred that manifested in that time frame was unprecedented in our recent history, and that anger has become an ongoing part of our national psychology. While it is true that foreign interference does happen in all elections, AI has given adversaries the tools that can create deeper and more extreme conflicts. AI is a potent social weapon, and it is much easier to arm people with that than guns.

 ## THE FIRST ATTACK

Like the early morning before the Pearl Harbor attack, a serene calm had spread across America. When the first wave of the AI attack came, America found itself unprepared. The calm was about to change in a dramatic manner. The stage was set for a new battle to begin.

Dates such as 12/07/1941 and 9/11/2001 signify the events when America suffered unprovoked attacks on the homeland. Both are remembered for the lives lost and the courage with which the nation fought back. Both events were not only attacks on American lives, but they also represented attacks on our institutions. Whether military and Congress, or commerce and trade, the enemies intended to shake America at its core. Along the same lines a massive strike targeted American institutions in the middle of the second decade of the twenty-first century. This raid did not kill people at the time when it was unleashed—but as years passed, it led to the loss of American lives on an ongoing basis. It left behind a divided nation, it created conditions for a potential civil war, and it destroyed the national spirit. But that attack went largely unnoticed. The frog was being boiled slowly, and it didn't feel a need to jump out of the pan. American was lost in its audacity.

Long before China came out of the shadows, America had to come to terms with the AI attack that left the country sizzling and scorching with political and social unrest. In fact, in some ways it can be argued that the American masses received their first introduction to intelligent bots in the form of a raid on their highest esteemed institution: democracy. The foreign meddling in the US election of 2016 was carved in the memory of many Americans—a testament to the power of bots. The foreign intelligent bots spewed hate and positioned themselves to create ideological conflict in the US.

Bots can do *that*! Many Americans wondered—and remained unconvinced—that bots can have such a control over them. They struggled to understand how bots can make them angry, resentful, bitter. After all, humans have their own minds and operate with their own values. *How dare someone propose that a foreign bot could alter my frame of mind or thinking power*—many questioned. Many Americans were convinced it could not have been bots—even though FBI agent Clint Watts testified before the Senate Intelligence Committee alleging that Russia used armies of Twitter bots to spread fake news. Intelligence was no longer confined to humans. A competing intelligent entity had been created. Humans were no longer in control of their minds—they were being socially engineered. This was a rude awakening. A grim recognition set in for some analysts: AI would be a force to reckon with.

That realization should have changed the business and agency calculus. But business consultant playbooks were not designed for this new wave. Their supply chain models were drawn for a world with a deterministic pedigree of overly simplistic causes and effects. Finance gurus imagined a world where humans made investment decisions. Still trapped in the counterterrorism mode, defense analysts piled up redundant reports on reanalyzing what had been already analyzed a million times. Political and inside-the-beltway intellect was developed and deployed to only respond to sensationalism. Intellectuals, journalists, and think tanks debated trivial and nonconsequential matters. Politicians created and re-created diversions, divisions, and distractions. Defense contractors submitted old technology RFPs and celebrated contract wins.

Totally oblivious to the industrial-scale nation-destroying metacognition at work in the background, America went about its business as if nothing had changed. But unbeknownst to many, the underlying reality of America had been materially altered. Signs of discomfort began appearing. A deep sense of anxious recognition manifested at the higher levels in the echelons. The American AI was no longer just about technological superiority, it was about the survival of the nation.

BATTLE II: COVID

And then the most unexpected thing happened. A dark cloud of pandemic engulfed the world. Of all the places it could have come from, the cloud rose from China and rapidly spread to the world. The Chinese understood the severity and acted quickly. With strong moves China put in place an aggressive program to combat Covid. The country mobilized significant resources and overcame the pandemic with impressive execution. America watched in horror as the virus spread through its states and cities. Overcrowded hospitals, morgues, and cemeteries became the talk of the day. Helplessness soared. That was when America suddenly realized its second vulnerability. Not only had the country underestimated the power of AI, but what became obvious was that the nation lacked the manufacturing and supply chain resilience to grapple with all the changes. With crippling shortages in toilet paper, hand sanitizers, masks, ventilators, medicines, and many other items of critical importance, America seemed like a country gasping for air. Hundreds of thousands perished as doctors and nurses struggled to reuse supplies. Apparently, those who had advocated sending manufacturing abroad did not consider such an event. Consultants who did both—enterprise risk planning and "move your business to China" consulting—stood on the sidelines as their models collapsed at the first test of a real risk. Suffering intensified across the nation.

As the picture became bleak by the day, some positive signs emerged. The services sector rapidly adapted to the digital economy. People worked from home, generating massive amounts of new data. With nearly everyone going digital for many types of work and personal tasks, AI got its unexpected second, and even more powerful, boost. All types of new digital data were now available for mining and training. Under the lockdown, as isolation intensified the need for social interaction, social media applications such as TikTok became the favorite release points. This meant more data for even more AI.

RISE OF DOMESTIC TENSIONS

Unfortunately, while the nation fought the pandemic, the broader rationality of the country became hostage to the daily battles of rhetoric among politicians. America was now fighting on multiple fronts—including an internal battle—and almost all her battles required AI in one way or another. As the government scrambled to build much-needed capabilities, recognition set in that the nation needed to mobilize to face the ultimate challenge. New RFPs were issued to build AI capabilities. America was trying to get its mojo back.

At the most critical juncture of when America needed absolutely clear leadership, when AI was emerging as the critical force to change the future of humankind, America was engulfed in the flames of domestic battles and violence. Every day consumed by the infighting was a day lost to build the AI potential of the nation.

The agony of Covid and the power dynamics of AI should have made two things clear for America: first, the country needed a revival and reorientation of its manufacturing and supply chains; and second, America needed sincere and clear leadership in AI. It had become obvious that China had both. What was also written on the wall was that these two factors—supply chains and AI—had now become one. Going forward they cannot be approached separately. Failure to approach them in an integrated, strategic manner meant a loss of competitive position in the world. America was not only in chaos, but now it was also in denial.

AI INDUSTRIALIZATION

The American supply chains began showing signs of cracking in early to mid-2021. This was not all due to Covid. Neither was it solely due to the aftereffect of Covid-related surge in demand. Right before Christmas 2021, President Biden made the following comments on a Zoom call:

> Earlier this fall, we heard a lot of dire warnings about supply chain problems leading to a crisis around the holidays, so we acted. A lot of recommendations of the people that you see on the screen here. I wish we were all able to do this in person.
>
> We brought together business and labor leaders to solve problems.
>
> And much—you know, the much-predicted crisis didn't occur. Packages are moving. Gifts are being delivered. Shelves are not empty. (Biden 2021)

Just few weeks after these comments, many parts of America started experiencing extreme supply chain shortages. With empty shelves at retailers, Americans complained, and on Twitter, #BareShelvesBiden started trending. The American solution to the supply chain problems was to throw in more money and hope the problem would be solved. President Biden touted his Bipartisan Infrastructure Law to push $17 billion to speed up and modernize American ports and for the Department of Transportation to give $200 million in grants to ports nationwide. No reference was made to AI—which should have been fundamental to determine both the modernization of the ports and the national supply chain planning and execution. The president and his staff were operating in the legacy world of the 1990s.

As if the inflationary pressures and Covid were not enough, America was in the grip of a national level supply chain meltdown. The delays at ports increased, and American supply chains began experiencing significant delays. The supply chains were built for efficiency and cost effectiveness and not resilience. From semiconductor shortages, which affected many other industries such as auto manufacturing, to the crisis at the LA port and trucker shortages, America was in the grips of a new supply chain dynamic. Years of neglect and an associated sense of invincibility had left the nation unprepared for major changes.

 ## CHANGE IN DEMAND PATTERNS

One of the reasons supply chain disruptions are expected to continue—even beyond the Covid times—is because the demand patterns are changing due to automation. This means that the way humans buy, what they buy, and how they buy is now changing, and that implies a new total demand pattern is emerging. The recommendation algorithms working in the background are shaping demand in unpredictable ways—and the more such demand patterns solidify, the larger the change will be. In other words, the change itself will drive more change as data from transactions will add to new learning and recommendations.

What remained unclear to many is that there is a deep, intrinsic relationship between AI and modern manufacturing/supply chain. In other words, AI and supply chain modernization and manufacturing are not two different pursuits. They are one and the same. They constitute the industrialization strategy at a national level. The new supply chains and manufacturing, if not built on the foundational platform of AI, will lead to disastrous results. The country would sink into chaos, and investment waste would leave America uncompetitive.

Rebuilding supply chain and manufacturing and the pursuit of AI should be undertaken as an integrated strategy. This means rebuilding the national capacity in a manner where American dependence on adversaries is minimized with AI-led innovation in supply chain and manufacturing. This is what we call the superspeed of relevance. The superspeed of relevance—the main message of this book—is based on rebuilding American leadership in manufacturing and supply chain with AI. The result is a resilient, self-reliant, powerful, and reliable supply chain. It also achieves national security goals—all while improving the standard of living and economic performance of our nation.

This book is about introducing this paradigm and showing how American government and American firms can adopt the most powerful and revolutionary transformation in the history of humankind—and come out of it successful and more powerful. But there is a critical dilemma. America had already started its journey for developing AI, and the current plans, strategies, and their execution have run into major problems. Numerous reports have pointed out this alarming trend—but no one has shown where the gaps are and how to fix the problems. None of the solutions proposed consider the existing conditions. The current plans function oblivious to what is transpiring in the nation, ignoring the chaos that now exists at all levels—and a lot of that is the aftereffect of AI. The existing paths to build the AI nation ignore ground realities and fail to confront the most critical issues. No one wants to say the truth or to challenge the existing power structures. No one wants to tell the emperor that he stands naked. In the absence of confronting those issues, it will be impossible for America to gain the competitive edge the country needs. We are committed to have that difficult conversation in this book.

GREAT-POWER COMPETITION: HYPED OR REAL OR WHO CARES?

Like the exuberantly decorated Christmas trees, the White House loves to create grand narratives that not only fascinate people but also help facilitate driving the acceptance of policies and strategies. One of those is the term "great-power competition" (GPC). The term has been used to describe various periods of power struggles between powerful adversaries.

Scholars have offered at least two criticisms of GPC as being an undesirable term (Cooper 2020). First, some scholars and researchers are uncomfortable with the usage of the term for unworthy or undeserving opponents.

This, they argue, gives too much credibility to an opponent who is not really a competitor. It elevates their status in the eyes of the world, they claim, and such an undesirable boost has consequences. It becomes its own truth and gives an unnecessary edge to the unworthy competitor. Within that line of reasoning, it is argued that using the term for Russia and China obscures the fact that these two are very different types of competitors and that the Russian power is nothing as compared to that of China. Furthermore, the liberal use of the term can create an impression that this competition is only about power and not values. The 2017 National Security Strategy (NSS) report claimed that "great power competition" is back "after being dismissed as a phenomenon of an earlier century." However, the terminology was changed in the 2018 National Defense Strategy (NDS) report that stated it as "the reemergence of long-term, strategic competition by. . . revisionist powers" (Trump 2017).

Within the above criticism category, some feel that even China does not deserve that status and it is possible that China is not as powerful as we have been led to believe. They argue that the data provided to us about China's rise is selective or architected. In a rather strange case of such selective offering of data, International Monetary Fund's (IMF) head Kristalina Georgieva was accused of boosting China's ranking by influencing a report when she worked at the World Bank. Based on the allegations, during her tenure as the chief executive officer, she applied "undue pressure" on World Back staff to make the ratings favorable for China in the "Doing Business" report (Martin and Donnan 2021). She maintained her innocence and denied any wrongdoing— but that did not stop many US congressmembers to criticize both China and the World Bank.

An investigation pursued and a report on the allegations was issued. While the authors of the report, lawyers at WilmerHale, exonerated China from having done anything wrong, Senator Marco Rubio lost no opportunity to lambast China and said, "No one should be surprised that the Chinese Communist Party uses its influence to corrupt individuals and institutions. It is in the CCP's organizational DNA to do so. Those complicit should be held accountable, and free nations need to seriously reevaluate the role we allow Beijing to play in global institutions"(Martin 2021).

Senator Rubio also chaired the Project for Strong Labor Markets and National Development, a project of the US Senate Committee on Small Business and Entrepreneurship. A comprehensive report was issued by the initiative. The title of the report was "Made in China 2025 and the Future of American Industry." Even though the report was supposed to be about American leadership in business and national development, the report focused on China right from the beginning. Senator Rubio described the state of the American challenge in the following words:

> High-end goods made by advanced manufacturing were the very products that America was supposed to make more of due to our competitive advantages in talent and capital. Instead, these products are increasingly being captured by China. The "Made in China 2025" industrial plan announced in 2015 by the Chinese government makes their goal clear. China aims to become the global leader in innovation and manufacturing. This would be an unacceptable outcome for American workers. To drive our own development in a competitive, global economy, we must prioritize the high-wage industries of the 21st century, to the benefit of American businesses, workers, and their families. (Rubio 2019)

Senator Rubio's initiative seemed to indicate a bit of reactionary panic, either intentionally hyped or real, and made China look as if it were in the driver's seat of the American planning. In fact, in the 80-page report the word "China" appeared 602 times and "Chinese" appeared 145 times—while the word "USA" appeared merely 4 times, "America" 28 times, "American" 101 times, and "Americans" only 11 times. Such was the paranoia. The Chinese dread had consumed America, and it was showing.

The second criticism comes from a pool of scholars who are less concerned about the factual positions of GPC and more about the dangers of hyping up terms such as great-power competition. Emma Ashford warned against using the terms that are not clearly defined. In an article in *Foreign Policy*, she argued that America has already suffered the consequences of loosely defined terms—such as War on Terror (Ashford 2021). She points out that no one is bothering to define what we are competing for and why we are competing. Such terms tend to create narratives based on loosely defined goals and lead to chaos and quagmires—such as the two wars in Afghanistan and Iraq. For Washington's strategic community, they represent a "poorly theorized model of the world and of America's place in it," Ashford claimed. Is it liberal democracy that is being defended in this competition? Is regime change the goal? Is it only means to some ends (with ends not being defined)? Ashford points to the dangers of an ill-defined strategy. Ashford suggested that there is never a time when great-power competition does not exist as states are always maneuvering for power—hence we can easily reject the notion that the competition is somehow returning. If anything, she argues, all this means is that the US is in a state of relative decline after three decades of a US-dominated world. This means the power gap has shrunk, and these competitors—including China and Russia—can make some moves that they wouldn't have been able to make before.

Both of the above criticisms, however, have not stopped US Congress, the executive office, and the numerous agencies under the executive office to make a strong case for China and Russia as strategic competitors. The Washington strategy analyst community also does not seem to be majorly concerned about either defining the term or exploring the factual basis of the competition. For them, this offers a new product to sell. Like any other product life cycles, the product of *war on terror* reached its maturity and was facing a perceptual decline. Its long-awaited replacement—counter-proliferation—was not as sexy and too complicated to turn into a narrative that would be consumed by the masses on a daily basis. But GPC is different. It is a much simpler play that can be consumed by the masses and the government alike. It can have major spinoff paradigms of its own. And it can be hammered into many different shapes—based on audience targeting. A new product was born in the DC circles, and it acquired its own reality. Welcome to the era of the great-power competition.

THE MAKING OF THE DRAGON

Acknowledging the rise of China while embracing it with open arms, President Obama stated that "the United States welcomes the rise of China" (Li 2016). Cheng Li, director at John L. Thornton China Center and senior fellow at *Foreign Policy*, believes that President Obama's background, his lack of experience with China, and his gullible idealism made him less distrustful or wary of China. Despite the overtures by President Obama, President Xi responded with a certain level of confidence in 2015 and referred to the relationship between China and the US as a "new type of great power relations."

Looking back now, it appears that when America embraced China with open arms, the strategic intent was a bit different than what really transpired. Most importantly, it was not any president's gullibility or naivety—but perhaps the emergence of a new phenomenon that strategy analysts did not consider. China was supposed to be the production backyard for everything uninteresting, everything unworthy of being produced in a developed economy, everything too blue-collarish. China was supposed to become one supersized factory of sweaty workers, oily machines, forklift trucks, workshops, warehouses, and conveyor belts. In contrast, more advanced nations—specifically the US—were seen as the ones that will lead the services industry, conduct the white-collar work, own the capital and financial markets, drive innovation, run the information technology industry, and be the gorilla economy that will consume the items produced in the developing nation factories. That model would have worked for decades to come. But China played its cards very differently than what policymakers and planners had anticipated.

China not only became the manufacturing center but also acquired and developed the innovation potential. Whether the innovation capacity was acquired through intellectual property theft or via internal capability building, China advanced its economy differently than what US strategists had assumed. That is why the shock expressed by Senator Rubio (see the previous section for his quote) was so high. As if in a state of disbelief, Senator Rubio complained that America was supposed to produce the high-end products, but instead, China is doing that and that China is doing both "manufacturing and innovation." A deep feeling of regret and despair was evident in his words.

Apparently, the planners who pushed for the pre-GPC China strategy did not take into account the inherent potential of people to reinvent themselves. The perception bias—as depicted in the words used in the movie *Ocean's Eleven*, "the little Chinese guy"—can paint an image of a compliant, submissive, and subservient China, a China that was eternally grateful and mesmerized to embrace the grand opportunity for bringing its massive population out of poverty and into a burgeoning middle class. A country known for its longstanding policy of strategic patience was not expected to draw a different course for itself than what was being given to it. But China was about to surprise everyone.

The US had not only lost its manufacturing edge, but also its technology and science leadership had been compromised. At a global stage, it appeared that the US was sliding, and its decline was accelerating. And that is where President Xi saw a once in a lifetime chance to make the ultimate move for China—which could be considered as the greatest move ever in China's entire history. Jude Blanchette—who describes himself as an American Sinologist— holds the Freeman Chair in China Studies at the Center for Strategic and International Studies (CSIS). Previously, he was engagement director at The Conference Board's China Center for Economics and Business in Beijing and has firsthand knowledge of the inner workings of the Communist party. While discussing China's shift from strategic patience to an assertive nation, he points out that "Xi has consolidated so much power and upset the status quo with such force because he sees a narrow window of 10 to 15 years during which Beijing can take advantage of a set of important technological and geopolitical transformation, which will also help it overcome significant internal challenges" and that President Xi sees a "perceived shift in the global balance of power away from the United States" and what President Xi called "profound changes unseen in a century" (Blanchette 2021). Blanchette has beautifully described the strategic calculus of President Xi. Notice the two drivers: *technological* and *geopolitical*. While geopolitical can be categorized as a "perceived shift," clearly President Xi noticed that the technological shift is as real as it gets.

Consequently, the new China was not aiming to be a regional power—it was aiming for the biggest prize: the ultimate global leader. This China was no longer the subservient state that would play by other people's rules. It was ready to challenge and change the rules of the game. It was mastering the ultimate technology: AI.

US power may have declined. But the decline was not that steep that it would have given President Xi a reason to conclude that China's decades long strategic patience should come to an end. The claim about the geopolitical decline appears contrary to the obvious power projection capability the US possesses and a credible military and powerful economy to back it up. It is rather clumsy to view the US as weakened or critically wounded due to either the Iraq or the Afghanistan quagmires. Neither lend themselves to draw parallels with the Vietnam or the Korean wars—and even those wars did not critically wound the US. In the Afghan and Iraq wars, the American frustration and fatigue happened more due to its inability to define what victory means rather than actual on the ground losses. Reinforced by scandals of corruption and exploitations by defense contractors, the war-related exhaustion had set in and had become an unnecessary distraction. However, at any level, that was not sufficient to conclude that an opening had risen to dislodge the leader. Despite its shortcomings, the state of the union was strong—both domestically and internationally.

It is highly unlikely that the Chinese decision to project its power was based on some analysis that showed a weakened America in terms of its military, political, economic, or soft powers. The American influence was strong in all continents and in all major allied countries. From military to economic power, and from soft power to political power, there was no near rival. American relationships with allies, whether by choice or compulsion, were strong. Whether it was Trump or Obama, the global fascination with America never declined. And neither did the obvious American power. The US military power was strong. From naval fleets to air superiority and from military mobility to intelligence, the US faced no global parallel. Add to that the economic power, and the picture becomes even clearer. Foreign direct investment was high. Capital was coming into the US, and American markets were performing well under both Obama and Trump administrations. And despite all the idiosyncrasies and unique communication style of President Trump, the power dynamics of the US continued to be strong. The economy performed, and the military strengthened.

A great proof of the above argument is that regardless of the power transition dynamics, change of the administration, and apparent policy clashes that may show a great divide among Republicans and Democrats, the Biden policy mirrored the Trump policy. So much so that in September of 2021, Fareed Zakaria seemed perplexed when he noticed that President Biden seems to be more Trump than Trump himself (Zakaria 2021). The reality was that America had not weakened, and neither had its power declined in the above areas.

Then the natural question is: What really happened that made President Xi realize that a window of opportunity has opened up to dislodge and unseat the uncontested leader of the world? The answer lies in understanding the technology dynamics and not just any technology—the game changer was the artificial intelligence (AI) technology. All other types of powers—military, economic, political, soft, and others—now rested on AI. A loss in AI competitiveness would trigger an across-the-board loss in power.

THE IT THAT WASN'T IT

At the turn of the century, the American leadership in the information technology sector was so evident that there seemed no need to even question that part of the US economy. After all, America was the uncontested leader in the Internet technology. So much so that Internet and US companies became synonymous, and terminology developed around them—for example *google* something, *tweet* something. A sense of invincibility was apparent. With Big Tech acquiring more power than many state institutions, America felt secure about its leadership in the technology. This confidence in the invincibility of the tech sector allowed President Trump to make political overtures to other sectors—such as the coal industry, trucking industry, and the broader energy sector. *The tech sector can be placed on cruise control, and America will be just fine* was the mantra that belied many presidencies and that also gave President Trump the flexibility to schmooze the rust belt. No one was worried about underperformance from the American tech sector. But AI was not the normal run-of-the-mill IT. It was different. For one, the regular IT is developed *for* data—as it stores, manipulates, analyzes, and processes data. But AI (specifically machine learning) is developed *from* data. This distinction between *for* and *from* often confuses people and makes non-technology people believe that IT trained professionals can develop AI solutions. But AI is its own specialization and requires very different skills than programming.

As the IT sector in the US developed rapidly, it began to create some noticeable problems. On one end, Big Tech became too big to manage and control—as President Trump discovered when his own Twitter and Facebook accounts were blocked. On the other end, due to this black-hole effect that sucks everything around it—Big Tech became the competitor of and the buyer of new start-ups. American start-ups and the national innovation potential began declining. Companies were being launched—but mostly designer firms to sell to the established Big Tech. Innovation translated into building a designer firm developed with the sole purpose of filling a small functionality or a feature gap in the Big Tech software offering. Venture capitalists specialized in funding those firms. Media outlets, recycled management teams, VCs, and a whole gamut of characters became proficient in flipping the designer firms. While the American innovation declined, the M&A deal flow increased. The financial innovation and designer-tech firm launch replaced pure-technology or science-based innovation. Fareed Zakaria noticed the trend as early as in 2015 and repeatedly warned about the declining entrepreneurship and innovation capacity of America (Zakaria 2015). In 2016 Zakaria pointed to a risk-aversive new American generation tarnished by the Great Recession and which lacked the adventurous spirit of their baby boomer ancestors (Zakaria 2016). This generation wanted complacency and certainty. The explorer mindset was replaced by the idler mindset. As the power of Big Tech magnified while the innovative potential of the nation declined, both Trump and Obama administrations felt helpless to do anything to reshape the deeply ingrained competitive dynamics of the tech sector. The new American superpowers (Big Tech) became untouchable. Congressional investigations and inquiries became media circuses as tech entrepreneurs and CEOs dropped tech buzzwords on congressional leaders who seemed ill-prepared to handle the new terminology and concepts.

The litmus test of the above problem was evident when Biden picked his head of FTC. Her biggest qualification was her strong opposition to the unrestrained Big Tech monopolization. Clearly, in the upper echelons of the government, the anticompetitive risk of Big Tech must have been raised to the red alert level for Biden to pull a young and determined academic out of Princeton and given her the reins of the FTC. Chair Lina M. Khan's mandate—it seemed—was to rein in Big Tech's ambitions.

Unlike the highly motivated Chinese new generation, the American new generation did not care about the AI revolution. It meant nothing for them.

The Clinton/Gore-era marketing of tech revolutions was nowhere to be found. Big Tech and then other software companies pushed terms such as cognitive, intelligent, augmented, and automation, but neither rose to become a clear national mandate. No one was able to mobilize resources and rally Americans to respond to this revolution. If anything, more naysayers, critics, and futurists emerged than pragmatic evangelists.

Despite being at such a critical juncture of human history, the federal funding in R&D as a percentage of GDP remained lethargic and continued to decline.

For the younger generations, America had been turned into the tech user nation as opposed to a tech developer country. Gen X and gen Z Americans quickly figured out how to make big money from becoming social media influencers and Internet sensations. But few were inspired to become AI experts or launch AI firms.

THE OPPORTUNITY OPENS UP

Collectively, all of these signs were way too obvious to ignore. It is likely that this is what led President Xi to realize that the opportunity to strike had emerged. America was now trapped in its own mess. The technology that was developed to bring people together, social media, had created an addiction and a mass hysteria. A different type of an opium war had started—but this time America was the target. A country that had lost its innovation potential, whose people had become fatigued and risk averse, whose leaders had lost people's trust could now be challenged. The calculus was simple—while America's military and economic power were intact, a decline was on the horizon. A self-absorbed nation mired in its own hysteria will take a long time to adjust its course. By that time China will be well past the leader, President Xi may have concluded.

With meticulous planning, which is characteristic of Chinese strategy, it would not have been hard for China to recognize that the AI transformation simultaneously enhanced productivity in three areas:

Discover: AI can speed up discovery and drive innovation. It can create new solutions.
Predict: AI can predict better. Consider all the gaps and losses that happen in both civilian and military activities because of our inability to resolve uncertainty.
Automate: AI can automate not only physical work but also cognitive work. The ability to automate total work implies no need for human workers.

Think about autonomous cars and driverless trucks—these vehicles offer physical automation (mobility) and cognitive automation (driving).

When viewed collectively, the three enhancers form a cycle known as the DPA cycle (discover, predict, and automate). This cycle, when perfected, can unleash tremendous productivity. Faster discovery means greater innovation, better prediction means less errors and more optimal solutions, and automation means all aspects of human work getting automated. This is the formula for productivity on steroids. When implemented, it has the potential to shift the productivity curve to a new height. And this made President Xi's gamble all the more worthy for China.

 ## VICTORY LIES IN LOSING THE GAME

Just as Clinton/Gore inspired an entire generation of Americans to launch the Internet era, President Xi led a similar vision-setting transformation for the Chinese in AI. Unlike American youth, Chinese young people began acquiring AI skills in hordes.

Kai-Fu Lee explains this revolution in his book *AI Super-Powers* and calls it the Chinese Sputnik moment (Lee 2018). The trigger event that inspired the AI revolution was a game of go. This game was played in 2017 between the world champion Ke Jie and Google's deep learning software known as AlphaGo. Go was considered one of the most profound strategy games in ancient China. AlphaGo, a deep learning algorithm-based software developed by DeepMind of Google, systematically defeated Ke and won the match. Like the Sputnik moment for Americans where the Russian launch of Sputnik initiated a national response in America, AlphaGo, a Western technology, beating the go master represented a national wake-up call and challenge. A year before Ke lost the game, AlphaGo had defeated a Korean master and over 280 million Chinese viewers had watched that game. The response was overwhelming. One game of go had mobilized a nation—and the Chinese technology community, investors, government, scientists, and entrepreneurs united to start a new era in China's scientific development. The forces of social constructivism and sensemaking were at work here. As Americans would have switched the channel to watch a baseball or basketball game—with sheer luck a game of go gave China a new national identity and launched a technology revolution.

One way to understand the impact it made would be to imagine if somehow the worst-performing NFL team recruited a new player—except the player was a cyborg—and this player won every game and took the team to win the Superbowl. Every pass he got turned into a touchdown. Every kick he made ended up in the goalposts. Imagine how this would have created a huge social awareness and sensation in America about cyborgs. People would talk about it at dinner table and in offices. Children would carry its pictures. Young people and students would want to create one. Grown-ups would want to own one. All other NFL teams would want to buy one. Professional teams from other sports—such as basketball, hockey, and baseball—would explore if they can recruit those as well. And companies across the US would become excited about recruiting and making cyborgs. You get the point. This is what happened in China.

The combined potential of the three capabilities of AI meant a new economy, a new technological revolution, a new type of machines, a new type of productivity, a new paradigm, and a new country. The path for the Chinese progress was clear.

The calculus for President Xi was obvious. Employing a strategy composed of AI-centric transformation, the state power of China can increase exponentially—and if played right, American power can decline. In fact, China would have concluded that the damage done by the Russian bots was sufficient to get the snowball rolling. China recognized that the American academic system has become commercialized and technological innovation is dominated by a handful of large companies. Start-ups are funded to become designer firms to be sold to large firms. The monopolization of the tech sector will be unbreakable—or at the very least take decades to end. An open political system that functions based on lobbyists and special interests will not lend itself to be easily swayed to start performing again. Rampant legalized corruption will not end overnight. The political rhetoric will become vile. Political campaigns will become too divisive. Social discontent will amplify. Racism, ethnocentrism, religious extremism, and dozens of such ideologies that coexist with their opposing forces in a liberal democracy can be extracted and deployed on the front lines. The inertia in America will keep the country trapped and paralyzed in its domestic struggles. China, on the other hand, can be positioned to run faster and without such burdens can sprint ahead of the competitor. The wolf warrior-ism was the only way out. This was not the time to take a back seat. The strategic patience was over. China will come out of the shadows. The American AI now had to find its way under the shadow of a towering great-power competitor.

AMERICA FIGHTS BACK, BARELY

Unfortunately, the timing for the AI surge could not have been worse for America. American politics had taken an unexpectedly bitter turn. The political rhetoric heated up, and the national attention focused on daily bickering, insults, and domestic conflict. The two terms of President Obama and then the era of President Trump became the battlegrounds for ideological struggles. A state of hopelessness and indifference consumed American youth. In the absence of great visions or aspirations, mediocrity descended in collective consciousness. Indifference and depression worsened with Covid. TikTok and social media commanded the attention of American youth. Entertainment consumption peaked. Shows such as *Game of Thrones* and Marvel's movie series captivated America. The nation was losing its ability to think critically. Andrew Yang, 2020 Democratic Party presidential candidate (withdrew during the primaries), proposed giving a monthly universal basic income (UBI) of $1000 to offset job losses due to automation. He termed it "Freedom Dividend." Who needs to innovate when one man can create a weapon like the Ironman suit! Who needs to work when leaders were proposing $1000 monthly checks that can be considered as some type of an AI relief fund! At a collective social subconscious level America felt protected by Ironman, SHIELD, the Avengers—and pacified with a promise of guaranteed income and stimulus packages. Kennedy's "ask not" and Clinton/Gore era's "information highway" became a distant history. On one hand, America was in battle with itself; on the other hand, it was immersed in a delusional state—America needed visionary leadership. But none came.

All the avenues necessary to mobilize a strong and viable response to regain the competitive leadership position seemed to be broken. Mired in its domestic troubles, Covid, inflation, ideological battles, and nepotism, America faced a long-term competitive existential threat.

POPULAR NARRATIVE

At the government level, the entire focus shifted to China, but at a masses level the understanding of the China competition—especially as it relates to AI at its core—was totally absent. Average Joe or Jane did not know that their economic and social well-being and the national security of their country was now dependent on winning the AI battle against China. They had no clue that America was now engaged in a full-fledged plan B strategy against China.

Perhaps intentionally, the population was kept in the dark. No communications took place to inform the public about the presence of a major threat to the US competitive position. No appeals were made to rise above the ideological battles. No requests were made to unite in the face of an adversary. No challenge was issued to the nation to come out of its complacency. No efforts were made to use either fear or excitement to motivate the populace.

Creating a narrative requires showing people something more or different from what they have seen. For example, Americans knew of Saddam Hussain as a brutal dictator, but his invasion of Kuwait gave the story a new spin. When combined with Saddam Hussain pursuing nuclear weapons—which obviously turned out to be false—the narrative became far more personal for Americans. Note that we are not justifying lying to the American people or recommending that Americans should be misled. We are simply giving an example of how fear is often used to create a national narrative to mobilize the population.

The invasion of Ukraine by Russia offers a more recent example of how the anti-Putin narrative took shape rapidly in America. Over 80% of Americans support increased economic sanctions against Russia and 42% support direct military action (Agiesta and Edwards-Levy 2022). This suggests that short of a direct attack on Taiwan by China, it is hard to imagine the American populace turning against China.

The Golden State Warriors minority owner and former Facebook executive Chamath Palihapitiya claimed on his All-In podcast that "nobody cares about the Uyghurs" (Jones 2022). Perhaps he was implying that the Uyghur narrative does not work in America. For one, in many political circles in America, the anti-Muslim messaging was used to create an impression of Islam as a force opposing the West. This went on for two decades. This dehumanizing narrative of Muslims shaped the perception of a large part of the population, and hence the Uyghur narrative may not lead to getting sympathy from America. Second, many Muslim-majority countries such as Pakistan, Iran, and Turkey who are usually vocal about Muslim issues in other countries are not talking about the Uyghur issue. In fact, many US allies are also mute about that. Third, President Trump's national security advisor John Bolton said that during a private meeting with Chinese President Xi Jinping, President Trump expressed approval of a concentration camp for Uighur Muslims (Bolton 2020). Fourth, there are many allies of the United States that subject their own populations or populations in their dominion to atrocities and harassment. This shows that it will be hard to drive support in America about the Uyghur-related narrative.

The same goes for Hong Kong and Taiwan. The fatigue the nation experienced after being at war for two decades has created an America that may not care about what happens on the other side of the world. The rise in anti-Asian crimes in America also points to the dehumanization of the Asian population. This implies that it will be hard to find significant empathy or sympathy across the nation to mobilize a national level response to the China challenge.

Shaping the narrative comes with a challenge. The American population genuinely believes that America is still at the forefront of the world, that American values and principles are intact and will safeguard America's leadership position, and that the American institutions are immune from subversion undertaken by foreign or opportunistic domestic forces. If the population is told that America is no longer in the leadership position, that our values and principles and the integrity of our institutions has been compromised or weakened by the adversaries, it will create an even greater psychological shock at a social level. However, considering the threat, would it make sense to communicate to Americans that America is not invincible and every generation must play a role to keep the country as a leader?

The narrative of the China threat has still stayed at the government level and not trickled down to the populace level. While policy publications such as *Foreign Policy* and *Foreign Affairs* fill their pages with China, the intensity of that is still low in the popular media or culture. This is perhaps a sign that the China-US rivalry is not being viewed as a cold war—but only as a technological rivalry. This was not how things happened in the Cold War. From cities to rural America, the nuclear fallout drills and bunkers shaped a social psychology that was fully aware of the Soviet threat. Movies such as *Red Dawn* helped shape the mental image. But when it came to China, the American perception is still somewhat favorable. "Made in China" has not become unpopular in America. America has not become anti-China to a point where people will cringe at the mention of the name or where a masses-level boycott happens for Chinese products.

 ## INFLATION AND FAILING SUPPLY CHAINS

In November of 2021, Janet Yellen said that "the pandemic has been calling the shots for the economy and for inflation" (Williams 2021). She then talked about the relationship between inflation and getting the pandemic under control. This sentiment was rejected by many who felt that inflation was not related to the pandemic but to overly aggressive monetary and fiscal policies. The *Financial Times* reported that the US Treasury secretary Yellen acknowledged that reversing the Trump-era tariffs on China could release some inflation pressure for the Americans (Williams 2021). Despite such an acknowledgment, no efforts were made to reverse the tariffs, and the Biden administration continued the Trump-era China policy. This was a clear indication that the tariffs were not just political or economic—they were about creating a more level playing field with an adversary who had surpassed America. Unfortunately, Americans were expected to endure higher prices for their government's failure to compete effectively with China.

The inflationary pressure was not about pandemic-related supply issues—although they exacerbated the situation. It was about the demand: the lethal combination of a fiscal policy that was driving the economy by constantly increasing the government's share of purchases with a monetary policy that was on steroids. The expansionary monetary policy created a surge in demand. This placed tremendous burden on supply chains and production capacity. A simultaneous reduction in supply when combined with an uncontrollable demand unleashed a sudden rise in prices. As America entered 2021, the country began noticing that inflation was rising. By the end of the year, it had become worse.

 ## THE AMERICAN AI PLAN

To build an American AI plan, government should have first taken an inventory of the above factors. These factors were not independent of AI. In fact, AI was at the core of all those developments. Just as any strategy development process starts with looking at the broader picture and understanding the environment, the American AI Initiative should have also developed in accordance with the environmental factors.

Technological change cannot transpire effectively and positively without the associated changes in economic and institutional variables, complementary technologies, social sensemaking and socially constructed meanings, economic structures, property rights, and private incentives. The American AI plan was greatly deficient.

 ## REFERENCES

Ashford, Emma. 2021. "Great Power Competition Is a Recipe for Disaster." *Foreign Policy*. April 2021. Available at: https://foreignpolicy.com/2021/04/01/china-usa-great-power-competition-recipe-for-disaster/.

Agiesta, Jennifer, and Edwards-Levy, Ariel. 2022. CNN poll: "Most Americans Want US to Do More to Stop Russia, but Most Also Oppose Direct Military Action." [Online]. Available at: https://www.cnn.com/2022/02/28/politics/cnn-poll-russia-ukraine-us-aid/index.html.

Biden, Joe. 2021. "Remarks by President Biden in Meeting with the Supply Chain Disruptions Task Force." [Online]. Available at: https://www.white house.gov/briefing-room/speeches-remarks/2021/12/22/remarks-by-president-biden-in-meeting-with-the-supply-chain-disruptions-task-force/.

Blanchette, Jude. 2021. "Xi's Gamble." *Foreign Affairs*. July/August 2021.

Bolton, John. 2020. *The Room Where It Happened: A White House Memoir.* Simon Schuster.

Bush, George H. W. 1991. "End of the Soviet Union." *The New York Times*. December 26, 1991. [Online]. Available at: https://www.nytimes .com/1991/12/26/world/end-soviet-union-text-bush-s-address-nation-gorbachev-s-resignation.html.

Cooper, Zack. 2020. "Bad Idea: 'Great Power Competition' Terminology. Defense360 Center for Strategic and International Studies.' [Online]. Available at: https://defense360.csis.org/bad-idea-great-power-competition-terminology/.

Cripps, Karla, and Deng, Shawn. 2021. "China Debuts Bullet Train That Can Operate in Extremely Cold Temperatures." CNN. January 12, 2021. [Online]. Available at: https://www.cnn.com/travel/article/china-bullet-train-cold-weather-fuxing/index.html.

Jones, Dustin. 2022. "Co-owner of NBA's Warriors Slammed after Saying 'Nobody Cares about the Uyghurs.'" NPR. [Online]. Available at: https://www.npr.org/2022/01/17/1073705516/co-owner-of-the-nbas-warriors-lambasted-after-saying-nobody-cares-about-the-uygh.

Lee, Kai-Fu. 2018. *AI Superpowers: China, Silicon Valley, and the New World Order.* First Mariner Books.

Li, Cheng. 2016. "Assessing U.S.-China Relations under the Obama Administration." Brookings. [Online]. Available at: https://www.brook ings.edu/opinions/assessing-u-s-china-relations-under-the-obama-administration/.

Martin, Eric. 2021. "Republicans Chide IMF Chief over China Data Manipulation Report." *Bloomberg.com*. September. [Online]. Available at: https://www.bloomberg.com/news/articles/2021-09-17/republicans-slam-imf-chief-over-china-data-manipulation-report.

Martin, Eric, and Donnan, Shawn. 2021. "IMF Chief Risks Weakened Authority after China-Linked Probe." Bloomberg.com. [Online]. Available at: https://

www.bloomberg.com/news/articles/2021-09-17/imf-chief-risks-undermined-authority-after-china-linked-probe.

Rubio, Marco. 2019. "Made in China 2025 The Future of American Industry." [Online]. Available at: https://www.rubio.senate.gov/public/_cache/files/0acec42a-d4a8-43bd-8608-a3482371f494/262B39A37119D9DCFE023B907F54BF03.02.12.19-final-sbc-project-mic-2025-report.pdf.

Stieb, Matt. 2020. "Leaked Recording of Melania Trump: 'Who Gives a F**k about Christmas Stuff?'" *New York (Intelligencer)* [Online]. Available at: https://nymag.com/intelligencer/2020/10/melania-trump-who-gives-a-f-k-about-christmas-stuff.html.

Trump, Donald. 2017. "National Security Strategy." [Online]. Available at: https://trumpwhitehouse.archives.gov/wp-content/uploads/2017/12/NSS-Final-12-18-2017-0905.pdf.

Williams, Aime. 2021. "Yellen Says Inflation Will Stay High until Covid Is under Control." *Financial Times.* November 14, 2021.

Zakaria, Fareed. 2021. "Biden's Policy Is More Trump than Obama." [Online]. Available at: https://www.cnn.com/videos/tv/2021/09/19/exp-gps-0919-fareeds-take-bidens-foreign-policy.cnn.

Zakaria, Fareed. 2015. "American Innovation Is in Trouble." *Washington Post.* [Online]. Available at: https://www.washingtonpost.com/opinions/fareed-zakaria-the-need-to-renew-american-innovation/2015/01/01/b0f0d864-913b-11e4-a900-9960214d4cd7_story.html.

Zakaria, Fareed. 2016. "Why Is the Number of U.S. Start-Ups Falling?" *Washington Post.* [Online]. Available at: https://www.washingtonpost.com/opinions/why-is-the-number-of-us-start-ups-falling/2016/05/19/53fe8e04-1ded-11e6-9c81-4be1c14fb8c8_story.html.

CHAPTER THREE

The Containment Strategy

B RIAN D. BLANKENSHIP AND Benjamin Denison study the great-power competition dynamics at Miami University and Tufts, respectively. After significant research on the Trump administration's claim that America is now fully embracing the GPC policy and the required capabilities and attributes of a credible player, they concluded that America is nowhere close to having a legitimate and well-thought-out comprehensive policy to be an effective competitor. If it is indeed a competition, American is not ready. Blankenship and Denison conclude:

> We contend that many of the long-term trends shaping America's power base, along with the Trump administration's domestic and foreign policies, are working against the United States' ability to successfully engage in the kind of great-power strategic competition being envisioned in the NDS and NSS. With a fiscal policy that has been dominated by tax cuts more than investment in physical and human infrastructure; stagnant military budgets lacking in robust investment in modernization and future capabilities; and a foreign policy that has alienated core allies and fostered distrust of American leadership among US strategic partners, efforts to pursue the goals of the NSS and NDS are unlikely to succeed. (Blankenship and Denison 2019)

While recognizing the deficiency, Blankenship and Denison draw out a battle plan for what it takes to be a true player. The plan had an internal and an external rebalancing actions. The internal balancing required increasing military spending, growing the domestic economy, increasing state revenues, investing in technological innovation, and building infrastructure and human capital. The external balancing required building and maintaining formal military alliances and informal partnerships, obtaining foreign-basing rights, enticing local partners with arms transfers and foreign aid, and working through international institutions.

Performing any of the internal or external balancing acts efficiently and more effectively would require AI. Consequently, the technology that gave China its power is the only remedy to respond to the American national crisis. How quickly can the US mobilize resources and snap out of its complacency is the real question. The American response required two levels of activities to sustain and enhance its position. The defensive capabilities—which include all the political, social, economic, and other capabilities required to sustain its position—to catch up in areas where China is moving ahead and to counter the influence of China.

As we highlighted in the previous chapters, plan A for America had failed. America was losing the AI battle on the domestic front, and it was clear that the national plan would not sustain American leadership in AI, so America needed a plan B.

Plan B, it appears, was architected to confront the rise and expansion of Chinese technology and technology-led expansionist policies. Plan B will be played out in the global theatre. This is the only chapter where we will take a deeper dive on plan B. The rest of the book will focus on the domestic plan.

It is important to note that plan B is not something that needed to be invoked if the competitive distance between the leader and the nearest competitor was not closing fast. It is deployed when the leader's position is threatened.

There are many advantages that America has in plan B. First, unlike the OSTP-led planning where a few scientists developed a national plan without even understanding or using the fundamentals of strategy, strategy methods, and strategy processes, in plan B America had vast experience and truly knowledgeable people who knew what they were doing. America also has existing relationships, strong soft power, and enough forward-deployed resources. American experience from winning the previous Cold War provided a treasure full of wisdom and guidance.

THE NEW LEADERSHIP

The incoming administration of President Biden barely got a chance to celebrate the election victory, and the tide turned against it. During the last several months of the Trump administration and before the elections, the mainstream media was obsessed with the Covid deaths. CNN ran a running measure that displayed Covid deaths in real time. Switching back and forth between reporting stock market indexes and Covid deaths, it was as if the deaths were a source of some performance celebration. On one hand it was increasing the national anxiety about Covid, and on the other hand it was dehumanizing and making such a large loss of life seem like the daily mood swings and reporting of the stock market. This ticker tape of Covid deaths continued in the mainstream media and then somehow miraculously disappeared as soon as the new administration took office. After a dip, Covid cases began mounting again and daily deaths crawled back to 2020 levels, but the media was no longer obsessed with it. There were no indexes, nor any sensational coverage. But instead of Covid deaths, the mask mandates and Covid restrictions became the battle cries. The game was reversed—it was now the GOP trying to discredit and destabilize Democrats—demonstrating that neither party really cared about the rising deaths.

As if the Covid catastrophe were not enough, America decided to pull out of Afghanistan in an erratic manner. The world watched in disbelief as the Taliban, the enemy against which America had declared war two decades ago, ascended victoriously back into power. The American inability to conquer and manage Covid along with the Afghanistan debacle created a perception of weakness. On the twentieth anniversary of 9/11, the Taliban raised their white flag as Afghanistan's national flag was brought down. The courageous act of ending the war in Afghanistan—which had been a drain on the American economy—was tarnished by the chaotic pullout. America demonstrated that even when the upper echelons of government do get the strategy right, flawed execution can hamper progress and leave the nation embarrassed at the global stage. The same was happening with the American AI Initiative.

The perception of the world about America was changing. Is America no longer at the helm of the world? The world wondered.

PRESIDENTS MEET AND GREET

A few months after the Afghanistan debacle, and after several weeks of back and forth between the American and the Chinese diplomats, the Chinese and the American presidents decided to meet. Significant maneuvering had taken place before that. A previous meeting in Alaska had exploded with both parties walking away furious at each other. Several small-scale follow-up meetings attempted to repair the relationship between the two giants. But the American style of reaching out to China was from a position of perceived power—a power that China seemed unwilling to acknowledge. Whether that power was real or simply a bluff, China did not show any overt signs of distress. America sent ships, mobilized military drills, and formed the QUAD (Australia, India, Japan, and the US)—but was not able to evoke any meaningful reaction from China. The problem with show of force is that failure to back it up exposes your cards to the adversary. And that was perhaps what China was reading between the lines. Now it was China's turn for the bluff.

When President Biden and President Xi finally met in November of 2021, the atmosphere was cordial. The meeting received wide media attention, and even though it was announced in the media that the more than three hours of discussion was professional, courteous, and positive, the events in the following weeks seemed to suggest that the US and China had not resolved their differences at all. American congressmembers traveled to Taiwan, and China, in response, issued various threats. The Biden-Xi meeting, it seemed, was the last-ditch effort to narrow the differences between the two powers. But concealed in that meeting were some strange signs of American frustration and fragility.

What was missed by the media, and is equally important, is the time of the meeting. The meeting started at 9 p.m. and continued past 12 a.m.—that is Washington, DC, time. For President Xi, it was normal office hours. While we don't know President Biden's bedtime, it seemed like an awfully late time to have such an important meeting. The Chinese media used that as an example of American desperation to have the meeting. From his body language, President Biden appeared less confident, even somewhat agitated, while President Xi seemed far more relaxed. The opening message of President Xi was strategic, elegant, and addressed to the world. The opening message of President Biden seemed very tactical and addressed to China. President Biden had a thick file in front of him and stacks of paper on the side while President Xi had a tea kettle, cup, and what looked like a milk pot. The implicit messaging was clear. President Xi was using every opportunity to show who was in control of that meeting.

FROM DECOUPLING TO RECOUPLING AND BEYOND

As America reemerged after the prodigious debacle of the Great Recession, unharmed and to a large scale unscathed, a debate raged in the higher echelons of economics. This debate was not much visible to the public and to some extent stayed as an intellectual argument within the academic circles—but often splashed out in popular media especially during the times of great change. It was about whether the dependence of the developing countries on developed countries has been diminished to a point where economic crashes in developing countries no longer affect the economic performance of the developing countries. Alternatively stated, in the first decade of the twenty-first century, have the developing economies become self-reliant and independent to an extent where they are shielded and protected from the economic shocks that originate in the developed nations? Various manifestations of the debate explored economic resilience, economic power, institutions, structures, and economic potential that can shield the developing nations from the periodic exuberances and the financial extravagance that has become a habitual indulgence of the rich nations.

The debate came to the front when *The Economist* took a stab at explaining the phenomenon and made a bold claim. In March of 2008, *The Economist* published an article that argued that decoupling had happened and that "as the American economy struggles to stay aloft, the developing world is learning to spread its wings" (Economist 2008). This claim was derived from two arguments: first, that trade with the US is only a small part of the Chinese GDP; and second, the investment in the developing economies continued despite demand slowdown in the US.

This did not go well in many circles and as the year unfolded was proven wrong by the economic data. Paul Krugman reacted strongly to the claim of decoupling and pointed out that:

> And not long ago everyone was talking about "decoupling," the supposed ability of emerging market economies to keep growing even if the United States fell into recession. "Decoupling is no myth," The Economist assured its readers back in March. "Indeed, it may yet save the world economy."
>
> That was then. Now the emerging markets are in big trouble. (Krugman 2008)

Foreign Policy called the prediction made by *The Economist* one of the worst predictions of the year (Keating 2008). The data showed that the adage that "when America sneezes, the rest of the world gets a cold" was still applicable. The context of the word "decoupling" seemed to encapsulate both the performance of financial markets and the general business performance as measured by the GDP and the associated supply chain operating performance of firms in an economy.

Then, the word "decoupling" was being used in the sense that developing economies are no longer dependent on the developed economies. Lately, and ironically, the term has come to signify the need for America to reduce and eliminate its economic dependence on China. The tables had been turned. Instead of a weaker, developing country trying to break its dependence on America, America was trying to do that with China. Perhaps unconsciously, but this use of the term is an acknowledgment that another country has now achieved a status powerful enough to create a certain level of dependency for the US—and hence a need to break that dependence. The burden of such a dependency has become overwhelming. And the US is feeling crushed under that burden.

Decoupling therefore is a survival mechanism. It is a game move where a country runs its economy in a manner where it is no longer dependent on the economic performance of another country.

Willet et al. have explained the different forms of meanings attributed to the term "decoupling" (Willett et al. 2011). They explained that the oil shock of the 1970s took America by surprise. American masses, who were generally shielded from sudden economic shocks emerging from developing economies, had to quickly learn about the global economic interdependence. By the 1980s America developed a more balanced view of interdependence on developing countries, but that was limited to managing the commodity shocks and did not elevate to the level of macroeconomic policymaking. The self-dependence concept tried to take shape in the Asian economies but the late 1990s financial crisis crashed any hopes of flying solo. After 9/11 when America entered a recession, emerging economies (China and India) continued to perform; thus the decoupling evidence continued to mount. On the financial markets side, Goldman Sachs and Morgan Stanley pushed the idea of decoupling. It was not until 2008 when the decoupling debate took a different turn, Willett et al. (2011) explain. The crash in the US had a global contagion effect, and emerging markets followed the decline. The financial system had become one. The deregulation, computerization, reduction in transaction costs, and free flow of capital across borders had created a truly global market. This market was not immune to what happened in one part of the world. It was connected like the body of an organism. The recoupling camp overpowered the decoupling camp, but with the passage of time, decoupling came back into fashion. Was it possible that decoupling in financial markets was becoming its own phenomenon vs. economic decoupling in general? In other words, while capital flowed freely across economies to be invested in various opportunities, was the actual trade dependence declining? The technological containment strategy needed both. On one end it requires diminishing the operational and market access capabilities of the adversaries, and on the other end it increases the cost of capital and reduces the capital flow. American plan B focused on both aspects.

 ## DECOUPLING, RECOUPLING, AND RE-DECOUPLING

Gina Raimondo, US commerce secretary under Biden, could not resist stating the obvious about China: "We want access to their economy, they want access to our economy," and she added that she would commit to push for US companies to trade with China. "There is no point in talking about decoupling," Secretary Raimondo said (Williams 2021). On the same day in a different interview she talked about the US needing to work with allies such as Europe to slow down China's "rate of innovation" (Macias and Tausche 2021).

From the outside, US strategy and policy had started to appear chaotic. It seemed that Gina Raimondo was on one hand stating her desire to maintain and even improve the trade bridges between China and the US but on the other hand intended to downgrade China's innovation. And this is not an exactly unworthy, undesirable, or unattainable goal from the US perspective. As Gina Raimondo herself pointed out in her interview with the City Club of Cleveland that the GDP of the autocratic governments has now exceeded that of liberal democracies, it could make sense for the US to take such a rise seriously (Raimondo 2021). Delivered two days before the 20th anniversary of 9/11 and a week after Americans observed the shocking withdrawal from Afghanistan, Secretary Raimondo gave an exhilarating talk at the City Club of Cleveland. She requested the venue, and the City Club of Cleveland was thrilled to have her present an important policy speech. Strangely, the venue for such an important event was rather awkward as her extremely relevant and crucial speech got less than 1000 views in the 90 days after the speech. A critical speech as such should have invited hundreds of thousands of views, if not millions, but it was as if Americans were no longer paying attention to what was being communicated by the Department of Commerce. Worse, the DoC did not consider that such a strategic policy speech needed to be shared with Americans in a more popular forum. Clearly, the need to inform Americans about the AI-centric competition, the rise of China, and the American response in the great-power competitive scenario was not being communicated as it should have been. This was an extremely personal and consequential message for Americans.

Dressed in an ocean-blue jacket with a matching necklace, Secretary Raimondo seemed passionate and animated about selling her vision for investing more back into the US economy. Behind her were a largely invisible American flag, a very visible Department of Commerce flag, and a globe displaying Eurasia. She made a strong case for essential investment back into the economy, of reskilling workers, of making the economy more equitable, and of fighting climate change. This, from her perspective, constituted Biden's signature Build Back Better plan.

As she spoke, the backlog of cargo ships had started to pile up at the Los Angeles port and inflation started creeping up with no end in sight. The supply chains were failing, and the American economy was melting rapidly. American policy and policymakers remained detached from the on-the-ground reality and considered inspiring and reaching out to America as unworthy goals. America stayed uninformed and uninspired—and was about to get slapped with another policy debacle of the government.

THE SHIPS WITH EMPTY BELLIES

Arizona State University is a leader in supply chain management and within ASU, Professor Dale Rogers is a legend himself. If you saw him, you would think that his second job is of Santa Claus—white beard, white hair, large round face with glasses, and a caring look. Whether he brings gifts for children on Christmas is not something we are sure about, but we do know that he possesses a treasure wealth of information on American supply chains and his country can truly benefit from his knowledge. We got the opportunity to get his thoughts about our topic of interest. Sitting on what seemed like a gaming chair, Professor Rogers's home office looked as the Hollywood depiction of a professor's office. With stacks of books and a large white board that served the dual purpose of displaying family pictures and writing on one side and what looked like a worn-out and semi-retired office chair on the other, Professor Rogers talked to us about the American supply chains, AI, China—and he pulled no punches. "This whole supply chain mess that America is experiencing is not due to Covid. The origin of this problem are the tariffs instituted during the Trump administration and then carried on by Biden. I was hoping they would have read the 150 years history of tariffs. They don't work! The decision was all political. And today the entire country is suffering because of that."

We were fascinated with his articulation of the problem's origin. "America has been told that this is all due to Covid, but you are saying tariffs are the real culprits. Can you explain to us what is transpiring?" We asked him.

Professor Dale explained: "In 2019 Oakland port was the 4th largest port in terms of activity. By mid-2020 it fell to the 9th position. Now you would wonder that how is it possible that Los Angeles ports are backed up with ships waiting months to unload and a port not too far is experiencing decline in activity. Well, the reality is that the Oakland port was designed to be an exports port and while US is getting more stuff in from China as year over year imports with China are up by 31%, US exports to China have declined. The levels are so low that the Oakland port is now used much sparingly than it was in the past. In the past ships would first sail to Los Angeles and unload, and then they would go to Oakland to pick up loads for the journey back. Now not only would they wait for months to unload, but due to the thinning of the exports back to China, they'd just turn around and leave without a full load. The two factors increase the cost of shipping because Americans are now paying for the roundtrip of shipment when they should only pay for one way. Add to that the waiting times because LA port is not very efficient, and now Americans are paying the cargo companies for the delay times. So much for tariffs! I don't think they thought through it. It seems to be a very reactive and political decision—but it didn't stop at Trump, the Biden administration is also moving ahead with it."

Professor Rogers raised an exceptionally powerful point, and he gave us a unique perspective. The China policy was not delivering results on the domestic front. If the intention was to slow down the Chinese progress, we ended up hurting ourselves more. If the intention was to retard the Chinese innovation, the country is no longer dependent on American innovation. If the intention was to increase power, it didn't happen. If Professor Rogers's analysis is correct, Americans had become a victim of our leaders' miscalculation. "The problem does not end at the LA or Oakland ports. As the freight comes in, a large part of that goes to Chicago's Union Pacific Yard. With underdeveloped infrastructure and delays to unload the freight, we experience more incremental costs. And just as with Oakland, the trucks and trains returning back to the West Coast do so with less than full loads. What do you expect? The costs of shipping a container load from China to California is now $18,000 to $20,000—that's about 9 to 10 times increase than it was just a year ago."

As we listened to Professor Rogers, we recognized that the emergence of AI has truly set unprecedented dynamics in motion. American competitiveness needed some breathing room, and an open economic conflict with China, while inevitable at some point, was probably launched prematurely and with little strategic planning. The AI technological revolution was showing its mark. The domino effect had started. In Professor Rogers's words, "Our strategy seemed very capricious. You know the saying that 'when you ask time from an American, he would see his watch; when you ask a Chinese, he would go to his calendar'—they have a long history, and we should have understood that. For thousands of years, they have been inward focused, and there was no need to create economic insecurity that would have forced them to focus externally. Now they look at the choices we make and are probably saying this is no way to run a world-class economy."

The conversation had turned serious and somewhat depressing, and one of the co-authors could not resist asking, "Professor, is there any hope? Based on what I understand you said, America needs a new infrastructure, while it rebuilds new supply chains and that while it tries to outperform China in technology. Is it even possible?"

"Of course, it is possible. But we need the right leadership at the top. We need smart, knowledgeable people who can do great things. I was born right after Eisenhower won his election. Those were the times of great leadership. Now I feel we don't have any. This seems and feels like a very different America than the one I was raised in. But regardless, I believe we can turn things around."

"How so?" one of the co-authors asked.

"Let me give you an example. I was at a conference in Laredo, Texas. The conference was on Latin American logistics. Several presentations were made, and they were in Spanish. I don't speak Spanish. As the mayor of Laredo gave his presentation, it was also in Spanish. He paused at one point and looked at me and asked my thoughts on what he was talking about, and I had no clue what he had said." Professor Rogers laughed and the mood lightened. There was optimism in the air, and we couldn't wait to hear the examples of America bouncing back into the leadership position. "The Latin American Logistics Organization is an initiative where we are enabling American companies to build strong supply chains by looking south rather than east or west. For example, China's progress included a Belt and Road plan that stretches from Beijing to Europe. We need a similar program that links us with Central America companies. Nike, for instance, which has invested more than $100 million in El Salvador. Adidas is also looking to invest $80 million or so there. And now Dell is considering refurbishment business going to Central America. China doesn't even want that business. They are not even taking recycling back. So we have come up with the idea of building a network of capabilities in Central America. This can start as a low-tech operation and slowly mature it to move to high tech. After all, go back 50 years and check how Singapore was back then. It takes time, but we have to start somewhere. This can help us build supply chains that are not only closer to us but also they meet national interests."

"Are there any risks that such plans can falter?"

"Yes. The risk is that we are a democracy, and democracies can sometimes be too slow to react. For example, it is a bureaucratic nightmare to make improvement in and around ports. We must overcome that type of inertia." In an article in *HBR* that Professor Rogers co-authored with two other co-authors, the authors emphasized the importance of enhancing near geography alliances:

> But the United States can't achieve these goals alone. They will require it to collaborate and strengthen trading partnerships with countries in North America, Central America, and South America and build a reliable, cost-effective land-based transportation network that connects the three Americas. Only with strong partnerships and a Pan-American transportation network will the United States be able to bring manufacturing home from Asia. This reconfiguration would benefit all involved: Creating jobs and promoting political stability in poor countries in the Americas would also build wealth in these nations and slow migration from them to the United States. (Vakil et al. 2021)

We felt that Professor Rogers made an extremely powerful point. With the right leadership America can achieve great things. He gave the example of several companies who are now actively engaged in decoupling. Policy is trickling down, but it is a risky game. Is it too little, too late? Is it too chaotic and unplanned? Is it just lip service and not genuine? Is there still hope that somehow the China-US conflict will just disappear overnight? That this is a bad dream and we will wake up one day and the world will be restored to a unipolar superpower structure? If American leadership does not return, would American democracy turn into autocracy?

ACT 1: THE BATTLE BEGINS

The stage was set to launch the first battle. As America woke up from what seemed like a bad dream, the American might and the playbook were deployed for both defensive and progressive postures. The AI protectionism began when Huawei was banned, followed by dozens of Chinese companies that were prohibited from operating in America.

Before China and the US entered the rivalry zone, the movement to support business in China hurled into the scene with the usual rumbling and roaring. Consultants, trade firms, and US multinationals pushed for more business with China, and analysts rated company stocks based on their China strategy. The China mantra was in full swing when suddenly this move to China came to a screeching halt. Huawei became the first casualty, followed by tariffs, sanctions, TikTok, and escalating tensions in the South China Sea.

Many attributed this change of heart to the peculiar style of President Trump. Blaming China as the job taker, currency manipulator, and IP stealer offered an easy target to arouse Trump supporters. But the new administration under President Biden did not project much love for China, either. Both Democrat and Republicans have made it crystal clear that America will no longer entertain what the US administrations believe to be unfair and heavily skewed policy that favored China at the cost of American prosperity and security. This change of status has not gone unnoticed in China, as the Chinese have also greatly increased the bluster and posturing.

As the rhetoric heats up, pundits and experts who lived through the actual Cold War may try to project a familiar pattern of the US-USSR-style rivalry. Some are even calling it Cold War 2. The imagery of Americans fighting wars in Vietnam and Koreas, bomb shelters, backyard bunkers, and school bomb drills is being used to project the new rivalry. But we beg to differ. We do not see it either as a cold war or a hot war—at least not yet.

We attribute this rivalry between the US and China to the "AI War." However, we do recognize that the AI War is not any less dangerous than a cold or a hot war and that it must be taken seriously.

Both China and the US understand that something fundamentally different is at play here. The advent of AI is not as simple as the rise of computing or the Internet. When humans create synthetic intelligence, they have essentially tampered with the evolutionary dynamics and redefined the course of the human civilization.

The regular information technology (IT) is no longer a competitive advantage for either companies or countries. Artificial intelligence and the legacy IT are widely different. In regular information technology, computer systems are designed *for* data (store, organize, process, and analyze). In AI, computer systems are designed *from* data (machine learning). Machines can learn, adapt, and accumulate experience. And that changes everything.

More than anything else, the greatest difference is that artificial intelligence is altering the scientific process itself. The creation and discovery of knowledge is no longer a linear process based on hypothesis leading to data accumulation and experimentation. It is now reversed, where data leads to an incessant and perpetual automated search for knowledge. Computers are the new scientists.

Intelligent systems can be deployed to automate work (e.g. robotics), reinvent finance, develop intelligent and integrated weapon systems, improve the national security apparatus, enhance intelligence and situational awareness, restructure supply chains, understand and influence social dynamics and political systems, accelerate innovation and scientific discovery, reshape manufacturing and distribution, redefine social norms and values, and advance business operations. AI is changing all aspects of a state.

AI, therefore, is the most critical capability for a country and the ultimate determinant of economic, military, technological, and soft power. The older advantages will become irrelevant as the new revolution allows countries to reinvent themselves. As the IT revolution did during the 1990s, the AI revolution will create winners and losers.

In this new era of AI War, the two primary and most advanced and strategic rivals are the US and China. And the first and perhaps most critical battlegrounds of the AI War are the supply chains of these countries.

As can be observed from the table below, in the opening scene of the AI War, the pattern of US interventions to block and tackle China's rapid advances in AI happened in the three arenas:

Drivers	US Actions
National strategy	▪ The US Commerce Department blacklisted 33 Chinese businesses—many of which develop artificial intelligence. ▪ The US also blacklisted Huawei and 68 affiliates and accused them of acting as proxies for Chinese espionage agencies.
Data and algorithms	▪ The US threatened to block downloads of TikTok and WeChat. Both TikTok and WeChat are sources of data that provide significant social media data. ▪ Restrictions were imposed on Chinese students studying data science in the US.
Processing power	▪ US placed restrictions on Semiconductor Manufacturing International Corporation.

Architecting and deploying the AI advantage also requires significant human capital in STEM (science, technology, engineering, and math)—and in terms of sheer numbers China has a significant advantage over the United States.

WHAT ARE THE DRIVERS OF THE AI LEADERSHIP?

The AI National Strategy:

> A national strategy of AI is developed by looking at multiple variables and focuses on industrialization, science, and technology. The AI-centric transformation is aligned with redesigned economic, social, and political structures and institutions.

1. **Data and data science:** AI systems are designed from data, and hence data becomes the key ingredient of systems. But getting data requires a comprehensive strategy that includes building data centers, building applications that collect data (for example, social media), integrating data across sectors (for example healthcare), improving telecom networks (for example, 5G or 6G), AI development platforms (algorithms), and building data science talent.
2. **Algorithms, models, skills:** This includes building capabilities by developing skills to deploy models and algorithms. It includes developing data science and automation talent in different types of machine learning including supervised, unsupervised, and reinforcement learning.
3. **Processing:** The third capability area is semiconductors and now the upcoming quantum computers.

This book shows how to build national and company capabilities to take maximum advantage of the decoupled economy.

WARNINGS WERE ISSUED

In October of 2021, *Financial Times* reported that US intelligence officials had launched a formal campaign to warn American firms about doing business with Chinese AI firms (Sevastopulo 2021). This was premised upon making it hard for China to gain access to American technology and to protect American intellectual property. The National Counterintelligence and Security Center (NCDC) was undertaking efforts to increase awareness about the Chinese firms in five sectors—of which AI was the first. The NCSC alleged that China was using various means to obtain intellectual property and data on Americans. In doing so, the NCSC's acting director Michael Orlando said that China was using an integrated front of Chinese companies, government, and academics to get its hands on American intellectual property. The civil-military dual role of AI made it even more dangerous. Orlando acknowledged that the narrative is still a hard sell for Americans. The *FT* article reported that Orlando did not mention which companies he was meeting with, but he gave the example that DNA data of Americans was being taken to China and that possessing such large data sets would give China incredible advantage. This was a unique operation. Even though NCSC was telling companies not to stop trade and business with China but only to increase caution, this communication by itself would result in increasing the transaction cost of dealing with Chinese firms.

American firms will be more wary, more cautious, and more concerned about dealing with Chinese firms. If the suggestions and warnings from NCSC were taken seriously by US firms, the work on alternative supply chain options would have already begun in many firms. However, to find such a narrative credible, Americans must believe that the Chinese rhetoric is not just posturing and that it is real and permanent. And that has yet to happen. The crackdown of Chinese firms started under the Trump administration and continues under the Biden administration.

The Department of Commerce placed several Chinese firms on the Entity List. As part of the stated policy, the Entity List's objective was defined as follows:

> The Entity List (supplement no. 4 to part 744 of the EAR) identifies entities for which there is reasonable cause to believe, based on specific and articulable facts, that the entities have been involved, are involved, or pose a significant risk of being or becoming involved in activities contrary to the national security or foreign policy interests of the United States.

> The list included companies (and individuals) not only from China but also Chinese or China-related firms operating from other countries such as Pakistan, Singapore, and Japan.

CHINA: Corad Technology (Shenzhen) Ltd.; Hangzhou Zhongke Microelectronics Co., Ltd.; Hefei National Laboratory for Physical Sciences at Microscale; Hunan Goke Microelectronics; New H3C Semiconductor Technologies Co., Ltd.; Peaktek Company Ltd.; Poly Asia Pacific Ltd., (PAPL); QuantumCTek Co., Ltd.; Shaanxi Zhi En Electromechanical Technology Co., Ltd.; Shanghai QuantumCTek Co., Ltd.; Xi'an Aerospace Huaxun Technology; and Yunchip Microelectronics.

JAPAN: Corad Technology Japan K.K.

PAKISTAN: Al-Qertas; Asay Trade & Supplies; Broad Engineering (Pakistan); Global Tech Engineers; Jade Machinery Pvt. Ltd.; Jiuding Refrigeration & Air-conditioning Equipment Co (Pvt) Ltd.; K-SOFT Enterprises; Muhammad Ashraf; Muhammad Farrukh; Prime Tech; Q&N Traders; Seljuk Traders (SMC-Private) Limited; and U.H.L. Company.

SINGAPORE: Corad Technology Pte Ltd.

During his last weeks in office, President Trump blacklisted several Chinese technology firms. The allegation against them was the dual-use of AI technology being deployed to violate human rights—especially in the Uighur Muslim area of China. The list included firms such as SMIC—a Chinese semiconductor manufacturing firm.

Despite the bold action by President Trump, many conservatives believed that this was simply a whitewash. Reuters captured these sentiments expressed about SMIC:

> It's a nice (public relations) line: "We're putting it on this bad guys' list," said William Reinsch, a former Commerce Department official, who said he imagines the agency was already blocking shipments of such technology to SMIC. "As a practical matter . . . it doesn't change anything." (Alper and Pamuk 2020/Reuters)

Republican Congressman Michael McCaul, ranking member of the House Foreign Affairs committee, echoed Reinsch's comments, saying he feared the rules were more "bark than bite": "I have concerns it undermines the intent, and may create an exception for malign actors to evade U.S. export controls," he said in a statement.

Clearly, certain voices from America wanted more than just blacklisting the Chinese.

In November of 2020, President Trump had placed 20 Chinese companies on the list where Americans were asked not to invest in them. In May of 2020, he had also asked the federal government pension funds to not invest in Chinese firms. President Trump's guidance was initially met with skepticism by the pension funds, but when it was made clear to them that the president was not playing games, they backtracked and supported the mandate. The escalation was real.

This implied two things were happening simultaneously. America was approaching decoupling from two angles: first, from the trade angle; second, from the financial side.

In June of 2021, President Biden added other restrictions on 59 companies as a continuation of President Trump's stance on Chinese tech and telecom firms. The presidential order banned Americans from investing in these firms. Investors were given time to divest their holdings or keep them but will be required special permission from US Treasury to sell their securities after one year. This included banning Americans from investing in funds that include these securities.

Among the defense companies on Biden's list are Aviation Industry Corp. of China, Ltd., which is one of the best known of the Chinese military giants; China North Industries Group Corp.; China Aerospace Science and Industry Corporation Ltd.; and China Shipbuilding Industry Co. President Biden's list also includes Hangzhou Hikvision Digital Technology Co., the developer of surveillance cameras and facial-recognition technology that US alleges has been deployed for Uighur persecution. Companies on Biden's list that weren't covered in Trump's initial ban include Zhonghang Electronic Measuring Instruments Co. and Jiangxi Hongdu Aviation Industry Co. Other companies included are: Proven Honour Capital Ltd.; Proven Glory Capital Ltd.; Shaanxi Zhongtian Rocket Technology Co.; Inner Mongolia First Machinery Group Co.; Changsha Jingjia Microelectronics Co.; China Avionics Systems Company Ltd.; China Satellite Communications Co.; China-based Costar Group Co.; Fujian Torch Electron Technology Co.; and Guizhou Space Appliance Co.

Many of the companies in Biden's order were already on the Trump administration's list, and they included both telecoms and semiconductor manufacturing firms. For example, China Mobile Communications Group Co., China Unicom Ltd., China Telecommunications Corp., Semiconductor Manufacturing International Corp., and Inspur. In December of 2021, the US blacklisted several Chinese companies including DJI and SenseTime.

Blacklisting was designed to increase the transaction cost for the Chinese companies and would make it difficult or even impossible for them to expand in the Western markets. It will slow down their revenue growth and affect profitability in lucrative Western or American markets. The associated financial blacklisting was there to increase the cost of capital for the Chinese firms and to reduce their access to capital. Another goal could have been to avoid the American know-how and intellectual property ending up in China; however, by that time Chinese technology in most areas had already developed to a point where there was no need to steal. In some areas, however, such as semiconductor manufacturing, China was still behind.

While technology protectionism may have been helpful and the growth of Chinese firms would have been contained, the access to financial capital is a different issue. Capital has truly become global, and the cost of capital would likely not get affected whether Chinese firms were raising money in New York or Hong Kong.

In an article titled "Chinese Companies Turn Table on US' Financial Decoupling Push" in January 2022 in a Chinese government-run media, the Chinese analyst Wang Cong claimed that the financial decoupling did not have any material impact on China. China, the analyst claimed, was able to take companies public in Hong Kong and American investors missed in the returns created by those IPOs. By that time there was no uncertainty in the Chinese circles that America would continue with this purge.

Throughout this back and forth with China, China had one hugely strong card in its pocket. For years to come, China would depend on its own markets and did not necessarily need to rely on foreign markets. The domestic growth in China was sufficient to drive powerful demand for Chinese companies. China is not Japan, and the 1980s playbook may not work with China. China is also not the Soviet Union, and the Cold War playbook may not work for too long. America must develop a strong domestic strategy.

The Chinese government also took actions to ensure that Western influence would not penetrate in China. The ideological carriers of soft power—movies, programs, games—have come under scrutiny in China. Additionally, the Chinese government also reined in the private education sites in China and the Chinese large tech firms.

It seems that President Xi was responding to an effective American strategy to contain China's technological prowess. Only time will tell whether the policy of containment works. China is down to basic maneuvers to guard against the advances. America has deployed every ounce of experience and capability to contain China, and America's experience from the Cold War is coming in handy.

 ## ALLIES AND ALLIANCES

The US has also become far more aggressive in developing and using alliances in the China containment strategy. American allies include not just the UK but also many Pacific regional players, including Japan, Australia, and other Pacific nations. The greatest prize for America came from India. One of the most powerful countries in the region, India came on the US side to confront China. A border skirmish with China rapidly developed anti-China sentiment in India. America possesses deep relationships on a global scale. These relationships have been nurtured and cultivated over decades.

The narratives about Uyghur issues, Hong Kong protests, and Taiwan are also helping the US cause an increase in China's transaction cost to conduct business.

 ## PLAN B IS WORKING, OR IS IT?

Plan B has certainly created higher transaction costs for Chinese firms. The Chinese firms would have to try harder and use other options to grow. One example of that was when Taiwan Semiconductor Manufacturing Company suspended chip sales to Huawei. The strategy of containment may be able to slow down innovation—as Secretary Raimondo longed for—but it would be hard to sustain that. The international growth options for the Chinese tech firms are becoming more limited. The American AI Initiative got some breathing room to find its glory. It all now depends on the domestic strategy. How fast can America rebuild its AI capability was on everyone's mind. America needed a miracle.

 ## REFERENCES

Alper, Alexandra, Pamuk, Humeyra, and Shepardson, David. 2020. "U.S. Blacklists Dozens of Chinese Firms Including SMIC, DJI." *Reuters*. December 18, 2020. [Online]. Available at: https://www.reuters.com/article/us-usa-china-sanctions/u-s-blacklists-dozens-of-chinese-firms-including-smic-dji-idUSKBN28S0HL.

Blankenship, Brian D. and Denison, Benjamin. 2019. "Is America Prepared for Great-Power Competition?" *Survival*. [Online]. 61(5), 43–64.

Economist, The. 2008. "The Decoupling Debate." *The Economist*. [Online]. Available at: https://www.economist.com/finance-and-economics/2008/03/06/the-decoupling-debate.

Keating, Joshua. 2008. "The Death of Decoupling." *Foreign Policy*. December 10, 2008.

Krugman, Paul. 2008. "The Widening Gyre." *The New York Times*. October 26, 2008. [Online]. Available at: https://www.nytimes.com/2008/10/27/opinion/27krugman.html.

Macias, Amanda, and Tausche, Kayla. 2021. "'U.S. Needs to Work with Europe to Slow China's Innovation Rate,' Raimondo says." CNBC. September 28, 2021.

Raimondo, Gina. 2021. "Strengthening America's Economy." [Online]. Available at: https://www.youtube.com/watch?v=pUgzXLEoJsQ&t=300s.

Sevastopulo, Demetri. 2021. "US Intelligence Officials Warn Companies in Critical Sectors on China." *Financial Times*. October 22, 2021.

Vakil, Bindiya, Linton, Tom, and Rogers, Dale. 2021. "The Case for a Pan-American Manufacturing Ecosystem." June 14, 2021. *Harvard Business Review*. [Online]. Available at: https://hbr.org/2021/06/the-case-for-a-pan-american-manufacturing-ecosystem.

Willett, Thomas D., Liang, Priscilla, and Zhang, Nan. 2011. "Global Contagion and the Decoupling Debate," in *Frontiers of Economics and Globalization*. [Online]. Emerald. pp. 215–234. Available at: http://dx.doi.org/10.1108/S1574-8715(2011)0000009014.

Williams, Aime. 2021. "US Commerce Chief Pushes China Trade Despite 'Complicated Relationship.'" *Financial Times*. September 28, 2021.

CHAPTER FOUR

The Presidents' Call to Duty

I T WAS DURING THE 1990s when the American leadership in shaping the future of the Internet became evident. Through that leadership America was also shaping its own future. At the forefront were the ambitious goals and vision of the executive branch. President Clinton and Vice President Gore saw the interconnected network of capabilities as fundamental to the development of the country. So much so that the term "information superhighway" was defined by the McGraw-Hill Computer Desktop Encyclopedia, published in 2001, as "a proposed high-speed communications system that was touted by the Clinton/Gore administration to enhance education in America in the 21st century. Its purpose was to help all citizens regardless of their income level. The Internet was originally cited as a model for this superhighway; however, with the explosion of the World Wide Web, the Internet became the information superhighway" (Wiki n.d.).

In his address at a 1994 conference in South America, Vice President Gore started his speech by reflecting on the words of Nathaniel Hawthorne, which VP Gore had read when he was still in high school. The words were: "By means of electricity, the world of matter has become a great nerve, vibrating thousands of miles in a breathless point of time. The round globe is a vast . . . brain, instinct with intelligence!" (Gore 1994). VP Gore explained that Hawthorne was inspired by the development of the telegraph, and he foresaw what

America was now poised to implement. VP Gore then asked the participants their help to create a global information infrastructure.

Those were the years when the executive branch created grand visions, and America trusted and was inspired by those visions. What followed was the greatest economy any country has ever seen. As the century turned, a new industry took shape and changed the course of human history. However, if we truly consider the words of Hawthorne, he touched on two concepts—the "interconnectivity" and the "intelligence." The Internet, for all its transformational power, could address interconnectivity—and could bring intelligence augmentation in terms of people acquiring knowledge and wisdom—but not become intelligent itself. For that to happen, something much more advanced than the Internet was needed. Something that VP Gore and the three administrations after his did not consider as part of the analysis. It was AI.

THE EXECUTIVE MESSAGING

In January of 1992 President George H. W. Bush gave his third and final State of the Union address, which was also his fourth and final address to a joint session of the US Congress. In that speech he talked about rebuilding schools to upskill Americans in computer science and suggested a tax credit for emerging technologies. He stated, "We must encourage research and development. My plan is to make the R&D tax credit permanent, and to provide record levels of support, over $76 billion this year alone for people who will explore the promise of emerging technologies" (Bush 1992). While this was a general reference to an emerging change in the economy, two years later President Clinton in his first State of the Union address to the nation gave a clear and powerful transformation plan.

President Clinton described Al Gore's vision for launching the Internet and said, "And the Vice President is right, we must also work with the private sector to connect every classroom, every clinic, every library, every hospital in America into a national information superhighway by the year 2000. Think of it: Instant access to information will increase productivity, will help to educate our children. It will provide better medical care. It will create jobs. And I call on the Congress to pass legislation to establish that information superhighway this year." President Clinton was right. Productivity increase did happen.

But notice the profound difference between how the two leaders—President Bush and President Clinton—talked about the transformation. One simply acknowledged that some change is taking place, while the other gave an entire plan, set a clear goal, and established the framework around which he could galvanize the nation. He used the term "information superhighway"—which helped with the branding and the messaging. It was descriptive yet mysterious. It combined two words that people already knew and could use their own imagination to envision a powerful future from the fusion of the two words. He didn't lay out the governance issues, the Internet safety issues, the values issues, the Internet ethics issues as the precursor to launching the vision for the Internet revolution. He didn't scare people about the downside of the Internet. He didn't begin his transformation pitch with fear-infusing narratives. He presented a vision for America that Americans were able to not only understand but also believe in. What came out on the other end was electrifying energy that placed America at the forefront of the Internet revolution and gave America a competitive advantage that even today remains intact. As the executive office inspired and guided the nation, America responded and experienced one of the highest rates of economic growth in the history of the nation.

President Clinton and Vice President Gore could have said that we would link local area networks with others such that we have a network of globally connected computers—and that would have meant nothing for the masses. They could have simply ignored the topic, or like their predecessor they could have just touched upon it lightly and vaguely as some emerging technology. They could have delegated it to some agency or created a special report-generation office to take ownership. They could have ignored the diffusion and industrialization potential of the Internet. But they owned the vision and led the change. The clarity, vision setting, planning, and communication not only gave America a new vision for transformation to the Internet economy, but they also inspired a nation to become the world's leading economic power by an order of magnitude. Even today, America remains the uncontested leader and the American control of and participation in the Internet owes a lot to the flawless execution of the government.

EXECUTIVE LEADERSHIP DROPPED THE BALL

The lesson learnt is that the passion and the energy with which a vision is communicated to the people are directly proportional to the results and participation of the masses. If the vision can inspire confidence, get commitment, and excite a large number of people, it can create a powerful technological revolution. This also shows that if we have leadership at the helm, we can accomplish great things. Most importantly, if we truly wanted to be the global leader in AI, we would have seen strong executive leadership—but what we saw was complete obliviousness to the greatest opportunity ever presented to America.

And if we consider AI to be bigger than the Internet, as Senator Ted Cruz reminded us in his Senate hearing on AI, we should expect even greater and stronger leadership from our presidents. But we saw none of that. In President Trump's over 56,000 tweets, we were not able to find a single reference to artificial intelligence and in State of the Union addresses there were no references to artificial intelligence, machine learning, deep learning, or intelligent automation. President Biden's record is a little better but only slightly.

Let us look at the complexity and extent of the situation once more. AI is the most powerful technological, scientific, and mathematical revolution ever experienced by humankind. It is literally designing intelligence. It will determine the competitive potential of countries, companies, supply chains, and sectors. It is the ultimate competitive advantage. It is the greatest form of capital that blends human, physical, and knowledge capital all in one. It is what will stimulate discovery, innovation, and research and development. It is what will secure the nation and create national security. It is what will keep America great or build back better. But despite all that, our presidents (and vice presidents) did not have the time, the vision, or the inclination to inspire America to embrace and advance this powerful transformation. They could not tweet or author articles about this. They could not give speeches about it. They could not come up with a plan to industrialize it. They could not give a roadmap to a community college in rural America to train the next generation on AI. They did not even bother to learn the basics about machine learning and its potential. They could not even talk about it as a layman.

The narrative coming from the presidents was neither motivational nor inspirational. In fact, it was nothing. It was equivalent to complete silence on a topic where America needed to be informed. And whenever conversation about AI arose, it was always somehow conditioned on or stitched to the governance and safety message. AI was presented as something to fear, something to be wary of, and something to be scared about. Why would anyone attach any importance to a fearful thing? No wonder Google employees staged a walkout because of Google's work with the Department of Defense. AI capabilities were not being viewed as essential for American success and prosperity or for national security. They were something to be worried about. This was not the case during World War II, when teams and teams of Americans and allies worked day and night to counter the German technology. With AI, there was no sense of nationalism. It is quite likely that if the AI messaging were done as a national need and in response to an existential threat, Google's employees would have viewed it entirely differently. They may have not staged a walkout. How a narrative is presented makes all the difference. The AI narrative somehow got mixed up in the ideological war going on in America.

TRUMP'S AMERICAN AI

In 2020 when President Trump visited the Centers for Disease Control in Atlanta, he reminded the world about his uncle being a super genius. The president said, "You know my uncle was a great — he was at MIT. He taught at MIT for a record number of years. He was a great super genius, Dr. John Trump." Then the president shifted his attention to himself and tried to establish that his uncle's scientific talent could have been a family trait. He continued, "I like this stuff. I really get it. People are surprised that I understand it. Every one of these doctors said: 'How do you know so much about this?' Maybe I have a natural ability. Maybe I should have done that instead of running for president" (Zilber 2020).

Whether President Trump was predisposed to be a scientific super genius would be hard to determine, but it is true that after two years of being in office he signed an executive order about AI. When it comes to a certain type of messaging, no one can beat President Trump. He has a gifted ability to communicate with his base. He can make his base feel as if they are running the White House with him and are participating in policymaking. But when it comes to major policy areas or to mobilize national resources, the Clinton/Gore team has no parallel. Al Gore had an uncanny ability to take on complex problems, break them down into meaningful solutions, develop narratives around them, and then present them in simplified messaging format to get public support behind those ideas. He did that with the climate change messaging and with promoting the information superhighway (Internet). And President Bill Clinton had incredible charismatic communication power that could inspire even his enemies.

President Trump had different strengths, and most likely his AI strategy was not his own idea or thinking but a result of what was communicated to him by the people who surrounded him. This included the OSTP (Office of Science and Technology Policy), an office in the White House that ran (and runs) the American AI strategy. Regardless of whether President Trump formulated the national AI strategy or not, his push to launch the AI efforts demonstrated his commitment to confront China. His role became even more prominent when America deployed plan B for Chinese technology containment. The Trump administration did not back down from placing several Chinese companies on the Entity List, blacklisting others, and asking Americans to stop investing in certain Chinese firms. President Trump also encouraged American allies to stop certain Chinese firms from entering their countries or doing business there. He went after the funds that had invested in or were planning to invest in Chinese tech firms. He forced firms such as TikTok to keep data in America and then pushed Americans to stop investing in Chinese tech firms. The Trump strategy on plan B was so effective that President Biden had no choice but to continue that, and Biden's Chinese technology containment strategy simply became an extension of the Trump plan.

On the domestic front, after two years of taking office President Trump reinvigorated American AI by signing an executive order about AI. At that time in 2019 there was still optimism about America's leadership in AI, and the positioning was about "maintaining" America's leadership.

A conference organized in May of 2018 became the precursor to the executive order. It was attended by over 100 people and brought together people from the government, industry research labs, and academia. The idea was to share research and development needs. In various breakout sessions, information was shared. But the large part of the conference, as documented in the OSTP report, contained remarks by Michael Kratsios, deputy assistant to the president for technology policy. In his remarks he pretty much repeated the so-called plan that represented the anchoring bias of the OSTP. The plan was composed of:

American AI leadership: In this Kratsios bragged about how America has great AI schools and that he visited Pittsburg where he saw Robotics Row start-ups that are part of the ecosystem surrounding Carnegie Mellon University.

Mr. Kratsios claimed that America is a leader—a statement that will soon be challenged by another committee report (discussed in Chapter 8). Then he touted that he, along with OMB Director Mulvaney, wrote a memorandum that directed the agencies: *For the first time in history, the memorandum prioritized R&D investment in autonomous systems, machine learning, and quantum computing.* This "first time in history" seemed to have been used excessively by the OSTP during the 2018–2020 time period. Most of these "first time in history" pat-on-the-back statements were either a stretch of the truth or meaningless in terms of their impact to successfully launch the AI revolution in America. They were a stretch because seven out of the eight strategies pursed by the OSTP were developed in the 2016 plan developed under the Obama administration. So much for the first time in history! They were meaningless because why brag about something that eventually led to the decline of American leadership in AI.

American workers: Kratsios then pointed out that the policy wanted to focus on American workers and to build the STEM potential. There was plenty of talk about the American workers, but no concrete plan was given to either retrain or protect the American workers.

R&D: He then focused on R&D, funding R&D, and building national capacity for research. Again, this was an area that represented the primary function of OSTP.

Regulations: He then talked about how the Trump administration would remove hurdles from research activities. He said:

> As we're making great strides within the Administration, to the rest of America often the most significant action our government can take is to get out of the way.

> Our Administration is not in the business of conquering imaginary beasts. We will not try to "solve" problems that don't exist.

> To the greatest degree possible, we will allow scientists and technologists to freely develop their next great inventions right here in the United States. (OSTP 2018)

This cliché of "the best thing the government can do is to get out of the way" is often used to signify that the government will not impose unnecessary regulations or that the agency does not have a mechanism, capability, or information to meet the needs of the target audience (researchers, private sector, others).

Mr. Kratsios also declared that he represented the United States in the G7 meeting where he recommended investing in R&D. His stance and message to the G7 validated that he and the OSTP were viewing the AI strategy from an extremely limited dimension of making R&D investments. He was pushing the concept of *build it, and they will come*.

In the same conference it was announced that to align interagency R&D priorities, a new committee known as the Select Committee on Artificial Intelligence would be formed.

In that conference, President Trump's message was straightforward. He said:

We're on the verge of new technological revolutions that could improve virtually every aspect of our lives, create vast new wealth for American workers and families, and open up bold, new frontiers in science, medicine, and communication. (OSTP 2018)

What he did not know was that his own OSTP would become the greatest barrier to innovation.

The Trump executive order resurrected the AI focus, which had been absent in the first two years of the Trump presidency. The bill was introduced as follows:

The Trump Administration is committed to strengthening American leadership in artificial intelligence (AI). Recognizing the strategic importance of AI to the Nation's future economy and security, the Trump Administration established the American AI Initiative via Executive Order 13859 in February 2019. This initiative identified five key lines of effort, including increasing AI research investment, unleashing Federal AI computing and data resources, setting AI technical standards, building America's AI workforce, and engaging with international allies. (Trump 2019)

In the typical promotional style of the Trump administration, the action steps included doubling the AI research investment, establishing the "first-ever" national AI research institutes, setting AI technical standards, providing regulatory guidance, establishing federal use guidelines, and creating new international alliances.

In January of 2021, the president authorized the creation of a National AI Initiative Office under the White House OSTP. This office was tasked with implementing the US national AI strategy. It was charged to coordinate policymaking and to bring government, private sector, academia, and other stakeholders together.

The executive action increased spending on AI 2021 budget 6% over 2020 budget to $142.2 billion in federal research and development. President Trump saw himself as the first president in American history who included AI as R&D investment. The National Science Foundation allocated an additional $50 million for AI—which took AI R&D at the NSF to more than $830 million. The Department of Energy invested an additional $125 million, the US Department of Agriculture $100 million, and the National Health Institute $50 million for new research on chronic diseases. On the defense side, DARPA was investing $459 million in AI R&D and the Department of Defense's Joint AI Center $290 million.

That was the time when the American AI Initiative was launched by President Trump – and which eventually became the United States national strategy for AI leadership.

The American AI Initiative directed federal agencies to prioritize artificial intelligence in their annual budget requests. The NSF, the White House, and the Department of Energy announced that $1 billion of awards would be used to establish AI and quantum information science institutes across the country. Six universities were tasked with the research. They included the University of Oklahoma at Norman, the University of Texas at Austin, the University of Colorado at Boulder, the University of Illinois at Urbana-Champaign, the University of California at Davis, and the Massachusetts Institute of Technology.

The national strategy was composed of only two drivers—invest more money and carry out more research. This was the professors' solution to a complex national capability-building strategy. From their perspective, all that America needed was more research, and all they needed to do was to open the banks.

Kudos to President Trump for supporting the bold investment plan for at least pushing the AI agenda. Clearly, what he pushed, however, was the OSTP agenda and not an American AI agenda. There was no link between the so-called plan and industrialization, adoption, diffusion, and productivity growth in America. It was all about research. The OSTP, which is run by professors and technologists, must have convinced President Trump to back up their agenda, and President Trump complied. Once again, it was hoped that the "build it, and they will come" mindset would win the day. The history of innovation shows that it never happens that way.

The Initiative also called for the development of the first-ever agency-by-agency report of nondefense AI R&D spending. This report identified $1 billion in nondefense R&D for FY 2020, establishing a benchmark for measuring nondefense AI R&D budgets in the future.

Despite President Trump's claimed genetic superiority to understand science, it is likely that the plan he implemented and approved did not come from him. Knowing President Trump's business background, had he really developed the plan, he would have certainly questioned how the R&D spending would drive returns on investment and how the technologies would find their way into industrialization, and that would have led to developing an actual plan. But that did not happen. This leads us to believe that President Trump did not spend much thought on the plan or critically analyzed it; instead, he must have relied on the OSTP to come up with a plan. Two years into the Trump administration, the OSTP must have known how to get President Trump to agree on things. The OSTP must have understood the internal workings of the new White House and would have known how to get the agenda approved. The art of the deal with President Trump would have been simple: praise him and show him how he could make his legacy—forming several claims of "first ever in American history"—and that would get him to pass anything.

The OSTP got its wish list, but America suffered. An R&D plan became a national strategy. Devoid of a corresponding industrialization, commercialization, and economic strategy, the agenda of the scientists became the face of AI. There was no corresponding business, economic, commercial, and industrialization strategy. All of that was shoved into a hypothetical public-private partnership where miracles would transpire and the R&D investment would somehow miraculously diffuse across the nation because a few business leaders, the OSTP, agency heads, and academics met twice a year to wine and dine and talk about AI. A disaster was taking shape. The fate of American future was being authored as its epitaph.

The mission of the OSTP did not call for developing a national strategy for something as profound as AI. This is how the OSTP describes its mission:

> The mission of OSTP is threefold; first, to provide the President and his senior staff with accurate, relevant, and timely scientific and technical advice on all matters of consequence; second, to ensure that the policies of the Executive Branch are informed by sound science; and third, to ensure that the scientific and technical work of the Executive Branch is properly coordinated so as to provide the greatest benefit to society. The Director of OSTP also serves as Assistant to the President for Science and Technology and manages the NSTC. (White House 2016)

The OSTP plans were being architected by coalescing the wish lists of bureaucrats and politicians on one hand and technologists and scientists on the other hand. What was missing was the industrialization concept of AI.

VIRTUE SIGNALING

While this was going on, another influential segment of the society jumped into the AI debate, and a third influencer group was created. This included the futurists, ethicists, AI governance champions, and values signalers.

There were many legitimate reasons to have these influences. First, there are genuine risks associated with AI, and having governance is an absolutely legitimate concern. Second, a society must reflect on ethics in every decision it makes and especially when a change as great as the AI revolution is taking place. Third, it is important to include different segments of society—especially social scientists—who can guide the development of technology beyond what technologists and scientists can envision or what politicians may desire. But all of that needs to be done sincerely, prudently, and with context. The way the OSTP led the social narrative of how AI was being created, it made AI appear evil, undesirable, and malevolent. No serious efforts were made to stop Big Tech from abusive policies related to AI. After all, it was Big Tech from which most of the AI ethics problems were coming. Whether it was gender or ethnic discrimination, exploitation to increase extremism, encouraging genocide in certain parts of the world, manipulation to buy products and services at higher prices, exploiting internal data to promote own merchandise at the expense of other sellers, and launching copycat AI products by copying them from smaller start-ups who shared their confidential information in hopes of partnering or getting acquired by the larger tech firms—all of these ethical violations were being done by the same firms who were in bed with the OSTP. The OSTP conferences were sponsored by the large tech firms, and in some cases executives from these large firms directly advised the OSTP. Even the semblance of propriety and independence was lost. The tech firms funded research programs in universities, where professors held private commercial interests in tech businesses, and the same universities were setting the strategy for investment in AI. The ethics and governance should have started at home first. The OSTP should have required governance and ethics from Big Tech before giving them a seat at the table.

PRESIDENT BIDEN AND AI

In July of 2019, during his election campaign, presidential candidate Joe Biden said the following in New York:

> I'll invest in research and development. The cornerstone of my presidency will be just that, so the United States is leading the charge for innovation around the world. There is no reason we should be failing or falling behind anyone, China or anyone else when it comes to energy, quantum computing, artificial intelligence, 5G, high-speed rail.
>
> Folks, we have the greatest research universities in the history of the world. We have more of them here than anywhere in the rest of the world combined. That we cannot ensure that our people are

ready for this transition that will inevitably accompany any new technology would be a disaster. We need the most agile system to accommodate these changes. (Biden 2019)

Here candidate Biden was making a commitment to invest more in emerging technologies, including AI. He points to the fearful trend of "failing or falling behind" China or anyone else. His words show that the concern had started to mount. But it also shows that President Biden, much like President H. W. Bush about the Internet or President Trump about AI, was treating AI as one of many emerging technologies, and his solution against failing or falling behind was to invest more. This implied that the only thing that was failing was the understanding that AI is not just any technology—it is the underlying force of all innovation, all economic and financial activity, all scientific discovery, and all national security. More importantly, America's falling behind and failing could not have been fixed by pouring more money into it.

Candidate Biden then quickly brought the issue of AI and 5G being tied to promote greater democracy and our shared prosperity. While it is understandable that for America this messaging had double value—on one end it showed that American AI technology is for good and will be used for good, and on the other end it created a perception of Chinese or foreign AI as evil or bad—this narrative also created a competitive differentiation for the American technology while providing a cover or an excuse for America falling behind in technology. One could now claim that the reason we are behind is because we take privacy, democracy, and human rights seriously and we do not approve of blatant solution-building using people's data for subversive purposes. This allowed the narrative of AI for good or responsible AI to flourish.

But there was a cost associated with that. Not only did it slow down the progress and make smaller companies question their solutions, but it also created a general fear of AI. The preexisting bias among the population about the killer robots got reinforced. People began thinking about AI as some type of a control device being launched by the government to control them. Hence, whatever the government was trying to accomplish by pointing out that *our AI is more ethical than their AI* did not do much—at least for the American audience. Would the Chinese believe that their AI is more evil than the American AI? Would foreign populations embracing Chinese technology believe that the Chinese AI is anti-democracy and does not deliver shared prosperity? That remains to be seen. But what we do know is that while the American AI strategy had a direct impact on Americans, it would not affect Americans to the point of them caring about the Chinese evil AI. Reminding Americans about the demerits of AI, about the risks, about the fears, about the evil potential was not helping in developing a positive or motivational perspective of the technology. Candidate Biden said:

> When it comes to technologies for the future like 5G, artificial intelligence, other nations are devoting national resources and dominating their development, determining how they will be used.
>
> We have to ensure that 21st century technologies are used to promote greater democracy, shared prosperity, not to curve freedom and opportunity either at home or abroad. As new technologies shape our economies and societies, we have to ensure that these engines of progress are bound by laws and ethics. We have done it at every technological turning point in our history. (Biden 2019)

A year later in July 2020 Mr. Biden again revisited the topic in Pennsylvania. There he promised to allocate $300 billion in his first four years to "sharpen America's competitive edge in the new industries where global leadership is up for grabs, like battery technology, artificial intelligence, biotechnology, clean energy" (Biden 2020). Clearly, Mr. Biden recognized that America was now no longer a leader in AI. His messaging from 2019 had changed. In 2019 he was merely pointing out the risk of America failing or falling behind—but by 2020 he was convinced that the global leadership was now up for grabs. America was no longer a leader.

And after getting elected, he kept that message intact. In January 14, 2021, he gave a speech in Delaware on Covid and the economy and again mentioned America making historical investments in technologies such as AI— where the leadership was "up for grabs" and repeated the "up for grabs" term in a Washington, DC, speech a week later.

In the Munich Security Conference that took place on February 19, 2021, President Biden emphasized another dimension of AI:

> We have to ensure that the benefits of growth are shared broadly and equitably, not just by a few. We have to push back against the Chinese government's economic abuses and coercion that undercut the foundations of the international economic system. Everyone—everyone—must play by the same rules. U.S. and European companies are required to publicly disclose corporate governance to corporate governance structures and abide by rules to deter corruption and monopolistic practices.

Chinese companies should be held to the same standard. We must shape the rules that will govern the advance of technology and the norms of behavior in cyberspace, artificial intelligence, biotechnology so that they are used to lift people up, not used to pin them down. We must stand up for the democratic values that make it possible for us to accomplish any of this, pushing back against those who would monopolize and normalize repression. (Biden 2021b)

President Biden's messaging about technology had now taken a China angle. Now the original narrative of good AI vs. bad AI was once again invoked but with the focus on China. The Chinese government was touted as abusers and Chinese companies as lacking governance and their technology not following behavioral norms. The problem with this narrative was that firstly behavioral norms for AI were not well defined at an international level and secondly America had no way to declare that our own AI was following the good norms. But regardless of dwelling on whose norms were good vs. bad, the most important insight was that once again the AI narrative was somehow connected with the evil AI storyline.

This mention of AI with reminding of ethics, values, and rights may have been a good strategy to create a competitive differentiation between American AI and Chinese AI, but it was stopping AI from being adopted and diffused in the population. It was a technology that came with anxiety and not fun. Imagine if at the launch of the auto industry the first introduction to cars would have come with a long list of cautionary requirements about drunk driving and its risks; it would have created social anxiety about cars.

The reality is that most of the evidence we have about AI being abused comes from our own Big Tech—and we have not been able to do anything to stop them. The Cambridge Analytica scandal did not happen in China or Russia, it affected America.

In March of 2021, President Biden held a press conference and declared that he is going to raise the research and science investment to close to 2% of the GDP vs. 0.7% because "China is out-investing us by a long shot because their plan is to own that future" (Biden 2021c). Clearly, the threat of China out-investing America was driving the Biden policy. A certain level of anxiety was evident.

In April 2021 President Biden addressed a joint session of Congress where he finally acknowledged that the competitive risk is real:

We'll see more technological change in the next 10 years than we saw in the last 50 years. That's how rapidly artificial intelligence and so much more are changing. And we're falling behind the competition with the rest of the world. (Biden 2021a)

President Biden in September 2021 made a statement related to security at AUKUS (a trilateral security pact between Australia, the UK, and the US), where Australian PM Scott Morrison and UK PM Boris Johnson were also present. At this point he was expressing the strategic deployment of AI on the defense side:

AUKUS will bring together our sailors, our scientists, and our industries to maintain and expand our edge in military capabilities and critical technologies, such as cyber, artificial intelligence, quantum technologies, and undersea domains. (Biden 2021d)

To counter China's growing footprint, President Biden was now reaching out to other partners and allies. Along the same lines, he announced at the United Nations General Assembly that America would work with its partners and that such work would ensure America's leadership in AI—and then he contrasted American technology ambitions with others who may use it to suppress dissent or target minority communities, most likely a comment directed toward China.

As new technologies continue to evolve, we'll work together with our democratic partners to ensure that new advances in areas from biotechnology, to quantum computing, 5G, artificial intelligence, and more are used to lift people up, to solve problems, and advance human freedom—not to suppress dissent or target minority communities. (Biden 2021e)

Later in the speech President Biden pointed out that he would not allow large and powerful countries to coerce smaller nations via technological exploitation.

Unlike President Clinton or VP Gore, President Biden did not seem to have a command on the technological revolution or that he wanted to understand AI in depth—but he clearly did know two things about it: first that AI will have a large impact on America's competitiveness and second that America was falling behind in it. But like his predecessors, his vision on how to fix the problem is limited by what he was told by the OSTP.

In July of 2021 President Biden had launched his version of the national AI initiative. This was now the third attempt to launch AI national initiatives by a president. The first was by President Obama in 2016. The unexpected results of the 2016 elections and its consequences implied a major reset where another attempt was made to launch a national AI strategy after what appears to be a two-year pause. That was under President Trump and where he signed the 2019 executive order. Before leaving office, President Trump augmented his February 2019 executive order by adding a layer of directives for responsible AI. After the Trump administration, President Biden launched the national strategy. The third time is the charm—but the path forward will not be easy.

But what do these "launches" and "relaunches" really mean? From an execution perspective, they meant that a website—usually composed of 5 to 10 webpages—is created, some committees are formed, the committees meet a few times, one or more reports are issued, and an associated legislation is often enacted or pushed. The committees are composed of the usual suspects—top university professors, Big Tech leaders, and government agency IT heads—all having a vested interest to make things appear better than they are. The OSTP provides the leadership for such initiatives. The committees meet and develop their own agenda—often based on their limited perception of the world or commercial interests—and then a request for information gimmick is employed to show participation and feedback from Americans. The plans are ratified based on feedback received from a handful of Big Tech firms, universities, and trade associations—all trying to push the singular agenda of "open the bank, and all problems will be solved."

The fact that year after year America is "falling behind and failing" (in President Biden's words) does not influence the overall strategy of launching committees, setting small websites, signing executive orders, wining and dining, issuing a report, and disengaging. The utter failure to create any type of industrialization strategy does not bother the participants. Professors with deep relationships with commercial interests participate without disclosing their conflicts. It appears that Big Tech participates with the sole interest of avoiding or controlling regulation and having government release more money. And agency heads participate because they must. This symbiotic relationship resides at the core of destroying America's leadership.

Along the same lines, President Biden signed an executive order and established yet another initiative that resulted in the formation of AI.gov—a critically deficient website that does nothing for anyone except talks about the most recent committees. Reports don't create strong nations, pragmatic leadership does. Making commercialized professors and tech representatives heads of these initiatives is like having fox guard the henhouse. Not only will they not know what needs to get done, they will most likely mess up and destroy even what they are trying to achieve. And that is exactly what is happening.

If you are an entrepreneur and you want to understand how you can embrace AI to enhance your business, the website doesn't guide you. If you are a food distributor, a consumer goods manufacturer, a publisher—the site gives you nothing on how to embrace AI. There is nothing that helps the country become AI industrialized. All these websites offer is a lot of mumbo-jumbo about why America should just throw in more money in research and about the fearmongering side of AI ethics, values, and governance. This would lead critics of the OSTP, like us, to believe that the fearmongering is being used as a tool to control the narrative from AI truly becoming democratized and from technology becoming socially absorbed in America. That would shatter the existing power structure, which is based on wealth concentration and Big Tech power.

THE IMPORTANCE OF EXECUTIVE LEADERSHIP

At this juncture, when AI is emerging as the most important force in the world, the executive leadership is even more important. Run-of-the-mill solutions and lip service are not enough.

Unlike the vision setting undertaken by Al Gore and Bill Clinton—both presidents Trump and Biden simply became the puppet of signing what was placed in front of them. What was being ignored were the American interests. The private sector had no representation at the table. Average Joe or Jane had no participation in the plan. The AI machine was working in the back—supporting the agenda and power concentration of a few at the cost of the country's combined future. A new rust belt was being created, and this time it would spread from the East Coast to the West Coast—with $1000 guaranteed monthly income being proposed for the masses—sufficient to cover their social media costs. What else would a person need!

The lack of leadership trickled down at different levels in the nation. From agencies to companies, AI adoption became a tactical and poorly administered project-by-project pursuit. That is why when asked about AI, Secretary of Defense Lloyd Austin gave a count of projects being pursued in the Pentagon. Those 600 projects would have included simple AI projects, such as reading forms and robotic process automation bots uploading data. They would have included chatbots or simple automation projects that will have no impact on America's leadership or industrialization potential. Those 600 projects would have been implemented with no associated data or sensor strategy. So much so that it is likely that in the DoD RFPs, acquisition specialists would not even know how to source machine learning projects.

As the situation became dire in America, the nation needed more leadership and not less. There was a greater need to pierce through the complexities, understand the existential threat, and develop an appreciation for what the AI revolution meant for America. But America remained oblivious to all that.

 ## A DIFFERENT AMERICA

Many would argue that Clinton/Gore got handed over an America that had already won the Cold War and that could now focus on itself. In fact, President H. W. Bush reminded Americans about that in his State of the Union address. Defeating the Soviet Union meant that America could focus on itself. Thus, it is fair to say that Clinton/Gore got the chance to build the American economy during a rare and opportune time when America stood victorious and jubilant. The 1990 Iraq War also left America proud and confident. The social noise was low. The force was working in America's favor.

Fast-forward to 2016, and we find an America that was tired and sick of never-ending wars. In Secretary Raimondo's words, ". . . economic woes also lead to extremism" (Raimondo 2021). Not only can such economic woes lead to extremism, but such frustrations can also be exploited by the opportunistic insiders and the adversarial outsiders.

But 2016 was a different year. AI, the most powerful technology ever created by humans, did not make it to the presidential debate. Instead, the size of the penises of the presidential candidates became an important issue. The lack of civility was mind-boggling. Major scandals had already increased Americans' mistrust in their government. With sexual misconduct of members of Congress and military generals to their active links with foreign countries, America seemed no longer in control. Infighting and bitterness were high. The Great Recession had devastated families, and millions were left behind. Two wars had taken their toll, and American attention was divided. Numerous social battles were raging—all enhanced and exploited by social media. Homes, offices, and businesses had become the battlegrounds. As if this were not enough, Covid landed in the midst of all that.

Clearly, Clinton/Gore got a nation that was far more at peace with itself, elated from a victorious hot war and the Cold War against the Soviet Union. That nation was receptive to change. But when Trump and Biden assumed presidencies, the nation's social psychological state was at a different level. Inspiring a nation to achieve greatness in AI would have taken a lot more than a mere mention in the State of the Union address. But the sad truth is that no attempt was made to even do that. It was as if the American leadership had accepted mediocrity at the strategic level.

When corruption becomes rampant in a country, the national will to achieve greatness diminishes. American will was broken, and the buck stops at the executive leadership at the helm.

 REFERENCES

Biden, Joe. 2019. "Biden, July 11, 2019." [Online]. Available at: https://factba. se/biden/transcript/joe-biden-speech-new-york-new-york-july-11-2019.

Biden, Joe. 2020. "Biden, July 2020." [Online]. Available at: https://factba.se/ biden/transcript/joe-biden-speech-dumore-pennsylvania-july-9-2020.

Biden, Joe. 2021a. "Biden, April 2021." [Online]. Available at: https://factba. se/biden/transcript/joe-biden-speech-joint-session-congress-april-28-2021.

Biden, Joe. 2021b. "Biden, Feb 2021." [Online]. Available at: https://factba. se/biden/transcript/joe-biden-remarks-munich-security-conference-video-february-19-2021.

Biden, Joe. 2021c. "Biden, March 2021." [Online]. Available at: https:// factba.se/biden/transcript/joe-biden-press-conference-white-house-march-25-2021.

Biden, Joe. 2021d. "Biden, Sept 2021." [Online]. Available at: https://factba.se/ biden/transcript/joe-biden-remarks-nuclear-submarines-australia-united-kingdom-september-16-2021.

Biden, Joe. 2021e. "Biden, Sept 2021, UN. Biden White House." [Online]. Available at: https://factba.se/biden/transcript/joe-biden-speech-united-nations-general-assembly-september-21-2021.

Bush, George H. W. 1992. "President Bush Address." [Online]. Available at: https://www.nytimes.com/1992/01/29/us/state-union-transcript-president-bush-s-address-state-union.html.

Gore, Al. 1994. "Information Superhighways Speech." [Online]. Available at: http://vlib.iue.it/history/internet/algorespeech.html.

OSTP. 2018. "Summary of the 2018 White House Summit on Artificial Intelligence for American Industry." [Online]. Available at: https:// trumpwhitehouse.archives.gov/wp-content/uploads/2018/05/Summary-Report-of-White-House-AI-Summit.pdf?latest.

Raimondo, Gina. 2021. "Strengthening America's Economy." [Online]. Available at: https://www.youtube.com/watch?v=pUgzXLEoJsQ&t=300s.

Trump, Donald. 2019. "Executive Order on AI." [Online]. Available at: https:// trumpwhitehouse.archives.gov/ai/.

White House. 2016. "Preparing for the Future of Artificial Intelligence." [Online]. Available at: https://obamawhitehouse.archives.gov/sites/default/ files/whitehouse_files/microsites/ostp/NSTC/preparing_for_the_future_ of_ai.pdf.

Wiki. n.d. "Information Superhighway." [Online]. Available at: https:// en.wikipedia.org/wiki/Information_superhighway#:~:text=The McGraw-Hill Computer Desktop,regardless of their income level.

Zilber, Ariel. 2020. "'Maybe I Should Have Been a Doctor': Trump Brags about His 'Natural Ability' for Science Because of His 'Super Genius Uncle' Who Was an MIT Professor and Claims CDC Officials Ask Him How He Knows So Much about the Coronavirus." Dailymail.com. March 6, 2020. [Online]. Available at: https://www.dailymail.co.uk/news/article-8084629/Trump-brags-science-knowledge-super-genius-uncle-MIT-professor.html.

CHAPTER FIVE

The Great Deception of the 2016 RFI

I N AUGUST OF 2018, the Trump administration directed the Select Committee on AI to refresh the previously developed 2016 National AI R&D Strategic Plan. A Request for Information (RFI) was issued to solicit public input. The result was the identification of eight strategic priorities—of which seven were the continuation of the 2016 plan. The overwhelming anchoring of the plan in the 2016 plan (seven out of eight strategies) shows that today's American AI plan is essentially the 2016 plan—which was developed during the Obama administration.

Apparently OSTP was not just pushing President Trump to support its agenda, it was also making sure that President Trump did not find out the AI-related activities led by his predecessor. Without that important information, President Trump can have many "first-ever" statements about his AI accomplishments. For example, the OSTP February 2020 report titled "American Artificial Intelligence Initiative: Year One Annual Report," says the following about President Trump being the first:

> President Trump made history when he became the first president to name artificial intelligence as an Administration R&D priority in 2017—and since then, America has never looked back. (Trump 2020)

However, the same office in 2016, stated the following about the Obama White House:

> On May 3, 2016, the White House announced a series of actions to spur public dialogue on AI, to identify challenge and opportunities related to this emerging technology, to aid in the use of AI for more effective government, and prepare for the potential benefit and risks of AI. As part of these actions, the White House directed the creation of a national strategy for research and development in artificial intelligence.

> This resulting AI R&D Strategic Plan defines a high-level framework that can be used to identify scientific and technological needs in AI, and to track the progress and maximize the impact of R&D investments to fill those needs. It also establishes priorities for Federally-funded R&D in AI, looking beyond near-term AI capabilities toward long-term transformational impacts of AI on society and the world. (Obama 2016a)

Based on the above, to claim that President Trump was the first president to "name artificial intelligence as an administration R&D priority in 2017" is a stretch of the truth. If the sentence implied that he was first president to do so in the year 2017, since both he and Obama were presidents that year, that is also somewhat misleading.

In fact, AI planning under the Obama administration seemed to have followed a more logical and evolutionary path than under the Trump administration. The Obama administration also looked into the economic aspects of AI and issued a separate report on that. The progression from big data to AI was a natural evolution, and it was important because it kept the focus on the important link between data and AI.

The 2016 plan became the foundation over which all future plans were developed. It is therefore worth it to determine the process that led to the formulation of the 2016 plan. This implies that it will be good idea to begin our analysis with the 2016 plan.

 ## THE OBAMA-ERA AI

President Obama's administration had already began preparing for AI. The administration published a report on big data and then took a systematic approach and started developing the AI plan. At least four conferences were organized to talk about AI. These included:

- May 24, 2016: "Legal and Governance Implications of Artificial Intelligence," in Seattle, Washington;
- June 7, 2016: "Artificial Intelligence for Social Good," in Washington, DC;
- June 28, 2016: "Safety and Control for Artificial Intelligence," in Pittsburgh, Pennsylvania;
- July 7, 2016: "The Social and Economic Implications of Artificial Intelligence Technologies in the Near Term," in New York City.

Then the Obama administration issued a report on big data, which was followed by the report on AI. This shows that AI had become a national priority in 2016 under the Obama administration—however, as the above titles of the conferences demonstrate, a large focus of AI-related narratives stayed on governance, safety, control, and social good. AI was being introduced to America from the prism of caution.

 ## THE PROCESS FOR FORMULATING THE 2016 PLAN

In an 2018 article by Lynne Parker, the director of the National AI Initiative, she describes the process of how the 2016 plan was created and to whom it was directed (Parker 2018). While American companies were investing a lot of money in consumer-centered AI and for short-term profitability, the plan was created to invest in building the long-term capabilities. The audience for the plan was US policymakers and federal funding agencies. The plan did not issue specific guidelines about funding programs for individual agencies and only gave a high-level perspective on high-priority funding areas. The plan was developed by the AI Task Force, which was a US interagency working group tasked by the Subcommittee on Networking and Information Technology Research and Development (NITRD). NITRD has representation of 20 agencies and coordinates funding for networking and information technology across the agencies. The process deployed to develop the plan was based on four steps. In step 1, the national priorities were analyzed and determined by doing a thought experiment on what the future with AI will look like and then linking it back to the Declaration of Independence. This was a vision exercise to paint a picture of the ideal future world with AI. In step 2, open areas of research were identified by understanding the research needs that were purely basic research–based, a mix of applied and basic, and applied only. In step 3, an RFI was used to solicit feedback. In step 4, the specific R&D priorities were determined, about which Lynne Parker writes:

> One additional point about the content of the plan is important to understand. Because R&D in AI primarily occurs within the discipline of information technology, the charge for the creation of the plan was directed to NITRD. Due to the fact that NITRD oversees (specifically) IT-related R&D coordination across the federal government, the content of the plan is exclusively focused on open IT-relevant issues for AI. Of course, the Artificial Intelligence Task Force recognized that AI benefits from a variety of perspectives across many other disciplines, including neuroscience, psychology, social and behavioral sciences, ethics, law, economics, as well as expertise from across the broad spectrum of application domains, including agriculture, transportation, and so forth. Research and development in these other domains is not included in the strategic plan, however, due to the IT-centric tasking of the task force. Nevertheless, a focus on IT-relevant issues still provides a useful foundation for considering priorities in AI R&D investments, and their potential benefits across a wide range of application domains. (Parker 2018)

Anyone with even a little strategy development background can see the dramatic mistakes being made in both the design and the development process of the plan. The plan was based on some pie-in-the-sky Hollywood sci-fi type of story of what the future of America would look like with AI, and then issuing an emotional, virtue-signaling call to tie that vision back to the Declaration of Independence as if the AI's terminator robots were ready to take over America. This exceedingly naïve vision of the future is then somehow used to determine the R&D priorities based on the overly simplistic allocation based on applied vs. basic vs. applied/basic research, and after doing all that, declaring, *Oh well, the plan is only about IT-related R&D.* So much for developing a strategic plan!

Note that the industrial needs, broad national priorities, competitive advantage and comparative advantages of the nation, industrialization maps, constraints, the state of the US government's current technology, change management, the narrative about inspiring and mobilizing American people, and hundreds of other such factors were not considered. Even if the plan was meant to be only for the government IT R&D, it was grossly deficient in terms of how strategies are developed. To call something like this a national strategy would be analogous to calling a calculator a supercomputer. More care and analysis go into developing a plan for opening a corner bakery than what went into developing what would eventually become the national strategy of AI for the United States of America—and then we wonder why China is leaving us behind. The most dangerous development that happened later was that somehow this plan eventually became the face of the national strategy and then shaped the American AI Initiative and continues to influence national strategies. This plan, which was grossly inadequate and did not follow any strategic process for development, would drive America's AI policy, legislative activity, funding, and presidential executive orders for the years to come. It would become the anchor on which all the future plans will be architected. America had just made its worst mistake. Every subsequent activity would now be based on the anchoring bias.

In 2016, the OSTP had already developed a general framework on what it wanted to do. The RFI is a mechanism used by the government to solicit feedback and guidance from various stakeholders. Unlike the serious feedback process undertaken by FDA or CMS to approve drugs or to evaluate their efficacy and reimbursement, the White House process to solicit the feedback was largely flawed and hugely biased (we will show that in our discussion below). It was a feel-good mechanism, a mere formality, which is typically used to ratify your own initial assumptions and ignore any dissent or criticism.

We do not believe that either any serious thought went behind analyzing the feedback or a sincere effort was made to at least bring in a large group of stakeholders to develop a strategy for the most important and critical strategy ever developed in the history of the nation.

The future of AI in America was to be built on RFP responses that the OSTP never really analyzed or most likely even read (as we will show below).

 ## THE RFI GIMMICK

To develop a policy response to the concerns about the benefits and risks of artificial intelligence technology, the Office of Science and Technology (OSTP) took a series of steps. These steps included organizing conferences and issuing a Request for Information (RFI) to obtain public opinion. The RFI stated:

> Like any transformative technology, however, AI carries risks and presents complex policy challenges along a number of different fronts. The Office of Science and Technology Policy (OSTP) is interested in developing a view of AI across all sectors for the purpose of

recommending directions for research and determining challenges and opportunities in this field. The views of the American people, including stakeholders such as consumers, academic and industry researchers, private companies, and charitable foundations, are important to inform an understanding of current and future needs for AI in diverse fields. (Obama 2016b; Obama 2016c).

The OSTP claimed that "many intellectuals, organizations, and academics had voiced concerns about the emergence of artificial intelligence technology and its impact on the social, economic, and political processes of human life." The following questions were posed in the RFI:

OSTP is particularly interested in responses related to the following topics: (1) The legal and governance implications of AI; (2) the use of AI for public good; (3) the safety and control issues for AI; (4) the social and economic implications of AI; (5) the most pressing, fundamental questions in AI research, common to most or all scientific fields; (6) the most important research gaps in AI that must be addressed to advance this field and benefit the public; (7) the scientific and technical training that will be needed to take advantage of harnessing the potential of AI technology, and the challenges faced by institutions of higher education in retaining faculty and responding to explosive growth in student enrollment in AI-related courses and courses of study; (8) the specific steps that could be taken by the federal government, research institutes, universities, and philanthropies to encourage multi-disciplinary AI research; (9) specific training data sets that can accelerate the development of AI and its application; (10) the role that "market shaping" approaches such as incentive prizes and Advanced Market Commitments can play in accelerating the development of applications of AI to address societal needs, such as accelerated training for low and moderate income workers (see https://www.usaid.gov/ cii/ market-shaping-primer); and (11) any additional information related to AI research or policymaking, not requested above, that you believe OSTP should consider. (Obama 2016c)

Even a cursory look at the above questions shows that the OSTP was least concerned about the industrialization of AI. The overwhelming focus was on governance, control, safety, public good, and so forth. It is rather strange that before even considering the diffusion, adoption, development, and industrialization potential of the technology, the strategic focus was being placed on risks and threats. As if the technology would somehow acquire a mind of its own and rise out of a computer and take over America, the fanatical adherence to safety and control were being pushed and projected as the primary concerns. This is not to discount the attention one must pay to ethical and governance issues of AI but only to point out that the public perception was being controlled with the negative dimensions of the technology vs. all the positive benefits. The reason for doing that was simple: Americans already carried the Hollywood-induced fear of the killer robots and the people formulating the AI agenda knew they could tap into that fear to appear as the saviors of humanity against the terminator. Their actions show that these heroes and so-called protagonists carried no sincere desire to truly solve the governance and ethics problems. But in their wisdom, this was the easiest way to engage people in the AI debate.

Secondly, one can observe that the questions mostly pertained to the supply side of AI—as if the demand side of the technology would somehow automatically appear through magic. When a strategy is based solely on the supply side, it will lack any link to the demand side and hence will not be able to either shape or respond to the demand side. The OSTP was not concerned about the demand side of AI. They couldn't care less about how the technology would be applied, who would use it, how it would be used, what are the national needs, which industries would use it first, and which industries needed to be informed or guided. All they cared about was how to build an AI field of dreams that was oblivious to the demand conditions.

After capturing the responses from the RFI, the White House issued its report in October 2016. As previously stated, this 2016 plan is the plan that would determine America's future, competitiveness, economic potential, political stability, social performance, and everything else that makes and gives nations their competitive edge. One would think that such a plan would have been designed and developed with the highest level of care, utmost responsibility, uncompromising meticulousness, and integrity. To determine whether such a process was put in place, we analyzed all the responses to the RFI and the plan itself.

 ## RFI COMMENTS

We analyzed all the RFI comments received in the public domain. Then we analyzed the report issued by the OSTP. Specifically, we wanted to determine the following:

- Who responded to the RFI? Who didn't respond?
- What does the composition of respondents tell us about their state of affairs?

- Were the responses sufficient to truly formulate and propose a strategy and policy position?
- Were the perspectives, viewpoints, and concerns of the respondents taken into account when developing the report?
- What were the key themes that emerged?
- Was there a conflict of interest, and did the government go far enough to ensure that the viewpoints were balanced and any conflict of interest was properly disclosed?
- Did the comments represent inherent bias of entities, and was that bias reflected in the responses?

 WHO RESPONDED?

Assuming that the RFI captured the requisite questions to achieve the goal of developing a broader perspective, our first task was to synthesize the data.

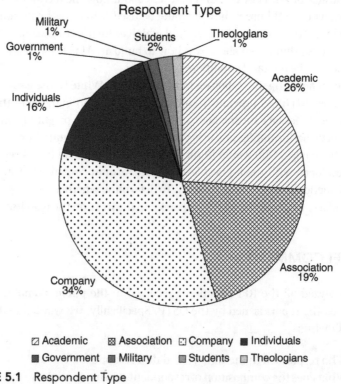

FIGURE 5.1   Respondent Type

While the OSTP reported that it received 161 responses in the final report, when we cleaned up the data, we found that there were 11 duplicates, or the same person doing two or more successive comments, and when we removed them, we were left with 150 comments. So while 161 entries were made, in reality only 150 comments were received. The fact that OSTP never knew that there were several duplicates shows that no one bothered to even read the responses.

Within the 150 comments, we segmented them into academic, companies, associations and nonprofits, students, military, US government, and individuals (Figure 5.1). The largest number of comments (34%) were received from companies, 26% from universities, 19% from associations (including nonprofits, and non-university affiliated institutions), 16% from individuals, 1% from military, 2% from students, 1% from theologians, and 1% from government.

We estimated that 8 comments were from Europe, 1 from Australia, and 1 from Asia, while 140 were from the United States (Figure 5.2).

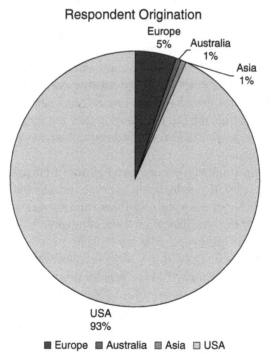

Respondent Origination

■ Europe　■ Australia　▨ Asia　☐ USA

FIGURE 5.2　Respondent Origination

Clearly, the fact that only 150 responses (with only 140 from the US) formed the basis for the most significant and powerful strategic revolution in the history of humankind shows that the OSTP was not really concerned about receiving any real data. They wanted to throw out something—without developing any deeper analysis or getting feedback from a large segment of society. It was more of a formality than a sincere effort to extract strategic help. It is likely that most people did not even know that an RFI was out.

 ## HOW MANY QUESTIONS WERE ANSWERED?

Since OSTP claims that it received significant feedback and based the national strategy on the feedback, it is important to see what type of feedback OSTP really received. The reason it is important to understand this data is to determine whether the comments actually captured the depth and breadth of the information request and whether the information received truly represents the social concerns and positions of the American population.

The White House posed 11 questions in the RFI, and roughly 55% of the respondents specifically referred to the questions while 45% simply left general comments without clearly referencing the questions. In question 11, the RFI did allow respondents to leave general comments so the free responses (FR) can be viewed as a response to question 11. For our purposes, however, we have classified such responses as a separate category since the RFI did specify that respondents should refer to the question they are responding to, and if a response was obtained that didn't refer to any question, we classified that in the free response category.

This shows that only a little more than half wanted to talk about what was being asked in the RFI. If you are doing a survey and only half of your respondents want to talk about what you asked them and the rest want to raise other issues, you must at least consider what those issues are.

The frequency of input received is shown in Figure 5.3. Free responses (68) were followed by "Public Good" (46), which was followed by "Safety/Control issues" (43), "Economic Impact" (42), "Legal & Governance" (40), "Research Gaps" (36), "Pressing Questions" (32), "Training Needs" (27), "Steps to Encourage Research" (26), "Training Datasets" (24), "Additional Input" (11), and "Market Shaping" (8). Even at this level, the least amount of information obtained was on market shaping. The market shaping question was important. It was about "accelerating the development of applications of AI to address societal needs, such as accelerated training for low- and moderate-income

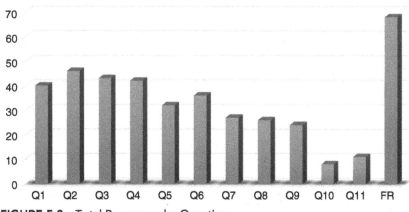

FIGURE 5.3   Total Responses by Question

workers," and it received the least input. Clearly, no one seemed to be concerned about low- and moderate-income workers. The eyes of the respondents were on the only thing they cared about: more funding.

The frequency measures the number of responses for each question from each representation category. This provides a perspective on whether the sample set is significant enough for the government to make an informed decision. Additionally, it determines whether enough information was collected for each topic. For example, academics, whose job is to educate and train people, were least interested in answering question 10, which referred to ideas about "accelerated training for low- and moderate-income workers" (Figure 5.4). Only one school, University of Memphis, addressed that question. This showed that all that the universities cared about was to get more money into their research and had absolutely no regard for national performance or to worry about training low- and moderate-income workers. This should have created a concern for the OSTP. The job of OSTP is not to wine and dine and attend Big Tech–sponsored conferences in luxury hotels. It is to serve the American people and to advise the president. Based on the above, the OSTP should have concluded that only a tiny fraction of the limited number of stakeholders who have responded show any concern for training "low- and moderate-income workers." This was a red flag.

Besides free responses, research gaps was the most popular topic among academic researchers, followed by safety/control and legal/governance.

Companies focused on safety/control issues, followed by social good/benefits, economic impact, and then governance issues.

Associations mostly focused on social good and governance issues.

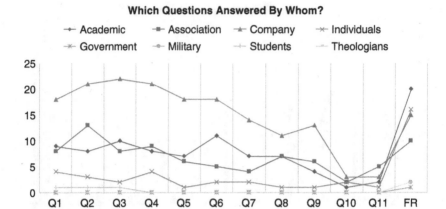

FIGURE 5.4 How Did Respondents Answer Questions?

 FREQUENCY OF QUESTIONS ANSWERED

This section shows how many respondents answered only one question, only two questions, and so on. This is a "coverage" measure and shows the comprehensiveness of the discussion that took place. While it is understandable that certain specialists (for example, a law firm commenting on the legal/governance issue) would comment only on their area of expertise, it is reasonable to expect that universities, associations, and companies would provide more comprehensive and broad coverage in their comments: universities because they are multidisciplinary, companies because business strategies are typically based on multidimensional research, and associations because they typically represent a broad member base and hence have the ability and the responsibility to collect multidimensional information.

Twenty respondents answered only one question, 12 answered two questions, 13 answered only three questions, while only 3 answered all of the 11 questions (Figure 5.5). Surprisingly, while 39 universities and university-based institutions participated, only one university (University of Memphis) answered all 11 questions (Figure 5.6).

Besides the universities, IBM and West Desert Enterprises were the two other respondents who answered all RFI questions. Only 22 respondents out of 150 answered more than five questions.

Clearly most universities chose to either not respond to any question or focus on a small number of questions.

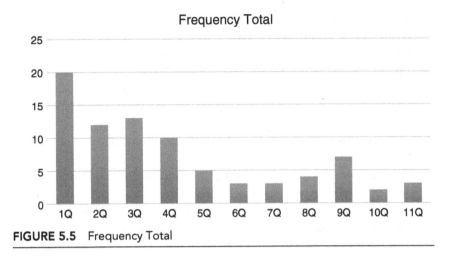

FIGURE 5.5 Frequency Total

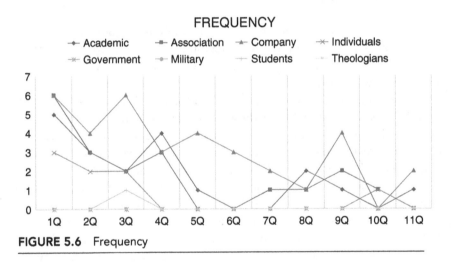

FIGURE 5.6 Frequency

 ## ACADEMIC INSTITUTIONS

- Universities submitted 39 replies.
- Future of Life Institute made three entries, and two of them were duplicates. MIT made three entries.
- George Mason University made two entries. Multiple researchers made entries from Johns Hopkins. University of Virginia also included an entry reference to another source.

- There were 19 comments that specifically referred to the questions in the RFI, and 20 came in the form of free responses.
- In total comments, 7 academic respondents attempted to market or sell their services, books, consulting services, or reports.
- Only one comment specifically disclosed a potential conflict of interest, but that was also done not as a means of disclosure but rather to show their credentials.
- Only one university, University of Memphis, provided comprehensive answer to every question.
- It is important to identity that many universities and some of the top programs were missing. Of the 18 top artificial intelligence programs in the United States, only one-third participated and two-thirds did not.
- Of the top 100 programs in the world, only 20% participated.
- Of the ones who did participate, only five universities responded to more than four questions.

American universities and research centers form the foundation of our nation's development and progress. Obtaining deep and thorough feedback from the universities should have been the top priority. But what happened was extremely disappointing. Of the nearly 4000 universities and colleges in the US (although *US News* included only 1452 schools in the 2021 rankings) only 39 responded to the RFI. Of those who responded, only one—University of Memphis—provided answers to all questions. So much for the feedback.

If OSTP really wanted to get real feedback, it should have gone to all schools. It should have knocked on the doors of community colleges and mid-tier universities and not just the elite schools. If the goal was to build the American AI capability, a college from a small town, a university from a rural area, a social sciences school, all should have been included in the planning process. But the OSTP was not designed that way. It was designed to be a representative of top schools who received large funds from companies and of professors who were engaged in building software companies to be sold to Big Tech. National interest or national strategy were not placed in the forefront.

It became obvious that in general the responses came from university computer science departments, and other departments were either not included or didn't respond. Thus, even though the goal of the RFI was to get information on social, economic, and governance/regulatory matters in addition to the technical matters, a vast majority of universities chose to focus only on the aspects of funding.

Unsurprisingly, to a large extent the questions of the RFI focused on governance, safety, control, and regulation, and the responses also concentrated on those aspects with an angle of funding. As if America was digging a dormant nuclear facility in the middle of a thriving city, the overly cautious tone belied the real intention: get more money. It would be analogous to launching the auto industry with a narrative based on the perils of drunk driving instead of making the automobiles, roads, infrastructure, economic impact of automobiles, understanding how manufacturing and distribution would change, how retail would develop with automobiles, how service industry would develop, and how people would travel and commute. What if the first question asked by the auto industry was about the ramifications of drunk driving?

George Mason University and Hunter College CUNY took the position of minimizing regulatory oversight and governance. Both strongly argued against any type of oversight, governance, and regulation unless clear evidence of harm exists.

A comment from the MIT Minsky Institute said, "Myself and a group met with Marvin Minsky at his house on 111 Ivy Street, Brookline, Mass., one night a week last fall. . . . We discussed what a 'Minsky Institute' might consist of and what its mission statement might be. Unfortunately, Marvin passed away before anything fully converged." Mr. Greenblatt offered to serve the Minsky Group as a central clearinghouse. Despite the response being irrelevant and nonsensical, it was MIT that later gained the central position in helping OSTP shape the strategy. Three years later when the czars of OSTP appeared in conferences, they were escorted by an MIT professor. This shows that the RFI feedback was either ignored or not even considered as the criteria to select advisors. In another comment from MIT, Mr. Lieberman said that the warnings are "overblown"; however, he acknowledged the need for safety research. The third comment from MIT (Brains, Mind, and Machines) didn't refer to the governance issue at all; however, it requested a major funding program by the federal government.

Nick Bostrom from the University of Oxford and author of the 2014 book *Superintelligence: Paths, Dangers, Strategies* (a book recommended by Bill Gates and Elon Musk—both heavily invested in AI) chose not to respond to the governance question directly; however, while addressing responses to question 3 and 6, he did touch on the governance issue. He wrote, "We believe that regulation of AI due to these concerns would be extremely premature and undesirable. Current AI systems are not nearly powerful enough to pose a threat to society on such a scale, and may not be for decades to come." In other words, on one hand he was increasing global anxiety about the dangers of AI while on the other hand, he was calling regulations premature and undesirable. He did offer the services of his group to be involved in the process, however.

On the governance issues, many universities did offer balanced and neutral analysis, and some provided several valuable ideas. Our analysis showed that the following institutions provided a balanced and valuable perspective on governance/regulation issues: Santa Clara University, Florida International University, University of Memphis, Hinckley Institute of Politics, Stanford University, University of Wisconsin, HKUST, University of Virginia, Texas A&M University, University of Michigan, University of Wisconsin–Madison, Washington State University, Brown University, University of Cambridge, University of Maryland, and UC Berkeley School of Information.

 ## COMPANIES

Of the nearly 10 million active companies in the United States, we estimate that only 50 companies responded to the survey.

Four of the submissions were from Alphabet/Google-related companies including Google, DeepMind, and Moonshot. Of the tech giants, Google, IBM, Facebook, and Microsoft participated while Amazon and Apple didn't (at least not directly). Oracle made an irrelevant comment. Nvidia made two comments.

Many other large software companies, such as SAS and Salesforce, did not comment.

Note: It is possible that software companies were represented by associations and hence decided not to comment directly. Although, we find it hard to believe that associations could have been able to collect, analyze, and synthesize data back from feedback from all of their member firms.

In the answers provided by large companies, we found Microsoft's comments to be balanced and looking at both sides of problems. Google-affiliated firms mostly addressed their capabilities and benefits. IBM answered all the questions. Facebook also focused more on its own capabilities and research.

In addressing the governance and regulation question, Skymind focused on the use of artificial intelligence to improve corporate governance vs. governance and regulation of AI technology.

Not only were dozens of sectors and potentially thousands of companies missing and not represented, but those who did answer the RFI provided little strategic insights. As with the academic institutions, the underlying message from companies was also, "Give us more money." Factors such as industrialization of AI were not considered. The term "AI industrialization" means adoption of AI in business and industry such that companies, industries, sectors, and government agencies are built around AI. Whether it is the automobile sector or the power sector, consumer goods or pharmaceutical, defense agencies or civilian, AI industrialization implies transforming the business models, operations, and products and services to make them compatible with AI.

Companies, particularly large companies, have powerful strategy departments. The questions asked by the RFI should have been covered by the strategy departments. But again, America was not involved in the OSTP so-called strategy development process—only a handful of tech firms (the sponsors of conferences) and professors (the seekers of research funding) were involved. This should be another red flag for the OSTP. Why were P&G, Kraft, Goldman Sachs, or Walmart not offering recommendations? Clearly, either they did not know about this or if they did, they did not find commenting on the initiative would make any difference. It was the OSTP responsibility to reach out to these firms and to get them to participate.

ASSOCIATIONS AND NONPROFITS

- Twenty-nine associations (nonprofits, trade, scientific, etc.) provided responses.
- Eight associations specifically addressed question 1, while five others touched on the issue in their comments.
- Of the ones that responded or commented on the governance/regulation issue, seven took the position that there should be no regulation/governance, six asked for light governance/regulation, and none asked for strong governance and regulation.
- The seven associations that took the same position as George Mason University and Hunter College CUNY (no regulation) represented trade interests of the technology sector. Several clearly disclosed that position. It is not clear to us whether the feedback provided by associations was vetted by their members before being submitted.

The anti-governance and anti-regulation sentiment is not surprising. Many of the associations are trade associations and serve the role of promoting the interests of their members.

Some of the associations that favored least or no governance and regulation include the US Chamber of Commerce, SIIA Software & Information

Industry Association, The Niskanen Center, The Internet Association, and Computing Community Consortium.

For example, the US Chamber of Commerce responded (Obama 2016b, p. 153):

> With these and many other questions in mind, companies like Google have established AI ethics boards, which go beyond legal compliance to examine the deeper implications and potential complications of emerging AI technologies. Regulatory questions also arise with the rise of any transformational technology. The misconceptions around AI increase the likelihood of reckless regulatory decisions. It is vital to recognize that AI is well covered by existing laws and regulators with respect to privacy, security, safety, and ethics. Placing additional undue burdens would suppress the ability for this technology to continue growing. The policy questions that AI and machine learning raise are not so radically different than questions raised by technology that has preceded it. It is important to remember that artificial intelligence is still nascent, and it would be a mistake to attempt to address the issue with broad, overarching regulation.

The reference to Google's ethics board is interesting, as the company has been unable to keep an ethics board intact.

Software & Information Industry Association (SIIA) commented:

> Automation has historically produced long-term growth and full employment. But the next generation of really smart AI-based machines could create sustained technological unemployment. Two Oxford economists estimated that 47% of occupations are susceptible to automation. An OECD study found that "9% of jobs are automatable."

> The Council of Economic Advisors (CEA) recently warned that AI could exacerbate wage inequality, estimating that 83% of jobs making less than $20 per hour would come under pressure from automation, as compared to only 4% of jobs making above $40 per hour. The CEA also documented a long-term decline in prime-age male labor force participation—from 97% in 1954 to 88% today—that could be exacerbated by AI.

> Despite these concerns, there is no real evidence that the ultimate impact of AI on the labor market will be any different from that of

earlier productivity-enhancing technologies. Studies have shown that labor market developments that some are blaming on computer technology and the Internet—like job polarization—have been a feature of the US economy since the 1950s. (Obama 2016b, p. 180)

The beauty of the above comment was that after providing significant empirical information in the first two paragraphs about the AI impact on labor market, the Association argues that "there is no real evidence" in the third paragraph of the excerpt above.

The Niskanen Center, a DC-based think tank, commented:

Some find the flowering of the technology alarming, and wonder aloud whether AI may lead to a Terminator-style future in which incomprehensibly intelligent computers destroy human civilization. Even moderate critics of AI warn that we now stand on the verge of a mass labor dislocation in which up to half of all jobs may be taken by machines. For now, however, these worries are extremely speculative, and the alarm they cause can be counterproductive.

In order to maximize the benefits associated with ongoing developments in AI, we recommend that policymakers and regulators:

1. Avoid speaking of hyperbolic hypothetical doomsday scenarios, and
2. Embrace a policy of regulatory restraint, intervening in the development and use of AI technology only when and if the prospect of harm becomes realistic enough to merit government intervention. (Obama 2016b, p. 183)

The Internet Association, which represented 40 of the world's leading organizations, commented and argued that existing policy frameworks can adapt to AI—a position that was proven incorrect based on the plethora of policy frameworks developed later on in America:

Before delving into policy specifics, the IA submits that it is advisable for policymakers to draw parameters around what artificial intelligence is and is not since this is an open debate that may trigger fearful policy responses where they are not needed. (Obama 2016b, p. 192)

Openeth.org talked about the products it is developing. The Leadership Council on Civil and Human Rights, ACM Special Interest Group on AI, the Center for Data Innovation, the Global Information Infrastructure Commission, the Application Development Alliance, and the Machine Intelligence Research Institute also touched directly or indirectly on the light governance issue. A comment claiming to represent truckers in America talked about the impact of AI on truckers and raised concerns about the economic well-being of the drivers. MITRE focused on the topic of safety and control and proposed to use its risk evaluation model.

The feedback from the associations should have been analyzed from many perspectives: first, which associations and scientific societies were participating and which were not and why not; second, what part of their feedback truly represents national interests vs. only being lobbyists for their members' causes; and third, why no association answered all questions and most only responded to questions about governance and regulation.

THE MIRACULOUS REPORT

One would assume the after receiving such a low, largely irrelevant, and mostly self-centered "just open up the bank" responses, the OSTP would have gone back to the design board and figured out how to truly engage and receive qualitatively and quantitatively relevant and actionable information, but that did not happen. The OSTP did not even consider the recommendations or the gaps that were pointed out in the 150 responses. Most likely they did not even read the responses, since—as already explained—the OSTP would have known there were 150 and not 161 responses. Once again, let us consider the following:

1. Out of 10 million American firms, only about 50 participated directly. Sectors other than the tech sector were mostly not represented. There were only a handful of Fortune 500 and, again, only a few tech firms.
2. Even most of the associations represented only the tech sector. There was little or no representation for other sectors.
3. Only 39 universities participated. The majority of American universities and schools did not respond.
4. Only two companies and one university responded to all questions.
5. Most common response was to increase funding (open the bank)—which is a completely expected answer from university research departments or from the tech firms whose tech investments can be subsidized by the government.

Clearly, what was lacking were the industrialization, diffusion, AI demand development, AI adoption, and AI communication—the factors that drive true national passion and energy to do great things. The OSTP plan was really a few professors and government employees—all apparently directed by or representing the Big Tech agenda—reaching to the conclusion that more money needs to be thrown into the AI pit. That was the extent of the plan. And this narrow thinking was going to cost America its leadership in AI.

 REFERENCES

Obama, Barack. 2016a. "Obama White House." [Online]. Available at: https://obamawhitehouse.archives.gov/sites/default/files/whitehouse_files/micro sites/ostp/NSTC/national_ai_rd_strategic_plan.pdf.

Obama, Barack. 2016b. "Obama RFI." [Online]. Available at: https://cra.org/ccc/wp-content/uploads/sites/2/2016/04/OSTP-AI-RFI-Responses.pdf.

Obama, Barack. 2016c. "Obama RFI 2." [Online]. Available at: https://obama whitehouse.archives.gov/sites/default/files/whitehouse_files/microsites/ostp/NSTC/preparing_for_the_future_of_ai.pdf.

Parker, Lynne E. 2018. "Creation of the National Artificial Intelligence Research and Development Strategic Plan." AI Magazine 39(2), 25–32. Available at: https://doi.org/10.1609/aimag.v39i2.2803.

Trump, Donald. 2020. "AI One Year Report." [Online]. Available at: https://www.nitrd.gov/nitrdgroups/images/c/c1/American-AI-Initiative-One-Year-Annual-Report.pdf.

CHAPTER SIX

The OSTP Obsession Continues

ONG BEFORE THE WORLD got shackled with the chains imposed by the pandemic, Washington, DC, was bustling with AI-related activities. In March of 2019, *The Economist* organized a conference on AI. It was strategically designed to announce the reappearance of artificial intelligence back at the national stage. The aftermath of the unexpected results of the 2016 elections had wiped out or steamrolled many initiatives. Those that survived went underground to try to take the pulse of the new administration before reemerging. Apparently, AI was one such initiative, and it had to wait for its turn behind other compelling priorities such as the coal, oil, and trucking industries. When it finally reemerged, it was brought back to life by a presidential directive signed by President Trump more than two years after he had assumed office. In February of 2019 the president signed the corresponding executive order.

The fact that it took the president two years to issue a directive that pretty much stated that America must maintain its AI leadership position was a testament to the complacency that surrounded America. As if it were something that America should have waited for two years, the power and potential of AI were ignored at the highest level, and when finally the president addressed the issue, it was too little, too late.

BETWEEN 2017 AND 2018

Besides hiding under the rock somewhere the entire 2017 and most of 2018, the OSTP did only two things. In May of 2018 it organized a conference to meet the industry, established yet another committee (known as the Select Committee on AI), and issued a memorandum on R&D budget priorities. For two years, the same two years when China developed AI at an incredible pace, the OSTP lost precious time to develop and implement an AI industrialization plan. For two years, the OSTP-led bureaucracy destroyed America's potential to move forward at the speed of relevance.

While the March 2019 conference was organized by *The Economist*, it was sponsored by Microsoft. It took place at the luxurious Four Seasons Hotel in Washington, DC. Under the exotic chandeliers and surrounded by art gallery–level artwork, the hotel projected power and prestige. Advertisement cards with Microsoft's name were neatly laid on the tables. Hundreds attended the conference. Excitement was in the air. Microsoft was launching a new AI business school, and the conference became the epitome of what was wrong with America's AI initiatives. Surrounded by commercial consultants wearing the cloak of professorship from top schools and staff of commercial sponsors, senior government officials appeared as the czars of AI. Short of being paraded around in a palanquin, the royal treatment the government officials received showed the symbiotic relationships that have become the symbol of why America lost its leadership position in AI.

THE EXECUTIVE ORDER AND PLAN WAS UPDATED

As the ideological debates raged and passions flared up across the country, the Trump administration needed to show progress.

On February 11, 2019, President Trump signed Executive Order 13859, which established the American Artificial Intelligence Initiative. This initiative broadened the scope of AI to the whole of government. And it greatly expanded the strategic responsibility of the OSTP. The OSTP observed that a lot of AI-related investment activity is happening in the industry, academia, and nonprofits; hence an update to its 2016 National AI R&D Strategic Plan was important.

Michael Kratsios signed the letter that introduced the updated plan. He wrote:

> In August of 2018, the Administration directed the Select Committee on AI to refresh the 2016 National AI R&D Strategic Plan. This process began with the issuance of a Request for Information to solicit public input on ways that the strategy should be revised or improved. The responses to this RFI, as well as an independent agency review, informed this update to the Strategic Plan. (Trump 2019)

The RFI that he referred to received a total of 46 responses, where 2 came from IBM. The responses included 20 from associations, societies, trade, and consortiums; 1 from a major consulting firm (Accenture); 3 from large tech firms; 2 from small tech firms; 2 from semiconductor manufacturers; 4 from individuals; 6 from universities; 5 from think tanks; 2 from Fortune 500 firms; and 1 from a legal institute. Needless to say, the number of responses was disappointingly low. It was as if the nation had become indifferent to AI and its potential. No one cared. The confidence in progress was lost.

The health care sector was heavily represented by associations—including radiology, clinical, and other representative associations. But AI is not just for health care. There was no or little representation from the financial, insurance, or food sectors, pharmaceutical firms, consumer goods, marketing firms, sports, entertainment, energy, construction, travel, transportation, telecom, and many other industries. Once again, the level of engagement and representation from industry was minimal.

Of all the possible universities only six (Princeton, Caltech, University of California San Diego and University of Southern California [joint comment], UT Austin, and Indiana University) participated. That is about 0.48% of *US News*-recognized universities and colleges, or 0.15% of all registered universities and colleges in America.

Despite such a disappointing turnout, OSTP paid absolutely no attention to the fact that there was no engagement from a wide spectrum of American society, that those who participated did not answer all the questions, that many just paid lip service, and that no one criticized or disagreed.

Once again, the plan was validated based on negligible representation from America. The emperor stayed naked.

Once again, the solicitation turned out to be nothing more than a formality, a check the box, an insincere bureaucratic ritual.

Once again, the thinking was shaped by Big Tech and a handful of universities that likely had relationships with Big Tech.

Once again, societies and trade associations lined up to influence the so-called strategy—which was essentially "open up the bank." Not an ounce of disagreement, no criticism, not even constructive feedback.

OSTP continued with its reckless posturing, which continued to hurt the American interests.

Granted, some technology and health care associations did claim to represent hundreds or even thousands of companies or individuals, but it is likely that those represented had no clue that the society of which they are a member is submitting comments on AI on their behalf.

It is hard to believe that Deloitte, PWC, Cap Gemini, Booz Allen, McKinsey, and other reputable consulting firms did not have any advice to offer. It is also not comprehensible that several emerging AI firms—such as DataRobot, Blue Prism, and UiPath—did not have any comments to give. It is hard to believe that the emerging government-focused AI firms such as NCI or Palantir did not want to share their thoughts about such an important area of American progress and future. The fact that Goldman Sachs or JP Morgan or Citibank or Procter & Gamble or Honeywell or General Dynamics did not have direct feedback showed that no real feedback was obtained. The reality is that either these firms did not know about the RFI or they simply did not consider the OSTP invitation credible and sincere or that their comments would make a difference. The fact that small and medium-sized companies from all sectors were not represented shows the shallowness of the effort. The most important strategy in the history of the country received no guidance or support from America. Why bother! They must have determined that nothing would change. If anything, this showed the mood of the country. No one really believed in the OSTP-led strategy. No one really cared. It was just another bureaucratic initiative—not something to get inspired by. There was no national awakening. There was no national commitment.

The responses to RFI had gone down from 150 (2016) to just 46 in 2019. Most of the comments from associations were valuable, although none challenged or criticized the OSTP plan. Accenture's Paul Daugherty, global chief technology and innovation officer, offered the following recommendation:

We encourage the Administration to focus on defining goals for investments made in AI, and in doing so, consider both the value and capabilities of AI. These five value levers are: Intelligent Automation, Enhanced Judgement, Enhanced Interaction, Intelligent Products and Enhanced Trust. A framework of five value levers can help prioritize quantifiable results and sustainable growth for AI R&D.

Due to the rapidly changing environment driven by emerging technologies as well as investments being driven in the private sector, we encourage the federal government to create a formal engagement strategy between the public and stakeholders to better identify and monitor investments, as well as anticipate risks and challenges in long-term R&D. The federal government would benefit from a formal advisory committee of stakeholders outside government, which would include industry, technical experts and consumer advocates. (Daugherty 2018)

In that above comment, Accenture was essentially pointing out that the investment goals remain undefined and hence inefficient allocation of capital can lead to waste, that quantifiable results matter, and that engagement outside the government is necessary. This comment captured what OSTP should have done but failed to do.

But none of that stopped OSTP from running around doing victory laps, celebrating some type of success. For five years of activities, what exactly did OSTP have to show for its efforts? A few conferences in luxurious hotels, a plan update composed of eight strategies, seven of which were left over from a previous plan, an unimpressive website, a few memberships in already developed international standards, over-obsession with governance-related fearmongering, and a few brag statements. That was the extent of the contribution made by the OSTP from an AI industrialization and adoption perspective.

With the newly launched AI Initiative, what was just an AI R&D and federal funding project would now become an AI national strategy. America just made its worst mistake in its AI journey. If America fails to recover from this mistake, decades from now when historians analyze America's decline and fall, they will point to this event as the primary reason behind the decline. This would be the parallel to the role of Rasputin in contributing to the credibility loss of the czarist government. An organization whose mission was to recommend R&D funding on science and technology was now running the national strategy of the country.

Most likely, President Trump did not know all the facts. Most likely, he sincerely believed in what he was being told. It was the responsibility of the OSTP to inform the president about the above facts.

It was OSTP that should have told the president the facts that only 46 responses have come for the RFI and that only about 100 people participated in the much-bragged 2018 conference. OSTP boasts that over 100 people (academics, government employees, industry professionals, and associations) attended the industry conference it organized in May of 2018. But remove the staff, the government employees, and the academics, and how many industry people would really have attended that conference? From how many industries? What were the qualifications of the people who attended, and what was their roles in their companies? The reality is that the OSTP never wanted to get real feedback. It was simply interested in one-way communication from a compliant audience whose role was to applaud and praise the OSTP. In return they would continue to receive fundings. The bank must stay open. It didn't matter if the nation goes down. It didn't matter that just about 100 people attended the industry conference on the biggest and most critical technological, scientific, and mathematical revolution in human civilization. But at least OSTP got the brag rights about the event.

 THE 2019 UPDATE, A CLOSER LOOK

Integrating the RFI responses from 46 entities and based on the directive given by President Trump, a new plan appeared. This plan was not very different than the 2016 plan. The document began by a letter that begins with:

> In his State of the Union address on February 5, 2019, President Trump stressed the importance of ensuring American leadership in the development of emerging technologies, including artificial intelligence (AI), that make up the Industries of the Future. (Trump 2019)

As a matter of fact, President Trump did not make any reference to emerging technologies or artificial intelligence in his February 5, 2019, speech. The closest his comment came to this topic was, "And I am eager to work with you on legislation to deliver new and important infrastructure investment, including investments in the cutting-edge industries of the future." To turn this comment into some type of policy statement of the government is purely embellishment.

From the OSTP perspective, they then presented on what they considered their challenge:

> The landscape for AI R&D is becoming increasingly complex, due to the significant investments that are being made by industry, academia, and nonprofit organizations. Additionally, AI advancements are progressing rapidly. The Federal Government must therefore continually reevaluate its priorities for AI R&D investments, to ensure that investments continue to advance the cutting edge of the field and are not unnecessarily duplicative of industry investments. (Trump 2019)

Note that the above statement refers to how they perceived their goal and challenge. It was to ensure that the federal government continues to invest in AI and does that in areas where there is no unnecessary duplication. While this was a respectable goal, the problem is that it is based on several assumptions.

First, it assumes that we are aware of not only how America is applying AI but also what is the best and most optimized application of AI across the US economy. This obviously requires having an industrialization perspective—which the OSTP did not have. Managed by scientists and technicians, OSTP was responding to the research needs of the US research community—and to some extent of Big Tech—and not to the industrialization needs of America.

Secondly it assumes that the investments made by the industry are in advanced technologies and not in technologies that are branded as AI but are really trivial, low-impact technologies.

Third, it assumes that diffusion of technology is happening and technology is being adopted.

Fourth, it assumes that the OSTP clearly knows how and in what areas non-government investment is transpiring.

Fifth, it assumes that there are no organizational constraints, change management challenges, and political considerations.

Sixth, it assumes that national knowledge and human capital are being developed and nurtured to take advantage of the investment.

Seventh, it assumes that there is a receptive and engaged population that is rapidly transforming innovations into practical applications.

None of that was included in the plan or even considered as variables that needed to be analyzed. The eight OSTP strategies turned out to be:

- Strategy 1: Make long-term investments in AI research;
- Strategy 2: Develop effective methods for human-AI collaboration;
- Strategy 3: Understand and address the ethical, legal, and societal implications of AI;
- Strategy 4: Ensure the safety and security of AI systems;
- Strategy 5: Develop shared public data sets and environments for AI training and testing;
- Strategy 6: Measure and evaluate AI technologies through standards and benchmarks;
- Strategy 7: Better understand the national AI R&D workforce needs; and
- Strategy 8: Expand public-private partnerships to accelerate advances in AI.

Strategy 8 was added as a new strategy. The RFI responses, as few as they were, suggested that OSTP takes a more proactive role in AI industrialization—which the OSTP probably translated as holding a few more conferences, wine-and-dine meetings, and issue more meaningless reports.

For the most part the plan seemed a self-affirming, self-praising, and self-directed plan—except it was hugely self-deceptive.

Making long-term investments in AI is not possible without truly understanding the sector-by-sector value chain needs of the entire economy. They cannot be deciphered without analyzing how sectors are being or will be redefined. They cannot be developed without understanding the impact of great-power competition, decoupling, a need to redesign American supply chains, economic performance expectations, or analyzing the various innovation trajectories and paths. Oblivious to all that, OSTP erected a plan that was based on the "field of dreams" thinking.

 ## HISTORY BEGINS IN 2018—REALLY?

To praise their accomplishments of organizing summits and conferences, the OSTP published a document titled "American Artificial Intelligence Initiative: Year One Annual Report." In that report, the OSTP bragged about its accomplishments.

Based on our research, one of the most factually inaccurate and blatantly false claims was made when a diagram titled "Timeline of US Government Actions to Advance the American AI Initiative" started the timeline in May of 2018 (Figure 6.1). As we have discussed in the previous chapter, the AI initiative was well underway during the Obama administration, and it was incredible that the start time was depicted in May of 2018. The most likely reason for this intellectual amnesia is that the Obama-era AI initiative was rebranded as American AI Initiative and relaunched as that in 2018. Ironically, the 2018 initiative was based on the same drivers as before.

After two years of following the base plan that was established under the Obama administration (2016), the Trump White House needed to show progress, change, and movement. Hence, when the 2020 report card was issued, it rewrote the history and made May of 2018 as the starting point of AI in America. Never mind that in 2019, OSTP (along with several other working groups and committees) had issued a report titled "2016–2019 Progress Report: Artificial Intelligence R&D"—and the 2016 plan was done under the Obama administration.

The story in the "Progress Report 2016–2019" depicted the National AI R&D strategy, which was composed of a total of eight strategies—seven from the 2016 plan and one from 2019 (Figure 6.2). Without any quantitative measures, the report pointed out the deployment of the strategies in various agencies. To the extent that the long-term investments were reported in the federal AI R&D budget by agencies, it does not clarify how it was deployed and what type of technology. Were chatbots considered R&D? Was RPA considered R&D?

The scorecard was really a measure of activities and not results. And it also created some concerns. For example, *the R&D strategy to make long-term investment* received a checkmark against it by agencies such as FBI, FDA, and GSA; however, the strategy 3 of *Understand and address the ethical, legal, and societal implications of AI* did not. In other words, the report said that FBI, GSA, and FDA had made long-term investments in AI without understanding and addressing the ethical, legal, and societal implications. That was a really scary insight—especially if we buy into the OSTP's ongoing obsession with what can be described as the killer robots' phobia. Of course, as one can expect, this was all some red tape bureaucratic check-the-box formality that was being tracked. It had no relationship to actual results. If it did, Chaillan would not have resigned and passed on the AI trophy to China (see Chapter 1).

The great denial by the OSTP continued. From the OSTP perspective, it got what it aimed for. A new AI initiative was established, more money was released for AI, and the large universities were promised big grants. Big Tech was happy, and that is all that mattered. The czars of AI now had an international limelight and a national strategy dominion.

AI R&D Strategies	AFOSR	Army	Census	DARPA	DHS	DoD*	DOE	DOT	FBI	FDA	GSA	HHS	IARPA	NASA	NIFA	NIH	NIJ	NIST	NOAA	NSF	NTIA	ONR	VA
1. Make long-term investments in AI research	X	X		X	X	X	X	X	X	X	X		X		X	X		X	X	X	X	X	
2. Develop effective methods for human-AI collaboration	X	X		X	X	X	X	X		X			X		X	X	X	X	X	X		X	
3. Understand and address the ethical, legal, and societal implications of AI		X		X	X	X	X	X							X	X				X	X		
4. Ensure safety and security of AI systems	X	X		X		X	X		X	X	X	X	X	X				X	X	X			
5. Develop shared public datasets and environments for AI training and testing				X	X	X	X	X	X	X	X		X	X	X	X		X	X	X	X	X	X

AI R&D Strategies	AFOSR	Army	Census	DARPA	DHS	DoD*	DOE	DOT	FBI	FDA	GSA	HHS	IARPA	NASA	NIFA	NIH	NIJ	NIST	NOAA	NSF	NTIA	ONR	VA
6. Measure and evaluate AI technologies through benchmarks and standards				X	X	X	X			X			X			X	X	X	X			X	
7. Better understand the national AI R&D workforce needs			X	X	X	X	X						X		X		X	X	X	X			
8. Expand public-private partnerships in AI to accelerate advances in AI		X		X	X	X	X		X	X		X			X	X	X	X	X	X			

FIGURE 6.1 AI History in Government

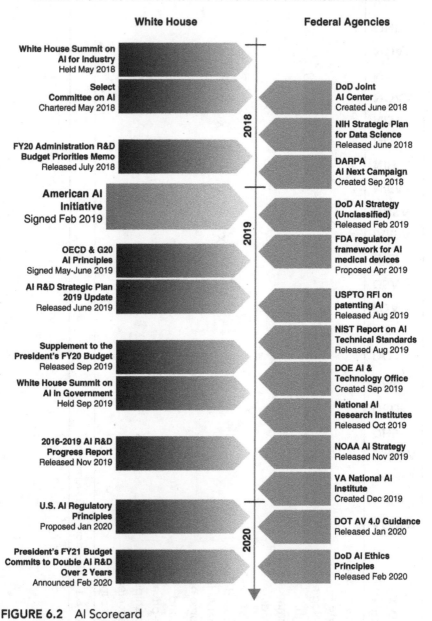

Timeline of U.S. Government Actions to Advance the American AI Initiative

FIGURE 6.2 AI Scorecard

THE THINKING WAS UPSIDE DOWN

A senior executive of Department of Defense's National Defense University commented, "Before I started teaching and when I was working in the government there used to be literally dozens of lobbyists for Enron and only one for Microsoft. Now it is swarming with tech lobbyists." One remarkable difference between the launch of the Internet and of AI is that at that time there was no parallel to what we now call the tech giants. These multitrillion-dollar market valuation firms exercise tremendous power over policy, and it is showing up in the national AI strategy. The problem with having influence from large tech players is that they apply resources and power to sway policy in their power. For America to pay the bill for R&D that will eventually end up with Big Tech (via hiring professors or coinvesting) was an easy policy. Why would they disagree with that. As long as the policy was being crafted by supply side dynamics only and other important stakeholders and constituents in the economy were missing, it favored such narrow policymaking.

The supply side thinking—build it, and they will come—is evident in the national strategy diagram released by the OSTP. In their thinking, AI needed to be founded on some broad foundations such as safety and security, data sets and environments, standards and benchmarks, AI workforce, and public-private partnerships (Figure 6.3). Then government money should be pumped to fuel research in long-term investments in building the core capabilities such as robotics and data analytics, along with investment in human-AI collaboration consisting of NLP (natural language processing) and visualization. Once these two layers of R&D focus areas for investment and the foundational capabilities are combined and funded, the applications would somehow flood the industry on the applied side.

This was a dramatic mistake. A mistake that could cost America its leadership, its economy, its military and civilian superiority, and its future. The major mistake was to ignore that products and services create and embed certain information about them as they pass through their life cycle. This information has components of how people assign meaning to it, social construction of meaning, and several other factors. The information travels back and forth—where the eventual use and application of the technology is used to guide the early development, and the development process constantly evaluates the current and future realities through the process. Technology and science-led teams—such as OSTP—tend to ignore how that information embeds in products and services. The designers of such strategies do not consider the nature of competition or the strategic goals of AI-based competition. In a competitive

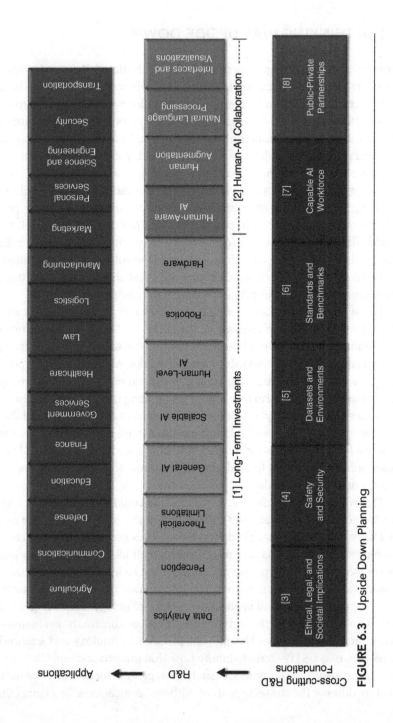

FIGURE 6.3 Upside Down Planning

environment where data and algorithms were defining success, speed was critical. The strategy must take into account several factors. For example, AI begets and attracts more data (for instance, an autonomous car collects more data every time it is out on the street), and learning is facilitated by additional data. There is a cost associated with acquiring and using data, and that implies that efficiency improvements in the underlying data processes would be key to making progress. Data is ubiquitous, and the same data can be used by different applications to learn different things in different ways, and having relevant data is critical. Unfortunately, the way the national AI plan was developed did not consider these issues. It was as if they took an inventory of different subfields in AI and, based on overly simplistic research assumptions, devised plans to pump money into them. That appears to be the extent of their strategic thinking.

This may result in creating new research insights, innovation, inventions, and, yes, we will see new models—but they have no way to reach to the world of the applied front. To assume that industry will somehow reach and deploy new AI technologies is based on an assumption that the R&D projects launched in universities and institutions will be picked up by non-tech small, medium, and large companies and is imprudent. It is likely that only Big Tech will commercialize or deploy these innovations to expand the functions and features of its own product suite. This will create even more monopolization and even further consolidation.

Let us look at some relevant variables:

- The process of commercialization of technology in America is complex. Applications in the industry require creating a vision for the intelligent alternative of the current business models, industry structures, and the emergent structures.
- The managerial resistance in companies and agencies without fully understanding and embracing technology will be hard to overcome. When you don't know a new technology, you will find it risky to adopt it.
- The industrial structure of America has now been consolidated into a few firms in each sector. Smaller firms do arise—but mostly to become fodder for the large firms.
- The dynamics of the AI competition are such that they have a snowballing effect. The firm that deployed a solution earlier will get more learning data faster, and its algorithms will learn more.
- The existing IT infrastructures in firms will create tremendous inertia. Most companies and agencies are already struggling with the legacy IT and infrastructure problems.

- The capital dynamics—the bedrock of our economy—have changed. Capital itself can contribute to opacity and can cloud transparency. This will necessarily affect the adoption part of the technology.
- The cost of capital of riskier players will be higher, and hence investors will flock toward firms with lesser long-term risk—and therefore, among companies trying to solve the same problem, the one with lesser financial and operational risk will have better access to funding. This will give an unfair advantage to Big Tech.

When you consider all of those factors, you recognize that what OSTP calls national strategy is essentially the R&D plan for America—and even that is detached from the economic realities of the country. This would be analogous to a company stating its R&D plan is its overall business strategy. While this could apply to an early-stage firm, it is well understood that R&D is only one part of the business strategy. All the other parts are missing from the OSTP-led so-called national strategy.

The presence of scientific development and pumping all this money will undoubtedly create a production frontier with many different options of deployment of technology. The problem happens in the selection process on what parts of the frontier will have the best possible economic value and productivity gain. Not knowing that answer simply means that while scientific and even technological collection of production possibilities will be expanded, it will not necessarily be applied to create national value. While the neoclassical model assumes that decision-making takes place in information-rich environments and the market forces somehow work to iron out the inefficient possibilities and help winners to emerge quickly, we now know that these assumptions are not entirely true. Especially if we consider the state of the economic structure today—dominated by few very large firms, with high concentration of wealth and power, and an investment model that literally dumps hundreds of millions of dollars in early-stage firms—we can recognize that fallacy of our assumptions. They are not connected to reality.

 ## GROUPTHINK ON STEROIDS

OSTP justifies the validity of its strategy by arguing that other countries have been inspired by the American national AI strategy. We find it hard to believe.

It is possible that some foreign countries are adopting and copying OSTP's strategy. But most likely that will be because those foreign countries may not know any better, and they will follow the American plan blindly. But for how long? Sooner or later the shallow strategy will shatter and expose OSTP's blunder.

Also, at this juncture it is worth it to analyze how China approached its AI strategy.

The Chinese plan is completely opposite to how OSTP approached the national strategy. The Chinese plan was based on first architecting the model of various industries and sectors from an intelligent and futuristic value chain perspective. Each sector was analyzed to determine all aspects of the value chain and what an intelligent value chain would look like. This plan was then expanded to analyze the enterprise capabilities at all levels in the value chain. It was then analyzed for what could be described as the integration points across sectors. Once that was clarified, determination was made to assess network, information, data, and integration needs—as well as identification of data sets within and across sectors. This was then followed by a parallel effort to coordinate research and development efforts by linking existing and future AI capabilities with the applied needs for the sectors and the economy. The why and when of industrial value chain formed the basis of AI strategy—which was then developed with the concept of the value chain of AI composed of multidimensional factors such as data, people, models, applications, problem-solution configurations, and other aspects. Finally, AI was architected for self-perception, self-cognition, self-control, self-adoption and feedback, self-learning, self-decision, and self-autonomy. Furthermore, the strategy for equipment and applications was linked with the enterprise strategy. This upside-down model compared to the OSTP's pie-in-the-sky is what drove China to accelerate and achieve their AI goals.

In the early stages of Chinese AI development there was less focus on AI governance and ethics, but that is rapidly changing. China is also developing AI governance and ethics frameworks. To what extent they will be integrated and adopted in AI applications and in society remains to be seen. In the US, however, as previously argued in the book, ethics and governance are being talked about a lot, but their actual implementation in Big Tech is still rudimentary. If Big Tech firms were serious about ethics and governance, then they would not need to spend tens of millions of dollars in lobbying efforts. Thus, the whole ethical and governance story seems to be less about the best interest of humankind and more about ostentation and pretension. The inordinate amount of time and energy spent on virtue signaling, ethics, and governance creates an unnecessary distraction. While all of those factors are critically important and should be pursued, it should be done sincerely and not just to create a distraction from AI adoption.

As we have argued elsewhere, it is possible that the focus on values gives the US an advantage as it increases the transaction cost of Chinese technology, but with China starting its own governance and ethics development for AI, the advantage may not last.

The detachment of R&D strategy and economics is at the core of the current national strategy.

It was the failure of this strategy that required America to incorporate plan B, which was to confront Chinese technological growth. Had this plan succeeded, America would have had no reason to institute plan B. Plan B comes with risk.

 ## THE CADRE OF ETHICISTS AND FUTURISTS

As soon as AI was in the center stage, an army of ethicists and futurists got a seat at the table. The ethicists' job was to discover and debate the ethical sides of AI and develop AI governance. The futurists were to paint what the picture of the future would look like and talk about the future of work.

Both of these groups acquired significant power in the popular culture and social platforms. With decades of sci-fi depicting AI as acquiring the power to destroy the entire human civilization, starting wars, destroying Earth, using humans to produce energy, and ruling humans, it was easy for the ethicists to find a receptive audience.

While the Hollywood depiction of AI risks was being promoted on one end, more relevant and serious issues of AI were being ignored. For instance, it was revealed that AI being used in the DoJ and health care was biased and prejudiced against African Americans. As soon as such cases were identified, the need for AI governance became evident. But instead of the government taking steps to establish an AI governance and compliance process where it mattered, especially one that deals with social injustice, the entire narrative was turned into a fearmongering quest to play with the American psychology. Google dismantled and recreated several ethics boards. Facebook was called to testify many times. Allegations were made about Amazon following uncompetitive practices. But nothing changed. The real and practical governance and ethics were missing.

Somewhere in Europe, a group (OECD) met and established some general guidelines for AI governance and ethics. Those general guidelines were picked up by various groups, and instead of conducting a proper investigation and looking into American priorities and social issues related to AI, the White House blindly accepted those guidelines via subscribing to them.

The guidelines do not establish a system of governance for AI itself. In other words, there was no mechanism of implementing the recommendations. No process was set up for audit, validation, punishment, and so forth. No legislative parallel was established. No corresponding policy was formulated. AI governance became a nice to have marketing slogan and a bumper sticker—but not much beyond that.

STRATEGY 8

In the DC circles the government, academia, and Big Tech collaboration is often presented as the triangular relationship necessary to drive results. For instance, in the 2020 document OSTP writes, "Concurrent advances across government, universities, and industry mutually reinforce an innovative, vibrant American AI sector" (OSTP 2020 p. iv)—but unfortunately it is likely that the term "universities" means a few universities (usually MIT, Stanford, and CMU), industry implies those who can afford to throw big parties and conferences and give significant marketing exposure to government officials (Big Tech), and academia means professors whose research projects are bank-rolled by Big Tech. While academia, industry, and government collaboration is absolutely necessary, unless done strategically and with a visionary leadership, it is anything but productive. A serious effort to do this is not driven by giving access to people who are the alma maters, friends, former colleagues, or club members of the czars of AI. That is what was completely different in the Clinton/Gore launch of the Internet. It was truly a revolution owned by the people and not just the few. Technological transformation was the bedrock of the Clinton/Gore presidency and Vice President Gore embraced, led, and evangelized the vision. There were large companies then also (although the power concentration was much lower), for example, Microsoft and IBM—but breathing space was created to launch companies such as Facebook, Google, eBay, and others. Now, we don't see that breathing space.

Today's politics, talent, and priorities are much different. A government official must never lose his or her sense of independence. It is hard not to be influenced by those sponsor conferences and events that place you in the lime-light. It is not easy to let go of the relationships from the universities or companies one had worked in. It is not easy to ignore the influence from those who fund the events and conferences that make you famous and give you the platform. But that is exactly what the government officials must avoid.

Surrounded by lobbyists and Big Tech partners, government officials get the royal treatment. Accountability, responsibility, and transparency become hard when the entire job becomes pushing some vague and unmeasurable agendas. The hype itself becomes the performance measure. These carefree jobs are independent of the responsibility that comes with true policymaking that happens with the recognition that your country's competitive potential is at stake.

The gravity of the situation apparently did not dawn on the czars of AI. In their happy-go-lucky style, they continued to celebrate victories as the American competitiveness melted away around them. In report after report, the White House claimed triumph. But the hollowness of those claims became evident when a long study that spread over two years highlighted that America is falling behind.

Interestingly, now there were two claims—both coming from the government: the OSTP office claim that America was at the forefront of AI and in a remarkably strong position and an alternative claim from a commission known as National Security Council of Artificial Intelligence that American competitiveness was in trouble. The day of reckoning was fast approaching.

REFERENCES

OSTP. 2020. "American Artificial Intelligence Initiative: Year One Annual Report." February 2020. Available at: https://www.nitrd.gov/nitrdgroups/images/c/c1/American-AI-Initiative-One-Year-Annual-Report.pdf.

Trump, Donald. 2019. "2016 AI R&D Update." [Online]. Available at: https://trumpwhitehouse.archives.gov/wp-content/uploads/2019/06/National-AI-Research-and-Development-Strategic-Plan-2019-Update-June-2019.pdf.

CHAPTER SEVEN

The Wake-Up Call

A MAJOR TWO-YEAR STUDY CONDUCTED by a newly formed commission on AI opened its report with these words. "Americans have not yet grappled with just how profoundly the artificial intelligence (AI) revolution will impact our economy, national security, and welfare." This statement referred to the American masses. One could ask that despite AI being talked about in magazines, blogs, news sites, and popular media, how is it possible that America has not grappled with the effects of the AI revolution? The answer lies in developing an appreciation of how societies make sense of technological changes. Being fascinated with technology is one thing, adopting it another. Being able to adopt a technology project is one thing, approaching technology-based transformation another. Experimenting with technology is something else, strategic diffusion something totally different. The commission's report was pointing to the fact that even though Americans were in general familiar with AI, they were missing the depth and breadth of the impact the technology will have on them, their country, their economic well-being, and their lives. This assessment was not only true for the masses, but it was also true for the American leaders.

Apparently, sensing that OSTP's whitewashing and self-praising passive approach to AI was creating an existential competitive threat to the US, Congress and the executive branch sponsored a different commission to study AI from a national perspective.

BARBARIANS AT THE GATE

By 2021, AI was no longer a new idea for America. Massive investment was going into the technology, the start-up scene was getting hotter by the day, and companies had begun to talk about AI. In 2019, and then in 2020, OSTP had already declared victory. If it were a scorecard, OSTP self-awarded straight As to itself. The eight strategies were considered necessary and sufficient, a largely superficial or opportunistic feedback mechanism had been architected, and there was no corresponding performance measurement system to measure the progress made. There was no critical thinking. There was no avenue for reflection. What was being measured and claimed as performance were the activities and not the results. OSTP patted its back in terms of introducing AI in American government, conducting a few conferences, and issuing a couple of reports that highlighted the eight strategies. There was no sense of urgency, no anxiety, no national inspiration, no *Sputnik* moment, no information superhighway–like mobilization. The strategy was as boring as a grocery shopping list.

While OSTP stayed in its bubble, greatly fascinated with its own eight strategies, another AI study was launched by the government. This one was sponsored jointly by Congress and the executive branch. As the results of the study were published, they painted a completely different picture from the rosy picture given by the OSTP. The bottom line of the finding: America was not ready for the AI competition.

Notice that the finding was not that America was lagging in the competition or losing to a worthy adversary. The finding was much more problematic: America was not even ready to play the game. The former interpretation would be analogous to an athlete who qualifies for the Olympics, participates in the events, makes it to the final, and then as the race draws to the final round, for one reason or another falls behind a better competitor. The second, and far more problematic, is where the athlete would not even qualify to be in the Olympics because the athlete was not prepared to do so. The warning was dire—but neither did it have any major impact on national leadership nor was it properly understood.

America seemed to be in a competitive disadvantage, and the report authors did not hide or cover up the findings. This project lasted over two years, and at the end a powerful report was issued.

THE FINAL REPORT

Recognizing an urgent need to perform a thorough investigation, Congress and the executive branch converged their forces to analyze and develop a realistic picture of artificial intelligence in America. A special commission was established to investigate AI in America. More than 700 pages of draft materials were posted for public review and comment, and 15 hours of deliberations were streamed online. The commission known as National Security Council of Artificial Intelligence was established as a Federal Advisory Committee. Headed by Google's former CEO Eric Schmidt (chairman) and Robert Work (vice chairman), the commission investigated and then issued a report. We start by first identifying some of the findings.

The report began by outlining its conclusions:

Despite our private-sector and university leadership in AI, the United States remains unprepared for the coming era. Americans must recognize the assertive role that the government will have to play in ensuring the United States wins this innovation competition. Congress and the President will have to support the scale of public resources required to achieve it.

The magnitude of the technological opportunity coincides with a moment of strategic vulnerability. China is a competitor possessing the might, talent, and ambition to challenge America's technological leadership, military superiority, and its broader position in the world. AI is deepening the threat posed by cyber attacks and disinformation campaigns that Russia, China, and other state and non-state actors are using to infiltrate our society, steal our data, and interfere in our democracy. The limited uses of AI-enabled attacks to date are the tip of the iceberg. (NSCAI 2021)

The above excerpt describes the problems that the commission observed. They acknowledged that America does have private-sector and university leadership in AI, and yet America remains unprepared. One might ask, how is it possible that America has private-sector and academic and research leadership and yet "remains unprepared"? Aren't these two—private-sector capability and academic research potential—the essential foundations of progress?

What else would one need? Where are the cracks? This was the first time that the OSTP-led field of dreams was being exposed. This was where five years of self-fascination was being challenged in a more objective manner. A sense of reality was emerging. It was also recognized that this naïve thinking that somehow public-private partnership would automatically result in progress was not delivering results. Clearly, preparing for the competition meant a lot more than just the two parties—academia and business—possessing talent. America was unprepared.

The second sentence clarified "the assertive role that the government will have to play." What does that exactly mean? Does it mean that the commission is asking the government to play a more active and invasive role? The commission was clarifying that the role played by the government was not good enough and that it lacked what needs to get done to drive true results. America was falling behind due to the passiveness and lack of leadership from the government. An assertive role is a role of leadership with clarity. It is not biased, and it is not self-serving. The commission added that China is not just any competitor. It is a competitor that possesses "might, talent, and ambition" to challenge America's technological leadership, military superiority, and its broader position in the world. This was an important sentence as it described the nature of the competition being technological leadership, military superiority, and the broader position in the world—which includes economy, society, soft power, values such as democracy, and institutions. The competitor had the resources and the motivation to unseat America. Later on in the report, the commission pointed out that "China is organized, resourced, and determined to win this contest." This was a powerful insight to bring attributes of competition into the picture. Unlike the OSTP planning, which lacked the competitive need and the urgency to drive results, the commission introduced a much-needed new perspective: America is not alone, America cannot be complacent, and America must work at the speed of relevance.

Lastly, the report attributed new types of risks to the nation that were emerging from the AI-related supremacy of the adversaries. Thus, not only a loss in AI competition will reduce and diminish the power of America, but it will also actually accelerate and intensify the decline. AI is not only the best defense, it is also the best offense.

 ## WHAT WAS HUSHED

While the report pointed out America's shortcomings and opportunities missed, the commission did not dwell into the root causes or drivers for those problems. That position is understandable.

The first was a hint toward the problems—some of which we have pointed out in the previous chapters. The commission reports, "While a competitive response is complicated by deep academic and commercial interconnections, the United States must do what it takes to retain its innovation leadership and position in the world" (NSCAI 2021, 11). We interpret these words to gently point to the nepotism and symbiotic relationship that exists in the tech sector and that destroys value for the country. But after stating that, the commission's report quickly moves forward to sidestep the issue by saying that the US must do whatever it takes. The above words in the commission's report are extremely important, and they should not be ignored. The commission says that a competitive response will be complicated due to deep academic and commercial interconnections and then adds that the US "must do what it takes" without suggesting what those actions should be. For a start, we strongly recommend that policy should not be developed by conflicted professors and Big Tech. We also recommend that this is not time to go easy on what's broken and who's responsible. The time to fix things is slipping fast. The commission acknowledges that but also hedges—most likely to not offend others. We don't think that should be a concern. This is an existential threat for national competitiveness, and it is important to be open and assertive about it.

The second part where the commission hedged was when the report acknowledged that previous warnings were ignored and that new warnings are now issued and if these are not heard, the United States will lose its leadership position. "This commission can warn of national security challenges and articulate the benefits, rather than explain why previous warnings were ignored and opportunities were missed" (NSCAI 2021, p. 19). The problem with this position is that while the report accepts the assertions that "the AI revolution was not a strategic surprise" and that previously issued guidance was ignored, it does not bother to dwell into the reasons why that happened. Most likely that was done for political expediency. Since commercial interests now dominate national interests, this has become the DC way of handling problems: identify the problem and then insist upon moving on without exploring the root causes.

This position typically ignores the root causes and the related underlying processes. It is easier to move the goalpost than to expose the performance gaps of someone. Again, the commission concludes that there were warnings that were ignored. And now there is a new warning issued by the commission, and a new guidance is provided. How can they be sure that the new warnings will not be ignored? How do they even know that the previous warnings were ignored? Perhaps they were not ignored, but the way work was done was clumsy and the execution was flawed? Perhaps the previous warnings were not understood or communicated properly? Perhaps the vision was poorly defined? Perhaps we failed to inspire people? Perhaps we lacked the managerial capacity? Perhaps the underlying organizational model, property rights, or the economic structure needed revision? Perhaps the strategy was not properly developed, articulated, or communicated? The commission accepted the blinders and refused to look deeper into the problem.

We believe that exposing and understanding the root causes was important. Unless we change those underlying conditions, every plan and goalpost move will have the same result. No warning can change things when the entire structure is designed to become an echo chamber of complacency, deception, political bickering, and exaggerations. The report refused to confront these issues.

We have taken a completely different position in this book. We are identifying the problems so that sincere and clear strategy can emerge from true leadership. We are not hiding or covering the problems. We are not hedging or evading.

The commission declared that:

> Despite exciting experimentation and a few small AI programs, the U.S. government is a long way from being "AI-ready." The Commission's business leaders are most frustrated by slow government progress because they know it's possible for large institutions to adopt AI. AI integration is hard in any sector—and the national security arena poses some unique challenges. (NSCAI 2021, p. 2)

This was the reality that America must face. The five years of the OSTP strategy had delivered the following: exciting experimentation and a few small programs. Not just that, the US government was far from being AI-ready—note the reference was not to AI-capable or AI-leader or AI-expert but to the basic requirement of being AI-ready. In other words, we were not even qualified to enter the arena. This was in stark contrast to what OSTP was feeding the two presidents and to America. The OSTP was claiming that America was at the forefront, prepared, a leader in all respects, and at the cutting edge. See Figure 6.2, and you would think that all agencies have now implemented long-term AI plans and that such plans are showing great results. After all, the majority of the boxes were checkmarked. This shows the cognitive dissonance of the OSTP.

Despite the two shortcomings of the commission's report—the reluctance to directly challenge the problems of the complex relationship between academia and commercial interests and the hesitation to explore and expose the root cause analysis of America's failure to rise to the top—the report gives a reasonable and accurate representation of the state of AI in America. We agree with the report's representation; however, there are five areas that the report did not cover, and our discussion below will complement the findings and the recommendations of the report.

1. MORE MONEY

The finding articulates that the buck stops at the president and Congress and recommends supporting the scale of public resources. Our approach to funding is different. While we agree with the commission to increase funding, we believe it is extremely important to develop an investment allocation model that uses multidimensional criteria to allocate money. Just as the OSTP did, the commission was also viewing the solution to the problem as throwing more money into AI, and everything would take care of itself. This represents the interests of the various research groups, Big Tech, which views this as subsidizing their research, and associations but is not necessarily in the best interest of the country. A plan for industrialization of AI must exist before money is thrown into the pit. The strategic orientation of investment must precede the funding. We must avoid the short-term, opportunistic mindset of OSTP: build it, and they will come. In Chapter 12 we show what would constitute a comprehensive plan.

We also disagree with this approach as this puts the cart before the horse. This recommendation style is symptomatic of the problem: everything is being approached from a short-termism. This also undermines what is the real role and responsibility of the president and Congress. Both should not be viewed solely as check writers. We must expect more from our leaders whose conduct, thinking, vision, communication, and leadership provides the inspiration that moves nations forward. The fundamental mistake of viewing Congress and the president as some bankers should not be repeated. Current and future presidents and members of Congress should receive comprehensive training on AI and the related economic and other drivers.

This spirit of just throwing in more money can work in less revolutionary times and when the competitive distance is wide. But when the competitive difference is short and technological lead has diminished, it is important to accelerate innovation in targeted domains first. This can stop the bleeding and give some quick wins. Innovations embed information and find their own paths and trajectories as they move through their life cycle. Information gets embedded at every level in the progression. The paths are adjusted and then readjusted. To bring greater certainty into innovation, one must incur more costs related to information. One must collect information about the future direction of the technology and embed that in the research and development process. When you are falling behind, you need to invest in getting greater information and not wait for technologies to fight their battles and follow the "survival of the fittest" path.

Second, AI itself can solve the innovation problem by applying AI to determine the AI innovation paths.

Third, it is important to provide information to industry to select and advance technology paths. It does not make sense to wait and allow the technology to find its path into adoption.

Fourth, the investment must be evaluated to ensure that it is indeed going into those technologies where the return on investment can be maximized. This handholding is important when things become tough.

2. THE FALLACY OF AVOIDANCE

The report highlighted a sensational finding that America was not ready for AI and then linked the conclusion to open up the bank so we can be ready.

Our position is different. We believe that the risk of not fixing the underlying issues and root causes that led to the previous warnings to be ignored is far greater than the risk of any foreign country overtaking America as a global leader.

But the report was not about fixing the underlying problems or root causes. It was about making a laundry list of things that needed to be improved and then suggesting some consulting-style fixes. America is faltering in AI and that government needed to allocate more funds to put the country back on track is the narrative that is certainly more accurate and reasonable than the OSTP's position, but we believe that the recommendations will not be helpful without an associated plan to fix the gaps. The gaps are in developing a solid and comprehensive plan and to stop viewing OSTP's plan as a national strategy. The OSTP must keep its focus on R&D and funding for federal AI. A new effort is needed to develop a national strategy, and it must be done outside of the OSTP.

3. CHINA IS IMPORTANT, BUT NOT REALLY

The initiative was clearly driven by a response to Chinese progress in AI and not so much to the organic development potential of AI in America. This lens of reactivity turned the final report into a document that seemed like a defensive strategy outlined to keep an invading army outside the city walls. Reminiscent of a plan to counter a siege, it lacked any forward thinking beyond fortifying the walls and fixing what's broken. There was no inspiration—just the basic defensive maneuvers. The China obsession was evident from the fact that the report uses the word "China" a whopping 604 times and "United States" 714 times. The word "America" (or "Americans") appears 184 times while "Chinese" appears 91 times. The report, it seemed, was just as much about China as it was about America. Whatever the report was expected to accomplish, from the outside it seemed like the commission members were pulling the ropes hung from the belltower bells to warn the city that it is under siege. There was no excitement. There was no vision. There was no inspiration. Just a boring battle plan to ward off the attacking army and fortifying the fortress.

We believe that while that level of realism and pragmatic thinking is important, the country also needs inspirational messaging to motivate Americans to develop and embrace AI. This requires building an American AI-centric identity.

The one thing we are trying to point out in our book is that America does not need to be either in a passive mode or a reactive mode. America needs proper leadership that is neither based on fear nor on paranoia. What is needed more than anything is the inspirational leadership that can inspire and mobilize the nation. Instead, plan after plan and report after report, we are simply creating plans that people will read but that will not inspire grassroots movement or mobilize the nation.

4. BELIEVABILITY

The authors of the report did not consider the change management and national identity–shaping transformation that will be needed for America. It requires a delicate balance. Americans believe in their country and its potential. They believe in American exceptionalism. They have been told about America's magnificent performance, its leadership, its strength, its power, and its ability to overcome difficulties. To suddenly find out that the country may not be a leader in less than a decade or that the nation is experiencing strategic vulnerability may confuse people or create unnecessary hostility against minorities or infighting. It can truly affect the psychology of the nation. This can paralyze the spirit of the nation to come together to emerge as an AI nation.

Even if true, the narrative that all of a sudden a new competitor rose from the East that will use a technology to threaten our economy, society, political stability, spiritual well-being, ideologies, intellectual progress, and other pillars of our country may also score low in terms of believability for the American populace, and hence America may not mobilize to rise to the challenge. Even the terminology used in the report, "infiltrate in in our society, steal our data, and interfere in our democracy," may sound extremely alarming for some people and not too threatening for others.

While every American was touched by the Internet, AI remains as an unknown. In the past American leaders have successfully inspired and motivated the nation. Current American leaders would need to discover a positive but pragmatic messaging to inspire the nation.

AI is not an easy technology to understand. Now consider that making the argument that AI is a powerful technology that will somehow tip the balance in China's favor (and by the way we have the world's most powerful tech companies) may not be believable for some people while it may really disturb other people, who may overreact.

So from a position of lacking trust, we push down on people a fairly complicated argument and expect people to be inspired by it. That's a recipe for disaster.

5. BREAKING DOWN THE SILOS

There are two major AI clubs in America. One could be described as the Silicon Valley club. The second as the DC club. Both have some similarities and some major differences.

Laying out the similarities between the two clubs is far easier than identifying the differences. Energized by the spirit of capitalism, both clubs are designed to create massive wealth for their members. Both clubs are trying to capitalize by developing AI capabilities for commercial and government clients. And both clubs are not necessarily approaching AI in terms of the national interests of the United States.

In terms of differences, the Silicon Valley club is composed of typical investors, celebrity-worshiping fans, plenty of foreign money, mostly West Coast–based academics and researchers, recycled management teams, dedicated nonobjective biased celebrity-pleasing media, tech celebrities and their fan clubs, and a unique culture.

The DC club is composed of investors (albeit of a different kind), academics typically from the East Coast universities, business leaders, retired military and government officials, former senators, governors, and congressmembers.

The Silicon Valley club's entrepreneurial constituency generally builds companies to fill the functionality and features gaps in the existing products of large firms. Occasionally they try to develop their own innovative business models, but as soon as their business models begin congealing, they are acquired by large tech firms. The goal of this club is simple: to create designer firms that can be positioned for sale to Big Tech.

The DC club is composed of systems integrators and government contractors who are also trying to embrace the new AI paradigm. To be accurate, due to the use of artificial intelligence in national security and weapons, the DC club was proficient in AI long before the field became prominent in Silicon Valley. The singular goal for this club is to win larger government contracts.

Caught in the midst of these two obsessions is the United States of America. These two clubs respected each other's space and kept a decent distance with each other, which allowed them to coexist. But the Silicon Valley firms started reading some obvious signs. As the economy was experiencing consolidation across major sectors, the growth opportunities were getting limited. Big Tech firms had two growth opportunities: first, to enter new sectors and redefine the competitive dynamics of those sectors with technology; and second, to go after the government business. Financial markets reward Big Tech on revenue growth, such that margins and revenue mix are often ignored. It did not matter where the revenue came from, what mattered was that they could show growth. And nothing beats the nice long-term government contracts.

Northern Virginia, Maryland, and areas in the DC suburbs suddenly saw a surge in Silicon Valley firms moving to the area.

The DC-area firms had developed powerful skills and domain knowledge to bring in new government business via RFPs and know how to navigate the complex world of government acquisitions (procurement). The government-focused technology sector is composed of both large firms (such as Boeing, Lockheed, GDIT, IBM, and Booz Allen), some midsize firms, and thousands of small firms. Many newly emerging AI firms—such as NCI—are now coming from the DC area. The nature of government contracting is such that it has created an ecological distribution parity where everyone gets something as long as they play the game. In this civilized jungle, the ecology calls for cooperation. The primes for major contracts could be small, so disadvantaged firms and larger firms would have to follow the lead of the small business. In other cases, large contracts awarded to giants necessarily require that some parts of the contract trickle to smaller firms. This natural order invites cooperation and has created a culture of cooperation. A far cry from the Silicon Valley's dog-eat-dog world where competitors are swallowed live and the game is played to eliminate each other, the DC club is designed to sustain each other. The DC ecology was about to get a culture shock as Silicon Valley firms began entering in the government space. AI is going to change the DC dynamics. Some of the DC-area firms have had long experience in AI. Their work on the national security and defense side required extensive machine learning work. Despite their performance record, they are not built like Silicon Valley firms.

On many AI RFPs the firms from the two clubs have to work together. Each brings some level of capability to win business. Both can learn from each other. This is something that should not be forgotten in the AI strategy. We believe change management of this type should be part of the national AI strategy.

Similarly, non-tech firms should not be excluded from the AI world. All AI planning must help move all sectors forward. This can be accomplished via engagement with scientific, professional, and trade societies.

Along the same lines, the acquisition and procurement staff of GSA and other agencies need to be retrained on how to procure AI. In December of 2021 the Senate passed a bill that directs agencies to retrain acquisitions staff. This is a good start. Congress should get far more involved in AI national strategy. The story of Congress is presented in the next chapter.

 REFERENCE

NSCAI. 2021. "Final report: National Security Commission on Artificial Intelligence. NSCAP." [Online]. Available at: https://www.nscai.gov/2021-final-report/.

CHAPTER EIGHT

Congress

O
N A SUNNY SUMMER day in Washington, DC, several congressmembers gathered near the Capitol building. There, they were going
to stage a spectacle to show their rage against a foreign country.
They were going to physically destroy a technological artifact of a foreign
country with jackhammers. If it feels as if something like this would have transpired in the recent past, it didn't. It happened in 1988. Japanese technology
was outperforming American technology. A subsidiary of Toshiba along with
a Norwegian firm had sold submarine technology to the Soviet Union. This had
angered the US congressmembers, and while Norway did not face any hate, a
group of congressmen staged a demonstration that many Americans will find
as reminiscent of the recent nationalistic fervor in the nation. The congressmembers placed a Toshiba radio on a stand. Then with sledgehammers they
demolished the radio. If that reminds you of a scene from the movie *Office Space*,
that was exactly what happened. One after another, they took shots at the
radio (Figure 8.1). The radio was shattered, but so was the American image in
many ways. It made Senator Daniel P. Moynihan, a New York Democrat, say
in anguish that the metaphor "Japan-bashing" would affect the American policies in the future and said, "The side with the commanding metaphor takes
the commanding position, and wins the debate" (Tolchin 1988).

FIGURE 8.1
Source: AP Photo/Lana Harris

But unlike post-World War II–Japan, over which America could exercise significant influence, China is a totally different animal. In fact, America has never experienced an adversary with the combined economic, military, technological, and strategic capabilities that China possesses. The battle against China cannot be won by gimmicks such as smashing a Chinese cell phone on the stairs of Capitol Hill. America needs a far more sophisticated strategy than either the overt symbolism or Cold War–style covert warfare. Most importantly, moving forward is not so much about pretention or drama but instead about serious, real, concrete, well-thought-out, clear plans and decisive actions.

THE DAWN OF ARTIFICIAL INTELLIGENCE

On November 30, 2016, Senator Ted Cruz organized America's first Senate hearing on Artificial Intelligence. It was named "The Dawn of Artificial Intelligence" (Cruz 2016). The hearing invited significant interest. Lines started forming outside the hearing room, and when the gates opened, all seats were taken. In a jam-packed room, the hearing began with Senator Cruz introducing the AI revolution. In his introductory remarks, he mentioned, "Many believe that there may not be a single technology that will shape our world more in the next 50 years than artificial intelligence. In fact, some have observed that as powerful and transformative as the Internet has been, it may best be remembered as the predicate for artificial intelligence and machine learning."

Sen. Cruz had invited five witnesses to the hearing, including Greg Brockman, cofounder and chief technology officer, OpenAI; Dr. Steve Chien, senior research scientist, Autonomous Space Systems Technical Group supervisor, Artificial Intelligence Group at NASA's Jet Propulsion Laboratory, California Institute of Technology; Dr. Andrew Futreal, professor in the Department of Genomic Medicine at the University of Texas MD Anderson Cancer Center; Dr. Eric Horvitz, interim co-chair, Partnership on Artificial Intelligence and managing director, Microsoft Research Lab; and Dr. Andrew Moore, dean of the School of Computer Science at Carnegie Mellon University.

Senator Cruz was up-front and clear about what was at stake. He stated:

> Today, the United States is the preeminent leader in developing artificial intelligence. But that could soon change. According to the *Wall Street Journal*, 'the biggest buzz in China's Internet industry isn't about besting global tech giants by better adapting existing business models for the Chinese market. Rather, it's about competing head-to-head with the U.S. and other tech powerhouses in the hottest area of technological innovation: artificial intelligence.'

> Ceding leadership in developing artificial intelligence to China, Russia and other foreign governments will not only place the United States at a technological disadvantage but it could also have implications for national security.

> We are living in the dawn of artificial intelligence, and it is incumbent that Congress and this subcommittee begin to learn about the vast implications of this emerging technology to ensure that the United States remains a global leader throughout the 21st Century. (Cruz 2016/Ted Cruz).

Senator Cruz's words showed that he was fully cognizant about the Chinese desire to compete head-to-head with America in AI and dethrone America as a leader. He warned about the results of the potential loss in the leadership position. In no uncertain words, he warned America that the nation must remain a global leader. This begs several questions:

- If it was known that AI was such a powerful advantage and mission-critical technology, then why did we not see a far more engaged Congress about this? Why were only one or two senators talking about it?
- Why was it not considered that the technology needed to be introduced to America in a positive and easy to understand manner, where masses could relate to it and get inspired by it?
- Notice that the witnesses came from the technical side. Why was there no representation from the policy or economic history side? Why were there no AI industrialization experts? Even though the focus of the investigation was on policy implications and impact on commerce, why were there no economists? As a side note, OpenAI, which was at that time a nonprofit, and was trying to position itself as an "AI for good" nonprofit, participated among others. Later, OpenAI became for profit and ditched the cloak of nonprofit.
- Why was the hearing so focused on the risks of AI without having a corresponding focus on the power of AI to transform the economy?
- Since most of the witnesses focused on three things—(1) increase funding, (2) technology, and (3) governance—why were other critical factors not considered as relevant?

Despite having such strategic clarity about AI as early as 2016, the American AI Initiative lost momentum in the later years. Five years later, it became clear that America had lost its position to China. Whatever Senator Cruz was trying to achieve did not work. The testimonies of the witnesses were unable to save America's leadership. One of the authors of this book attended the hearing and came out of it certain that without a corresponding execution plan, America would not be able to protect its competitive position.

The problem lay in listening to the technologists and not to innovation diffusion experts, industrialization experts, and technology historians. Technologists will simply state the obvious about how they see the world. In their world, the problem is about the technology they are working on, the problem they are trying to solve, about the data and the algorithms, and most importantly about the funding. In their world, if they can get enough money and resources, they can solve the technical problem. The question is, then what? Even if the technologists solve the technical problem, that does not mean that innovation will find its way in society or get implemented to maximize returns. All it means is that the researcher will be able to address the research problem.

You can call one technical expert or a million, the story would have been the same. More data sets, more money, more grants, more researchers, and more governance. The last one, governance, mostly for virtue signaling reasons to appear responsible—since responsibility was in fashion.

And the storyline during the hearings stayed the same. It was: AI is big, AI needs investment to maintain American leadership, give us more money, and it will build the American economy. The senators really did not require testimony from expert witnesses. The story line was standard and known in advance. Senator Cruz's own opening statement was probably far more insightful than any of the witness testimonies. No technologist could have added value at a national level without an associated innovation diffusion and industrialization plan. America did not need testimonies from technical experts and computer science department heads. America needed industrialization experts.

DIGITAL DECISION-MAKING

A year after Senator Cruz's hearing, on December 12, 2017, another US Senator, Roger Wicker (R-Miss.), who was chairman of the Subcommittee on Communications, Technology, Innovation, and the Internet, convened a hearing titled "Digital Decision-Making: The Building Blocks of Machine Learning and Artificial Intelligence." He invited Dr. Cindy Bethel, associate professor, Department of Computer Science and Engineering, Mississippi State University; Mr. Daniel Castro, vice president, Information Technology and Innovation Foundation; Ms. Victoria Espinel, chief executive officer, The Software Alliance; Dr. Edward Felten, PhD, Robert E. Kahn Professor of Computer Science and Public Affairs, Princeton University; and Dr. Dario Gil, PhD, vice president, IBM Research AI and IBM Q, IBM. Once again, the entire panel was composed of technology experts. And as expected, the core theme of the witness testimonies turned out to be the same: AI is big, more funding is needed, and good things will happen with more money. Within all that, experts also talked about the advancement in deep learning and other innovations, but the main point always came down to asking for larger grants.

It is hard to imagine what additional insights were obtained by Senator Wicker—except precious time was being lost. That was the time when America should have been working full-steam ahead to capture the AI industrialization edge—as China was doing. That was when the technology adoption should have been worked on as part of a larger industrialization transformation. That did not happen.

China was working with a very different plan. Research was being approached from an industrialization perspective and industrial applications from research. A symbiotic relationship between research and industrialization was incorporated with a structured and organized approach. Investment was being allocated wisely and systematically. Unlike other technologies, machine learning applications develop from data. More applications lead to more data and more data to more applications.

Besides those hearings, other AI-related initiatives were attempted in Congress.

 ## HOUSE GETS INVOLVED

In July of 2017 Congressman Delany published an article on *The Hill* after launching in May of 2017 a congressional caucus on artificial intelligence. Congressman Delany started his article by:

> One of the biggest problems with Washington is that more often than not the policy conversation isn't grounded in the facts. We see this dysfunction clearly on technology policy, where Congress is largely uninformed on what the future of artificial intelligence (AI) technology will look like and what the actual consequences are likely to be. In this factual vacuum, we run the risk of ultimately adopting at best irrelevant or at worst extreme legislative responses. (Delaney 2017b)

Congressman Delaney, a former entrepreneur, represented a Maryland district. His words are extremely powerful as he claims that legislative and policy discussions are not based on facts, and that is especially true when it comes to technology. He proposed that Congress must take a proactive role and established a caucus. He received support from Rep. Pete Olson, a Republican from Texas, making the caucus a bipartisan undertaking. Several other members of Congress joined the caucus. At the final tally, a total of 28 members of Congress joined it. The representation was from across the country.

Besides congressman Delaney, the caucus included the following: Pete Olson (TX-22), Jerry McNerney (CA-09), Don Beyer (VA-08), GK Butterfield (NC-01), André Carson (IN-07), Emanuel Cleaver II (MO-05), Suzan DelBene (WA-01), Mark DeSaulnier (CA-11), Nanette Diaz Barragán (CA-44), Debbie Dingell (MI-12), Anna G. Eshoo (CA-18), Bill Foster (IL-11), Josh Gottheimer

(NJ-05), Pramila Jayapal (WA-07), Henry C. "Hank" Johnson (GA-04), Ro Khanna (CA-17), Derek Kilmer (WA-06), Brenda Lawrence (MI-14), Ted Lieu (CA-33), Dan Lipinski (IL-3), Michael McCaul (TX-10), Bobby Rush (IL-01), Brad Sherman (CA-30), Darren Soto (FL-09), Elise Stefanik (NY-21), Steve Stivers (OH-15), and Marc Veasey (TX-33).

These congressmen and congresswomen included some of the most influential members in Congress. For example, congressman Don Beyer is chairman of the Joint Economic Committee, the Subcommittee on Space, and the Subcommittee on Research and Technology; and Dr. Bill Foster is a PhD in physics from Harvard. The sad part is that despite having a caucus composed of such a powerful group of people, the caucus did little to move AI forward. By the end of 2021, Congressman Delaney, Representative Olson, Representative Lipinski, and Representative Stivers were no longer in office.

The caucus was active between 2017 and 2018—and one year after coming together, the caucus was pretty much abandoned by the representatives. A website was created to report the activities of the group. A total of four press releases and six news/blog entries were made by the caucus. The last entry appeared in December 2018.

Representative Olson authored a blog entry and stated:

> The AI Caucus is the perfect forum for legislators to be educated on the applications of AI in various applications, understand the issues and policy impacts surrounding AI and to ask the hard questions concerning the matter. The caucus provides an opportunity to learn the benefits as well as gauge the risk versus reward in this emerging field. (Olson 2017)

Both Rep. Olson and Rep. Delaney referred to a comment made by Elon Musk in which the famous entrepreneur warned the world that AI is a potential existential risk for humankind. Neither one of them questioned the validity of that comment or considered the fact that if Mr. Musk actually believed that, then why is he building a company that specializes in AI. Another possible explanation could be that Mr. Musk was in a creative mood when he stated that. He has been seen in different moods and even gave an interview while smoking marijuana. He was also fined by the SEC for making irresponsible statements. Both congressmen seem to have taken the warning seriously and focus of the caucus turned to governance, control, and safety.

Congressman Delaney then conducted a few interviews—in one of which he interviewed a Stanford professor who was also an entrepreneur. Congressional hearings took place in late 2017 and in February 2018. Congressman Delaney once again warned the nation about AI. This time his tone was different, and one could see that the overall anxiety was increasing. Referring to deficit spending, he said, "It's as predictable a crisis as we've ever seen. This is almost certainly going to happen." And then he connected it with AI and said, "AI has the potential to make people healthier, create new jobs and connect communities. Government may not need to step in with regulations, but it will need to play a role in how these new innovations shape society. If we don't do it for this next wave of change, I fear the results will be very negative" (Delaney 2018).

Once again, we want the readers to understand the criticality of what was at stake. America was experiencing a powerful adversary. The primary mode and basis of competition was AI technology. The competitive loss implied significant competitive threat to the nation in terms of economic performance and in almost all other areas. More than any other time, that is when America needed a powerful and clear leadership from Congress—but that did not happen between 2016 and 2019, the critical and formative years of AI.

What is truly surprising is that the caucus seemed to have come to a sudden halt in December of 2018. The last press release was of Congressman Olson recognizing Congressman Delaney's contribution. Now that website stands as a relic in a museum reminding America that just when China was accelerating its AI adoption, expanding its footprint, developing AI with a high level of discipline, the American leadership was abandoning the caucus formed to focus on AI. The story of this abandonment will be preserved on the Internet. It became the story of withdrawal and relinquishment. A website will remind us of the good old days when there was hope. Now desolate, barren, and unattended, the site clings on as a reminiscence of a period when at least a bunch of congressmen and congresswomen attempted to make a difference. Both Olson and Delaney are no longer in Congress at the time of this book's publishing. Both left their mark—but what they did was not enough to move America forward in AI.

KILLER ROBOTS OBSESSION

AI is a complex technology. Unless you allocate some reasonable time to understand how machine learning works, it is counterintuitive to understand how a system rises out of data. But there is an easy part of AI. That is the governance, control, ethics, values, and killer robots part. While most people may not understand the functional aspects of AI, it is easy to view AI as some type of a terminator scenario. Hence, one way people can feel important and be part of the broader AI debate is by focusing on the killer robot scenario. By doing that you are in the limelight since you are talking about something that America already understands. And you can tap into the existing molds of monsters shaped over decades by Hollywood. If you are a congressmember, you can show your constituents that you care about them and the future of the world by being part of the "responsible" movement and saving them from the terminator robots. It was easy and it was popular. Hence, the overwhelming focus of Congress remained on the governance and ethics of AI.

Yet even as scandal after scandal erupted from Big Tech firms and their CEOs were pulled into hearings, no governance and ethics standards and frameworks were universally adopted by these firms. Despite so much attention being paid to governance, all the problems related to governance and ethics—for example, exploitation, manipulation, profiling—continue in Big Tech, but the government has not been able to influence them to change their ways. This shows that the entire governance and ethics posturing is superfluous and insincere.

So the governance and ethics posturing is problematic on two ends: first, it creates unnecessary and preemptive fear, and second, it does not solve the real problems of AI governance and ethics. It stays as virtue signaling and posturing.

 ## THE VIEW OF AI

In December of 2017, three senators along with two representatives introduced a legislation to promote an environment to advance and develop AI. The bill was called "Fundamentally Understanding the Usability and Realistic Evolution of Artificial Intelligence Act of 2017," or "FUTURE of AI Act." It was to establish a federal advisory committee to examine economic opportunities and the effect AI will have on American lives. The committee was expected to examine recommendations on investment, workforce, privacy, and ethics, although that never moved beyond the proposal step. However, it is important to analyze the statements made by various congressmembers and evaluate how AI-related meaning was being formed in America.

The press release about the bill stated the following: "AI technologies are evolving in capability and application at a rapid clip. Yet, the United States currently has no federal policy toward AI and no part of the federal government has ownership of the advancement of this technology" (Delaney 2017a). Notice that this was December 2017 and the OSTP had already issued the 2016 R&D—which was probably collecting dust somewhere as apparently the OSTP was trying to adjust to the new reality during the government transition. The fact that the initiative claimed that AI was growing in an orphaned state implied that OSTP was not viewed as credible or that their efforts were considered meaningless and unable to make a difference at any level. Within the proposed bill, one can observe the four perspectives of the legislators.

The first view was that *of transformation.* "We expect that artificial intelligence will be an incredibly transformative force for growth and productivity. We need to be ready for it," said Senator Maria Cantwell (D-WA). This implies that there was a clear recognition—at least by some congressmembers—that AI will be a powerful force for the economy, growth, and productivity and that America was not ready for it and the country needs to be ready for it. One of the most consistent themes of AI in America between 2016 and 2020 at all levels in the government is the "we are not ready." From the report analyzed in the previous chapter to congressional insights, there was a clear understanding that America was not ready. The sirens were sounding, and the red flags were being raised. Three years later when the National Security Council of Artificial Intelligence report came out, it too concluded that America was not ready. How many reports would it take to come to the recognition that we are not ready and we need to take actions to get America ready? This is the dilemma of AI in America. Wasn't a US senator's statement enough to know that we are not ready and we needed to have an action plan?

The second theme was of *preparing the society.* Senator Todd Young (R-IN) said, "Artificial Intelligence has the ability to drastically boost our economy. As Americans continue to interact with this technology every day, and as its capabilities expand, it's important that we study and prepare for AI's continued use in our society." You can observe that Senator Young agreed about the power of AI to boost the US economy but wanted to focus on how to prepare for AI's continued use in society. This motivation was a bit different as it was driven by how societies use technology and not how they develop technology.

The third theme was about *governance and ethics.* "While artificial intelligence holds the promise of providing goods and services more efficiently and effectively, increased automation has potentially broad negative impacts on our workforce and our privacy," said Senator Edward J. Markey (D-MA). "This bill serves as an important step in bringing together all stakeholders to better understand how this new technology will impact our lives. I thank Senators Cantwell and Young, as well as Representatives Delaney and Olson, for their partnership on this important bipartisan issue." Senator Markey was focusing on the governance part of AI. He showed his concern about the "broad negative impacts" and wanted to study that.

The fourth was about *action to advance AI*. Congressman Delaney, co-chair of the House AI Caucus, explained his reasoning for sponsoring the bill:

> "It's time to get proactive on artificial intelligence. AI is going to reshape our economy the way the steam engine, the transistor or the personal computer did and as a former entrepreneur, I believe the impact will be positive overall. Big disruptions also create new policy needs, and we should start working now so that AI is harnessed in a way that society benefits, that businesses benefit, and that workers benefit. This bill starts the process, by bringing together experts and policymakers. As co-chairs of the AI Caucus, Rep. Olson and I are shining a spotlight on these issues and this bipartisan bill makes sure that both Congress and the Executive Branch get engaged on this topic. I thank Senator Cantwell, Senator Young and Senator Markey for their leadership in the Senate."

Congressman Delaney emphasized the need to be more proactive and encouraged to bring together experts and policymakers.

Rep. Pete Olson said,

> "Artificial Intelligence has the power to truly transform our society, and as policymakers, we must be forward thinking about its applications. The AI Advisory committee will help ensure that the federal government enables growth and advancement in this exciting field, while empowering Congress to address potential AI issues going forward."

Rep. Olson was right that as policymakers needed to be far more engaged but wrong in the sense that AI was not a technology of the future. It was a technology of the present. It was happening then and there. It was rapidly progressing in China. America needed a strategy, and 2017 was wasted by the OSTP-led AI strategy. Another year was gone, and America was still not ready.

THE BILLS OF AI

Between 2013 and early 2022, 379 bills containing the term "artificial intelligence" were proposed in the US Congress (Figure 8.2). Of the 379 bills, only 21 made it to the end and became laws. Many were referred to the subcommittees. A total of 226 bills were from the House while 153 came from the Senate. In the Senate, Marco Rubio was the most active, pushing 14 bills in a seven-year period.

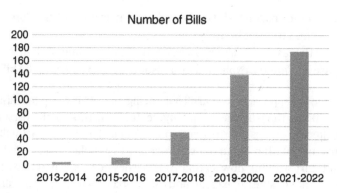

FIGURE 8.2

The data below shows the names of the representatives, their states, and the number of bills proposed by them:

Rep. Auchincloss, Jake [D-MA-4]	1
Rep. Baird, James R. [R-IN-4]	1
Rep. Banks, Jim [R-IN-3]	2
Rep. Barletta, Lou [R-PA-11]	1
Rep. Barr, Andy [R-KY-6]	2
Rep. Bass, Karen [D-CA-37]	1
Rep. Bonamici, Suzanne [D-OR-1]	2
Rep. Bourdeaux, Carolyn [D-GA-7]	2
Rep. Brady, Kevin [R-TX-8]	1
Rep. Brown, Anthony G. [D-MD-4]	3
Rep. Buck, Ken [R-CO-4]	1
Rep. Cardenas, Tony [D-CA-29]	3
Rep. Castor, Kathy [D-FL-14]	2
Rep. Castro, Joaquin [D-TX-20]	2
Rep. Chabot, Steve [R-OH-1]	1
Rep. Clarke, Yvette D. [D-NY-9]	2
Rep. Cleaver, Emanuel [D-MO-5]	1
Rep. Cohen, Steve [D-TN-9]	1
Rep. Comstock, Barbara [R-VA-10]	1

Rep. Conaway, K. Michael [R-TX-11]	3
Rep. Correa, J. Luis [D-CA-46]	1
Rep. Cuellar, Henry [D-TX-28]	1
Rep. DeFazio, Peter A. [D-OR-4]	4
Rep. DeGette, Diana [D-CO-1]	3
Rep. Delaney, John K. [D-MD-6]	2
Rep. DeLauro, Rosa L. [D-CT-3]	2
Rep. Dent, Charles W. [R-PA-15]	1
Rep. DeSaulnier, Mark [D-CA-11]	1
Rep. Deutch, Theodore E. [D-FL-22]	1
Rep. Dingell, Debbie [D-MI-12]	1
Rep. Doyle, Michael F. [D-PA-18]	3
Rep. Dunn, Neal P. [R-FL-2]	2
Rep. Eshoo, Anna G. [D-CA-18]	4
Rep. Flores, Bill [R-TX-17]	1
Rep. Franklin, C. Scott [R-FL-15]	1
Rep. Gallagher, Mike [R-WI-8]	2
Rep. Garcia, Sylvia R. [D-TX-29]	1
Rep. Gonzalez, Anthony [R-OH-16]	2
Rep. Green, Al [D-TX-9]	3
Rep. Green, Mark E. [R-TN-7]	2
Rep. Grijalva, RaÃºl M. [D-AZ-3]	1
Rep. Guthrie, Brett [R-KY-2]	2
Rep. Hastings, Alcee L. [D-FL-20]	2
Rep. Hinson, Ashley [R-IA-1]	1
Rep. Horn, Kendra S. [D-OK-5]	2
Rep. Horsford, Steven [D-NV-4]	1
Rep. Houlahan, Chrissy [D-PA-6]	2
Rep. Huffman, Jared [D-CA-2]	2
Rep. Hurd, Will [R-TX-23]	2
Rep. Issa, Darrell E. [R-CA-49]	2

Rep. Johnson, Eddie Bernice [D-TX-30]	7
Rep. Khanna, Ro [D-CA-17]	6
Rep. Kilmer, Derek [D-WA-6]	1
Rep. Kinzinger, Adam [R-IL-16]	2
Rep. Krishnamoorthi, Raja [D-IL-8]	1
Rep. Lamb, Conor [D-PA-17]	1
Rep. Lance, Leonard [R-NJ-7]	1
Rep. Larson, John B. [D-CT-1]	1
Rep. Lawrence, Brenda L. [D-MI-14]	2
Rep. Lee, Barbara [D-CA-13]	7
Rep. Lipinski, Daniel [D-IL-3]	1
Rep. Lucas, Frank D. [R-OK-3]	3
Rep. Lynch, Stephen F. [D-MA-8]	1
Rep. Malinowski, Tom [D-NJ-7]	1
Rep. Maloney, Carolyn B. [D-NY-12]	5
Rep. Matsui, Doris O. [D-CA-6]	2
Rep. McAdams, Ben [D-UT-4]	1
Rep. McCarthy, Kevin [R-CA-23]	2
Rep. McCaul, Michael T. [R-TX-10]	3
Rep. McCollum, Betty [D-MN-4]	1
Rep. McGovern, James P. [D-MA-2]	3
Rep. McKeon, Howard P. "Buck" [R-CA-25]	1
Rep. McMorris Rodgers, Cathy [R-WA-5]	3
Rep. McNerney, Jerry [D-CA-9]	3
Rep. Meeks, Gregory W. [D-NY-5]	1
Rep. Miller, Carol D. [R-WV-3]	1
Rep. Moulton, Seth [D-MA-6]	1
Rep. Neguse, Joe [D-CO-2]	1
Rep. Norman, Ralph [R-SC-5]	2
Rep. Nunes, Devin [R-CA-22]	1

Rep. Obernolte, Jay [R-CA-8]	2
Rep. O'Halleran, Tom [D-AZ-1]	1
Rep. Olson, Pete [R-TX-22]	1
Rep. Panetta, Jimmy [D-CA-20]	2
Rep. Pappas, Chris [D-NH-1]	1
Rep. Pascrell, Bill, Jr. [D-NJ-9]	1
Rep. Pence, Greg [R-IN-6]	1
Rep. Pingree, Chellie [D-ME-1]	1
Rep. Price, David E. [D-NC-4]	1
Rep. Quigley, Mike [D-IL-5]	2
Rep. Raskin, Jamie [D-MD-8]	2
Rep. Reed, Tom [R-NY-23]	1
Rep. Richmond, Cedric L. [D-LA-2]	1
Rep. Royce, Edward R. [R-CA-39]	2
Rep. Sarbanes, John P. [D-MD-3]	2
Rep. Schiff, Adam B. [D-CA-28]	2
Rep. Schweikert, David [R-AZ-6]	3
Rep. Sensenbrenner, F. James, Jr. [R-WI-5]	2
Rep. Sherman, Brad [D-CA-30]	2
Rep. Sherrill, Mikie [D-NJ-11]	2
Rep. Shuster, Bill [R-PA-9]	3
Rep. Simpson, Michael K. [R-ID-2]	1
Rep. Sires, Albio [D-NJ-8]	1
Rep. Slotkin, Elissa [D-MI-8]	1
Rep. Smith, Adam [D-WA-9]	3
Rep. Smith, Christopher H. [R-NJ-4]	1
Rep. Soto, Darren [D-FL-9]	2
Rep. Stefanik, Elise M. [R-NY-21]	1
Rep. Stevens, Haley M. [D-MI-11]	1
Rep. Takano, Mark [D-CA-41]	2

Rep. Thompson, Bennie G. [D-MS-2]	3
Rep. Thornberry, Mac [R-TX-13]	4
Rep. Tonko, Paul [D-NY-20]	3
Rep. Torres, Ritchie [D-NY-15]	1
Rep. Underwood, Lauren [D-IL-14]	2
Rep. Vela, Filemon [D-TX-34]	1
Rep. Wagner, Ann [R-MO-2]	2
Rep. Waltz, Michael [R-FL-6]	1
Rep. Waters, Maxine [D-CA-43]	1
Rep. Weber, Randy K., Sr. [R-TX-14]	1
Rep. Welch, Peter [D-VT-At Large]	1
Rep. Wexton, Jennifer [D-VA-10]	1
Rep. Wilson, Joe [R-SC-2]	2
Rep. Yarmuth, John A. [D-KY-3]	1

On the Senate side, the following data shows the names and states of the senators and the number of bills they proposed:

Sen. Bennet, Michael F. [D-CO]	2
Sen. Booker, Cory A. [D-NJ]	3
Sen. Brown, Sherrod [D-OH]	1
Sen. Burr, Richard [R-NC]	2
Sen. Cantwell, Maria [D-WA]	4
Sen. Casey, Robert P., Jr. [D-PA]	4
Sen. Coons, Christopher A. [D-DE]	3
Sen. Cornyn, John [R-TX]	1
Sen. Cortez Masto, Catherine [D-NV]	5
Sen. Crapo, Mike [R-ID]	1
Sen. Cruz, Ted [R-TX]	3
Sen. Ernst, Joni [R-IA]	4

Sen. Fischer, Deb [R-NE]	2
Sen. Gardner, Cory [R-CO]	5
Sen. Gillibrand, Kirsten E. [D-NY]	2
Sen. Graham, Lindsey [R-SC]	2
Sen. Harris, Kamala D. [D-CA]	1
Sen. Hassan, Margaret Wood [D-NH]	2
Sen. Hawley, Josh [R-MO]	1
Sen. Heinrich, Martin [D-NM]	4
Sen. Inhofe, James M. [R-OK]	5
Sen. Kelly, Mark [D-AZ]	1
Sen. King, Angus S., Jr. [I-ME]	1
Sen. Lee, Mike [R-UT]	1
Sen. Lujan, Ben Ray [D-NM]	1
Sen. Manchin, Joe, III [D-WV]	1
Sen. Markey, Edward J. [D-MA]	10
Sen. McCain, John [R-AZ]	2
Sen. Menendez, Robert [D-NJ]	7
Sen. Merkley, Jeff [D-OR]	3
Sen. Murkowski, Lisa [R-AK]	2
Sen. Ossoff, Jon [D-GA]	1
Sen. Peters, Gary C. [D-MI]	7
Sen. Portman, Rob [R-OH]	6
Sen. Reed, Jack [D-RI]	1
Sen. Risch, James E. [R-ID]	2
Sen. Rosen, Jacky [D-NV]	2
Sen. Rounds, Mike [R-SD]	1
Sen. Rubio, Marco [R-FL]	14
Sen. Schatz, Brian [D-HI]	4
Sen. Schumer, Charles E. [D-NY]	2
Sen. Scott, Rick [R-FL]	1

Sen. Shaheen, Jeanne [D-NH]	1
Sen. Tester, Jon [D-MT]	1
Sen. Thune, John [R-SD]	2
Sen. Tillis, Thomas [R-NC]	1
Sen. Udall, Tom [D-NM]	1
Sen. Van Hollen, Chris [D-MD]	1
Sen. Warner, Mark R. [D-VA]	3
Sen. Whitehouse, Sheldon [D-RI]	4
Sen. Wicker, Roger F. [R-MS]	7
Sen. Wyden, Ron [D-OR]	5

 ## THE SCIENTIST SPEAKS

Congressman Bill Foster is an Illinois representative from the 11th district. He has a PhD in Physics from Harvard and is certainly one of the most brilliant people to serve in Congress. His father, also named Bill Foster, was a Stanford-trained chemistry specialist who saw how the equipment created by his team led to loss of life in World War II and developed a feeling that he needed to make a change. He was from the South and has observed the way black people were treated in some cases, and this moved him to give up his science career and become a civil rights lawyer. Thus, Bill Foster is not only a brilliant scientist, he also comes from a background that truly cared about America and about true American values. He, we are confident, is among a handful of legislators—or perhaps the only one—who actually downloaded and played around with TensorFlow, Google's AI platform, went through tutorials, and applied algorithms. Congressman Foster talked about AI in one of his interviews with Barefoot Innovation Group. We believe his approach to thinking about AI was sensible, comprehensive, and at the right level of abstraction. He said:

> One of the first lines of defense that Andrew Yang and others come to is the question of universal basic income, and how will our economy work? I guess probably everyone is familiar with the old science fiction story about one person who owns the robot factory, and no one can compete of any job with the robots built by the robots in

his factory. We're within spitting distance of that, and whether the person at the top of the pyramid will be Elon Musk or Bezos, or whoever it is, there is that problem.

The problem is that an unregulated free market economy in that kind of technological universe will deliver all of the money to the one person at the top of the pyramid. Then the economy stops. From a circuit design point of view, there is not a continuous circuit for the money to flow. When that happens, there is not an alternative to reaching deep into the pockets of Elon Musk or Sergey Brin or whoever's at the top and redistributing the money at the base of the pyramid. And then let that money circulate in the human-to-human economy. Then that will persist until someone spends a dollar buying a McDonald's at a robotic McDonald's, and then immediately all the money will be distributed, pile up at the top again, and you will have to continuously redistribute it.

The interesting question, from a circuit design point of view, is what fraction of that wealth you will have to continuously redistribute. I suspect it may be smaller than people think. If you think of the whole world as a factory town where the factory is closed and all of the factory jobs disappear, and then think about that town, maybe 80% or more of the economy were not the factory jobs. They were the people, the restaurant workers and the realtors and everyone else who fed off of the money injected by the factory salaries. So it might be that with a number as small as 20% or perhaps smaller of injected money that the human-to-human economy will proceed in a very healthy state, the same way you could replace the factory wages with a UBI of the same magnitude and have all of the other businesses in a town survive well. Then there are some interesting observations along those lines. The first observation is that in Alaska, everyone gets something like $3,000 a year. That doesn't seem to have destroyed capitalism in Alaska. In Canada, everyone gets the equivalent of $10,000 a year in the form of universal health care. That doesn't seem to have destroyed capitalism in Canada, as well. Those are two interesting numbers. The real question is at what point does the basic income become so generous that people just sit around on their couches and take drugs and play video games. (Barefoot 2020/Barefoot Innovation Group)

Congressman Bill Foster's argument is based on a scenario that pretty much acknowledges that the money will continue to concentrate in a few pockets that sit right at the top of the pyramid and then redistributed via some trickle-down mechanism that will then keep the rest of the 80 percent fed via 20 percent receiving a universal income. Can you imagine this scenario for America where, other than a handful at top of the pyramids, the country just becomes the type of slum depicted in the movie *Elysium*? Many of the readers will shrug or even feel disgusted by the sound of it, and many would cringe at the thought of their children and grandchildren living in that world. But that represents the reality based on the math done by Dr. Foster. He provides examples, among which, based on his understanding, 95% of the investment trading jobs will be gone in 10 or so years.

The above scenario can turn out to be true—but only for a country that has concluded that it will transition into an Elysium city and not for a country that understands that the basic driver of human work is to overcome the survival dread, to exist, and counter the forces that threaten survival. Hence, as long as threats to human survival exist—viruses, asteroids, climate issues, volcanoes, nuclear threats, and so forth—there will be a need for human work. Humans will simply move to the next set of problems. But that will only happen to nations that view themselves in those terms, that display confidence and will to evolve, that have not given up on their people, that have not surrendered their prosperity and country to the hands of few billionaires, that do not constitute an economy that sucks everything from the lower parts of the pyramid, and that have committed to retrain, reskill, and redeploy their people instead of distributing a thousand-dollar monthly checks. In fact, those will be the countries that will make sure that such an Elysium city never materializes.

That is where the focus of the legislature needs to be. To advance AI they need to help create a country where everyone can be part of the prosperity promise. It is possible to accomplish that. Where there is a will, there is a way. And $1000 monthly checks is not the way of the future. Neither is ignoring the middle class and only focusing on the billionaires. The point is that these legislators must help create an economic and social structure that maximizes AI's potential and minimizes the negative aspects by addressing the negative aspects sincerely. The biggest problems associated with the negative aspects are social and cognitive meltdown due to epistemic oppression and concentration of wealth and power.

China has taken the steps to accomplish that. The country has reined in its Big Tech, and entrepreneurs such as Jack Ma, to ensure that their Big Tech's power does not exceed the state power. They have also come down hard on businesses that were threatening their ideological foundations. Clearly, America has a different value system, and the country should not emulate what China is doing—but it is important to understand that building the new world will necessarily require taking actions in the best interest of all citizens and not just the billionaires.

 ## 2020 AND BEYOND

By the end of the 2020, almost everyone was talking about AI in Congress. But the tone and messaging had changed. It was now about China and AI together and indistinguishable.

Senator Rob Portman (R-OH) had issued a warning by tweeting, "We cannot take America's AI leadership for granted. Right now, China is engaging in a full court press to unseat the United States' dominance in AI." What Senator Portman did not expand on is that unseating the United States' dominance in AI implies that America will lose its global standing in all other areas of power. His colleague Senator Martin Heinrich (D-NM), however, did touch on the impact of AI on America and said:

> Artificial intelligence—and the opportunities and challenges it will bring—will have serious national security implications. If we defer AI development to other nations, important ethical, safety, and privacy principles will be at risk, which not only harms the United States, but also the international community as a whole. I have been proud to work alongside Senator Portman to create bipartisan solutions and put into place policy, people, and potential for this new market to truly take transportation, health care, manufacturing, and national security to the next level. I will keep fighting for provisions like those that we secured in the FY 2021 NDAA to step up our domestic efforts and prevent the unethical use and proliferation of AI technologies around the globe, and right here in the U.S. (Heinrich 2020/Martin Heinrich)

Both of these senators worked hard to make the Senate aware of the need to make AI a central issue and included that in several important bills. But unfortunately, as we have pointed out before, you can't build a strong building on a weak foundation. Everything that happened was anchored in a weak start.

The Senate Caucus

Nearly two years after Representative Delaney's failed attempt to mobilize the House Caucus, in March of 2019 Senator Heinrich and Senator Portman announced the formation of the AI Caucus for the Senate. Senator Heinrich said:

> I am proud to announce the formation of the bipartisan AI Caucus in the Senate with Senator Rob Portman. Together, we will work with our colleagues to develop smart policy in a responsible way to ensure the United States remains at the forefront of innovation while maintaining important ethical, safety, and privacy standards. In the years ahead, it will be critical for policymakers to strike the right balance in developing the technology so that academia, private industry, federal agencies, and our national labs can harness the enormous potential of AI to the benefit of society and the American people. (Heinrich 2019b/Martin Heinrich)

This was an important milestone and much-needed change. One can ask several questions about this. First, when Senator Cruz conducted the hearing on AI in November 2016, he pretty much expressed a similar sentiment. Why did it take the Senate more than two years to launch this important caucus? Also, the Senate had the example of the AI caucus from the House. Again, why did it take that long? Those were the critical formative years of building AI. Second, why did we continue to belabor the same points over and over again: AI is important, we must harness its potential. The whole world knows that, and America needed to see some action.

After the formation of the caucus, it was as if a new level of consciousness and awareness had transpired at the Senate level. A month later, in a hearing before the Senate Committee on Armed Services, Senator Heinrich questioned then-US Secretary of the Air Force Heather Wilson and then-Chief of Staff of the Air Force General David L. Goldfein about how the Air Force, and the Department of Defense as a whole, were working to address the growing workforce needs as the military implements artificial intelligence initiatives. In the hearing, Senator Heinrich said, "Artificial Intelligence is going to be critical both on and off the battlefield. As you know, AI is not possible without good quality data, and AI is only effective if we have a workforce that understands how to take care of that data" (Heinrich 2019c). Here the senator was raising two important questions—first about the data science expertise and the second about the data. Secretary Wilson responded and acknowledged that there will be a huge shortage of data scientists and analysts over several decades and that it is a priority.

In response to the findings from the session, on May 16, 2019, Senators Heinrich and Portman introduced the bipartisan Armed Forces Digital Advantage Act, to modernize the Department of Defense (DoD) workforce by adding a recruitment focus and establishing military career tracks for digital engineering.

This showed what needed to get done in America. Ask the relevant questions, understand the problem, propose a solution, and then act on it quickly. Within two months America gained more velocity than in the last two years. The actions taken were commendable.

While the questions asked by Senator Heinrich and the actions taken were extremely relevant, the real answer lies not in hiring another HR professional to drive a wave of recruitment to hire more data scientists. Those are all tactical interventions, and they are important. However, to really address the question we must consider how to change the basic fabric of education in the nation so that the country produces data management and data science experts. The question is how the country can develop a national data strategy where it is understood what type of data will be captured, how, and why—and who will capture it, process it, and use it to develop new AI.

To address such concerns, in May of 2019, Senator Heinrich, Senator Portman, and Senator Brian Schatz (D-HI) proposed the National Strategy for Artificial Intelligence and called for $2.2 billion investment in education, research, and development. The three senators introduced S. 1558, the bipartisan Artificial Intelligence Initiative Act (AI-IA), which would organize a coordinated national strategy for developing AI and provide a $2.2 billion federal investment over five years to build an AI-ready workforce. The goal of the bill was to accelerate the responsible delivery of AI applications from government agencies, academia, and the private sector over the next 10 years.

In his introductory statement, Senator Heinrich said:

> Artificial intelligence—and the opportunities and challenges it will bring—are becoming seemingly inevitable. Now is the time to formulate AI workforces and policies to keep these innovations on a responsible path. The Artificial Intelligence Initiative Act would ensure that the United States establishes a national strategy for AI research and development and would invest $2.2 billion in R&D. Whether it's Silicon Valley, New Mexico or Ohio, or elsewhere across the United States, our high-tech companies, universities, and national laboratories are the foundation by which we lead and maintain an advantage in AI. But the gap is closing quickly, and the United States will only continue its leadership position if it acts with a sense of urgency and purpose. If

we defer AI development to other nations, important ethical, safety, and privacy principles will be at risk, which not only harms the United States, but the international community as a whole. When a new AI advancement is made—the AI-IA will have already put into place policy, people, and potential for this new market to truly take transportation, health care, manufacturing, and national security to the next stage of opportunity. (Heinrich 2019a/Martin Heinrich).

This was a good initiative. It recognized the need for urgency. In February of 2019, President Trump had already signed the American AI Initiative, and the OSTP had floated what they were calling the national strategy for AI. The above statement from Senator Heinrich seemed to indicate that a national strategy did not exist and that there was a need to establish one—including one for R&D. Was the government not talking to each other or Senator Heinrich did not consider the OSTP-led national strategy as a legitimate full-blown strategy for the country? We don't know the answer to this question, but we assume that the Senate was in action mode and had little patience for 2016–2019 indolence. The bill asked the president to establish and implement an initiative with respect to artificial intelligence to be known as the "National Artificial Intelligence Research Development Initiative." This is something President Trump did in the last weeks in office.

According to the information about the bill from Senator Heinrich's office, the Artificial Intelligence Initiative Act accomplished the following:

- Established a National AI Coordination Office (director and staff to coordinate federal AI efforts), an AI Interagency Committee (senior leaders across federal departments), and an AI Advisory Committee (non-governmental experts) to develop a National Strategic Plan for AI R&D and to facilitate coordination across government agencies.
- Required the National Institute of Standards and Technology (NIST) to identify metrics that may be used to establish standards for evaluating AI algorithms and their effectiveness, as well as the quality of training data sets ($40 million each year).
- Required the National Science Foundation (NSF) to formulate educational goals for addressing algorithm accountability, explainability, data bias, privacy, and societal and ethical implications of AI. The NSF will also request to fund research on both the technical and educational aspects of AI and to analyze the AI effect on American society through awarding up

to five new "Multidisciplinary Centers for Artificial Intelligence Research and Education." At least one of these five centers will have K-12 education as its primary focus, one will be a minority-serving institution, and all will include a lifelong education component ($500+ million total; five centers at $20 million per year for 2020–2024).

- Required the Department of Energy (DOE) to create an AI research program, build state-of-the-art computing facilities that will be made available first and foremost to government and academic AI researchers but will also be available to private sector users on a cost-recovery basis as practicable. The bill established up to five Artificial Intelligence Research Centers to include institutions of higher education and national laboratories ($1.5+ billion; five AI Research Centers at $60 million each per year for 2020–2024).

In 2020, Senators Heinrich and Portman introduced another bipartisan AI-related bill. This time it was for the Armed Forces Act to strengthen the Department of Defense's AI capacity by increasing the number of AI and cyber professionals in the department. Perhaps the most important contribution from these senators came in the form of obtaining advancements for AI in the National Defense Authorization Act for Fiscal Year 2021 (FY21 NDAA). Some of the previous versions of the legislations championed by Senators Heinrich and Portman were rolled into this bill, including:

- Artificial Intelligence Initiative Act (AI-IA);
- Artificial Intelligence for the Armed Forces Act;
- National AI Research Resource Task Force Act; and
- Deepfakes Report Act.

Pulling In Other Bills

The FY21 NDAA included a modified version of the Artificial Intelligence Initiative Act (AI-IA) aimed at boosting US leadership in AI research and development. The AI-IA included in the NDAA was tasked with creating a National Artificial Intelligence Initiative Office to coordinate ongoing AI R&D and demonstrate activities among civilian agencies, DoD, and the intelligence community.

The bill also established the National Artificial Intelligence Advisory Committee. This committee will provide expert advice to policymakers and the National AI Initiative Office. The legislation also tasked the National Science Foundation with examining how the present and future US workforce can better prepare for and integrate AI systems.

The bill directed the National Institutes of Standards and Technology (NIST) to develop and advance collaborative frameworks, standards, guidelines, and associated methods and techniques for AI. Such development of technical standards and guidelines were expected to promote trustworthy AI systems. Overall, the bill authorized $1.5 billion over the next five years for these critical AI initiatives.

The conferenced NDAA included some provisions from S. 3965, the Artificial Intelligence for the Armed Forces Act of 2020, previously introduced by Heinrich and Portman. The bill was aimed at advancing the Department of Defense's AI capabilities on two fronts: (1) requiring new hires in armed services to take additional tests to determine computational skills, which was an indication that the future of the military was about automation; and (2) guiding the armed forces to hire and develop AI professionals and data science experts.

NDAA also included a version of the National AI Research Resource Task Force Act (S. 3890) previously introduced by Senators Heinrich and Portman. The provision in the FY21 NDAA were to organize a task force to develop a detailed roadmap for the development of a national cloud computer for AI research. It was expected that the cloud would now enable researchers and entrepreneurs around the country to access supercomputing capabilities, which were previously restricted to national laboratories and universities. This will result in building a national research cloud.

Lastly, the conferenced NDAA included a version of S. 2065 originally introduced by Heinrich and Portman. The provision in the FY21 NDAA required the Department of Homeland Security to assess and report on the state of digital content forgery technology—commonly known as "deepfakes." This will help identify and assess the tactics employed by foreign governments, and their proxies and networks, for deepfakes to harm US national security.

In May of 2021, Senators Heinrich and Portman announced another bipartisan legislation. It was the Artificial Intelligence Capabilities and Transparency (AICT) Act. The AICT Act was proposed to implement recommendations of the National Security Commission on Artificial Intelligence's (NSCAI) final report. AICT's goal was to improve talent and accelerate adoption by agencies.

The legislation gave new authority and resources to the Department of Defense, Department of Energy, intelligence community, and Federal Bureau of Investigation in order to ensure the federal government is positioned to make the best use of rapidly evolving AI capabilities.

In May of 2021, Senators Heinrich and Portman also sent a letter to Director Sethuraman Panchanathan of the National Science Foundation, calling on him to ensure that the US remains a leader on AI, to establish AI institutes focused on ethics and safety, and to ensure that AI advancement is transparent, reliable, and in line with American values.

In October of 2021, Senator Heinrich appreciated the National Science Foundation (NSF) establishing a new theme prioritizing trustworthy AI as part of its National Artificial Intelligence (AI) Research Institutes. Senator Heinrich released the following statement:

> If our country is to reap the benefits of AI at scale, we must ensure that citizens and users—human people—have the trust and confidence in AI systems to actually deploy them. That's why I'm pleased to see the National Science Foundation embrace the need to prioritize AI research on safety and ethics and increase efforts to establish a new AI research institute theme focused on studying and enhancing the trustworthiness of AI. In recent weeks, internal research of major tech companies like Facebook have revealed that AI systems can have unintended consequences on its users, including significant ethical and safety issues. Funding this research in the public domain will go a long way to help address those problems. I look forward to providing congressional oversight to ensure NSF puts sufficient resources towards this critical Trustworthy AI research topic. (Heinrich 2021/Martin Heinrich)

The efforts by the Senate were showing results. America was finally getting to the point where the country needed to be in 2016. Was it too little, too late? Only time will tell. The problem was that instead of leaving the OSTP-operated failed 2016–2019 leadership, the new AI Initiative outlined in the William M. (Mac) Thornberry National Defense Authorization Act for Fiscal Year 2021 (to accompany H.R. 6395) ended up back with the OSTP. If the past is any indication of the future, it is unlikely that the decline of American AI will be stopped, let alone reversed. The anchoring bias of the 2016 plan was now deeply ingrained and rooted in the nation. Senators were working hard with what they were given. The agencies were adapting and trying to make sense out of a delusional national strategy on one end and a flurry of legislation that were hitting them on the other end—all while trying to do their best to serve America during the Covid times.

REFERENCES

Barefoot. 2020. "Transcript of Bill Foster Interview." [Online]. Available at: https://www.jsbarefoot.com/podcasts/2020/1/8/congress-physicist-house-ai-task-force-chair-rep-bill-foster.

Cruz, Ted. 2016. "First Congressional Hearing on Artificial Intelligence." [Online]. Available at: https://www.cruz.senate.gov/newsroom/press-releases/sen-cruz-chairs-first-congressional-hearing-on-artificial-intelligence.

Delaney, John K. 2017a. "Bill by Caucus." [Online]. Available at: https://artificialintelligencecaucus-olson.house.gov/media-center/press-releases/future-of-ai-act.

Delaney, John K. 2017b. "Time to Get Smart on Artificial Intelligence." [Online]. Available at: https://artificialintelligencecaucus-olson.house.gov/media-center/in-the-news/time-to-get-smart-on-artificial-intelligence.

Delaney, John K. 2018. "Delaney Comments." [Online]. Available at: https://artificialintelligencecaucus-olson.house.gov/media-center/in-the-news/us-needs-sharper-focus-on-artificial-intelligence-policy-lawmaker.

Heinrich, Martin. 2019a. "Heinrich, Portman, Schatz Propose National Strategy for Artificial Intelligence; Call for $2.2 Billion Investment in Education, Research & Development." Press Release. [Online]. Available at: https://www.heinrich.senate.gov/press-releases/heinrich-portman-schatz-propose-national-strategy-for-artificial-intelligence-call-for-22-billion-investment-in-education-research-and-development.

Heinrich, Martin. 2019b. "Heinrich, Portman Launch Bipartisan Artificial Intelligence Caucus." [Online]. Available at: https://www.heinrich.senate.gov/press-releases/heinrich-portman-launch-bipartisan-artificial-intelligence-caucus.

Heinrich, Martin. 2019c. "Heinrich Questions Top Air Force Leadership About AI Workforce Needs."

Heinrich, Martin. 2020. "Heinrich, Portman Secure Groundbreaking Advancements for Artificial Intelligence in FY21 NDAA." [Online]. Available at: https://www.heinrich.senate.gov/press-releases/heinrich-portman-secure-groundbreaking-advancements-for-artificial-intelligence-in-fy21-ndaa.

Heinrich (2021) Heinrich Encouraged by National Science Foundation Establishment of "Trustworthy AI" Research Theme. Press Release. [online]. Available from: https://www.heinrich.senate.gov/press-releases/heinrich-encouraged-by-national-science-foundation-establishment-of-trustworthy-ai-research-theme.

Olson, Pete. 2017. "Education before Regulation." [Online]. Available at: https://morningconsult.com/opinions/education-before-regulation/.

Tolchin, Martin. 1988. "'Japan-Bashing' Becomes a Trade Bill Issue. *The New York Times*. February 28, 1988. [Online]. Available at: https://www.nytimes.com/1988/02/28/weekinreview/the-nation-japan-bashing-becomes-a-trade-bill-issue.html.

CHAPTER NINE

AI for Agencies

O N A COLD FEBRUARY morning in 2021, one of the co-authors of this book received an urgent message from a government contractor executive. She, along with a group of several firms, was trying to respond to an AI-related RFP. She wanted Professor Naqvi to review the proposal before submission. When Professor Naqvi reviewed the RFP, he observed that both the questions and the answers related to the software quality were not applicable to machine learning (ML) systems. The RFP, Professor Naqvi recognized, must have been developed by the staff that was not trained in AI. Professor Naqvi explained to the executive that while the question seems to be for the post development, deployment, and production-related integration stage of ML, testing for machine learning application development is widely different than that of non-learning software. Since machine learning software develops from data, its development process is different. It requires training the learning algorithm. For example, among others, some of the issues in testing are:

- Understanding the features of data and initial testing for performance potential and informativeness of features (for example, calculating entropy) and studying mathematical characteristics of the data;
- Dividing data into development/training, cross-validation data, and testing data;

- Selecting various algorithms for testing and studying their performance;
- Understanding the population dynamics from which data is selected and its evolutionary features;
- Testing for human bias and data issues;
- Testing for overfitting or underfitting, understanding cross validation, variance and bias;
- Applying back-testing protocols where applicable;
- Testing model dynamics and dimensionality;
- Testing for stability in relation to population distribution changes;
- Testing for life cycle and testing for ethics and governance.

Once developed, production and deployment testing are performed using various data. The AI system becomes part of the existing technology infrastructure and is integrated. At this stage, deployment testing requires some of the testing that uses traditional approaches—but it is the last stage of testing and relatively less complex and more deterministic than the testing explained above. Unfortunately, this was not the only example where existing templates for non-AI solutions were being used to source AI solutions.

Since 2016, the government has sourced several AI projects. The process for sourcing starts when the government issues a request for proposal (RFP) for technology projects. Much of the sourcing is undertaken by GSA (General Services Administration). However, even though the process has been going on for years now, we noticed something peculiar about the RFPs related to AI. They were structured as if they were for legacy (non-AI) projects. In many cases the questions were posed as if they were for non-AI solutions. This implied that the buyer did not have a good understanding of what was needed to develop and deploy AI systems.

But that was symptomatic of something far more problematic. It showed that much of the AI adoption could be only because of the directives issued by the president or the OSTP assistant director. From an organizational and change management perspective, it meant people were rushing to embrace the technology just for the sake of doing it and to comply with the directive. They were not actually thinking, creating, designing, and developing new process maps. AI is not just about automating manual processes. More than anything else, it is about rethinking how work is accomplished and about finding new types of work. In other words, you are not just automating the existing process, you are also innovating the work itself. This also includes thinking and imagining how everything else that surrounds a certain type of work will change. This will become clear with an example. The autonomous car is not only automating driving, it is also increasing the efficiency and safety for driving. The autonomous machine does not drink alcohol, require sleep, or get distracted to answer phone calls. At an advanced level, the car will understand the personality and emotions of its drivers. But having an autonomous car implies that builders have to rethink about the capacity of the parking lots— since cabs could be out on the road constantly and that will make owning a car less desirable. It will also have an impact on organ donations since there will be fewer accidental deaths—the primary source of organ donations. It will require rethinking the energy strategy and developing the city infrastructure that is conducive for driving. And so on.

 ## THE AGENCY PROBLEM

It was mid-2017 and the nation had somewhat recovered from the 2016 election shock. As focus returned to building the American future, many people began thinking about AI. AI was the new thing, and its popularity was growing by the minute.

Justin Herman—also known as Justin (Doc) Herman from GSA—managed LISTSERVs (email mailing list) known as Public AI. In October of 2016, right before the elections, GSA created three new information-sharing initiatives, one of which was AI. The idea behind launching the digital communities was to provide a platform for sharing best practices and ideas for federal technologists and managers. A month later, America's attention was consumed by the elections and their aftermath. In the emails sent to the mailing list, Justin clarified the goals for the government.

He argued that customer service initiatives can be greatly improved by incorporating next-generation digital public services powered by government data and new advances in artificial intelligence. Public services can become more open, responsive, informative, and accessible. He foresaw that natural voice recognition systems will revolutionize citizen engagement via personalization and automated delivery. The government began organizing workshops, and demand from agencies exploded to learn and experiment with AI. Collaboration about best practices, security, policy, and privacy was encouraged.

As an early appreciator of AI, Herman recognized that some type of coordination across the agencies was necessary to drive adoption. He also realized that too many soft concepts are being spread about AI. Some people were talking about the future of work, others about consulting models, and yet others about governance-type models. He wanted to develop a no-nonsense and pragmatic perspective for the government. He has a powerful sense of humor and good people skills. Through that simple initiative of sharing information, he was able to bring public and agencies together on a single platform. One of the authors met Justin at a conference and found out that Justin had even bigger plans.

The government has many internal LISTSERVs where thousands of technologists share information. Justin wanted to not only bring internal government managers together but also connect them to an external ecosystem with the public, entrepreneurs, and other stakeholders. In August of 2017, Herman wrote in a blog entry:

> Open data and emerging technologies—including artificial intelligence and distributed ledgers, such as blockchain—hold vast potential to transform public services held back by bureaucracy and outdated IT systems. We are opening the doors to bold, fresh ideas for government accountability, transparency and citizen participation by working with U.S. businesses, civil society groups and others to shape national goals for emerging technologies and open data in public services. (Herman 2017/Digital.Gov/Public Domain)

By September of 2017, the interaction had increased tremendously.

Such initiative also led to the establishment of a database where use cases were listed by various areas. The use cases could have been provided by anyone. They could come from the public or an agency. The idea was to create a large collection of use cases via an "Emerging Citizen Technology Atlas," which highlighted and published:

- Federal use cases;
- Ideas/concepts;
- Programs;
- Resources;
- Events; and
- Media.

A little more than a year after the initiative started it had more than 2000 members and significant sharing of information was going on between managers across agencies. Herman continued to clarify that the focus of the initiative was on pragmatic aspects and urgency. In his communication he continued to push for more practical projects and not some futuristic Johnny

5 from *Short Circuit*–type innovations. This focus on what's important now in public service and the associated sense of urgency drove the initial adoption.

This avenue opened up opportunities for agencies to collaborate with each other as well as with the private sector, where AI start-ups and emerging firms were encouraged to showcase their innovation and technologies. In one of such sessions organized by the group was a keynote from Nvidia, which focused on the most practical, real-world uses of AI.

As ideas of innovations develop, they tend to retain the initial conditions that led to their creation. In other words, at the inception of major transformations, social and cultural information is embedded and carried forward in subsequent growth trajectories of innovations and ideas. As early as 2017, as agencies paid attention to AI, the concept of interagency collaboration, crowdsourcing ideas, and pragmatic technology focus solidified. What was also embedded in the social construct was the need to do something quickly, to show results, to bring in technology innovation, to be practical and pragmatic, and to develop use cases that can be turned into products quickly. As two-way communication between the government and public was opened, there was no shortage of ideas. But what that was also doing was to shape the concept of what AI is for the government. Economic historians have pointed out the complexity of embracing technology in times of rapid technological changes. The interpretation of what constitutes a particular technology goes a long way to define the future of the technology and its adoption.

This government initiative, while commendable, also meant that the thinking was largely focused on doing something now and doing something practical. At that time the social perception or social construction of what AI was either too vague and Hollywood like, or too basic, such as robotic process automation (RPA). Machine learning was complicated for most people to understand and required building new skills, getting access to data sets, and developing a different vision of the future than what simple automation entailed. Without a comprehensive vision, the dominant design at a social and cultural level in the government, the common denominator turned out to be RPA. This was the automation that everyone understood, and it was composed of digital bots automating simple repeatable manual tasks. RPA quickly became the face of AI in the government.

One can appreciate the position Herman and his colleagues were in. There was a lot of talk about AI, but no concrete efforts were made to achieve the transformation. There was push from the top—both from the OSTP now playing an active role to push the agencies and from the agency heads.

No comprehensive strategic plans existed for agency transformation with AI. There was no meaning given to what AI is at a cross-agency level. The level of AI competency was different in different agencies. Even the senior leaders did not understand how to empower their agencies with AI. It was a buzzword, and there was enough buzz around it, but no practical steps were being taken to move forward. It is at that time when people like Herman came together and began formulating a plan to push the AI in their agencies. They were not concerned about the grand plans or strategies. They did not care about what the robots would look like five years from that time. They wanted to see AI in action. They wanted to see results. They wanted to be able to say that the US government was getting AI. Hence, the tactical adoption of AI in the government preceded any strategic thinking—that is if strategic thinking ever entered in the process.

In this case we don't blame Herman or his colleagues. They did what needed to get done. Just as a combat team that was not rescued and left to die, and the team had to apply tactical adaptation and improvise to survive, government employees such as Herman were filling the vacuum created by the lack of leadership from the executives. This is not the ideal way to go about a change as powerful as AI, but it was the best they could do.

First, the pressure to do something and to do something now forces people to think about the simplest, low-hanging opportunities. Hence, they don't try to solve complex problems or even think about broad opportunities, they do what they need to do to make it look like things are moving forward.

Second, the urgency places pressure to recruit or bring in a supplier quickly to show progress. This does not give enough time for the buyer to properly determine their acquisition needs and the capabilities they need or should seek in a supplier.

Third, the term "practical" is often used to signify the opposite of strategic. The action orientation unleashed by pragmatism is viewed as an antidote to passive ivory-tower strategic orientation. While it is true that action is better than analysis-paralysis state or a state of perpetual passiveness, what is also true is that practical actions without strategic orientation and deeper thinking can lead to inefficient adoption of technology. You feel as if you are moving ahead, but in reality you are static or falling behind. The activity itself, and not the associated results, creates a deceptive measure of progress.

Fourth, the sharing of information across agencies, while helpful, does assume that the best outcome would be limited by the collective knowledge frontier of the agencies. In other words, the learning from each other would only be as good as the most advanced player in the group. While it is true that learning can generate ideas and new ideas can emerge via sharing of information, the style and processing of information greatly constrain this type of creativity.

Fifth, the interaction of the people—both government employees and outsiders—creates the model that defines what is pragmatic and practical. People's backgrounds, their vantage points, their experience, and their political considerations greatly affect what business models they form and how they form them. When groups consider these matters, they tend to look at the common denominator or constraints and opportunities. This implies that models that emerge are the best political models and not the best functional models.

Sixth, at the early stage of technological revolution development, suppliers and entrepreneurs also do not possess the broader strategic models. They function with limited information, often trying to solve a small problem. Their resources are limited, and in many cases their products and services are not fully developed. Based on their marketing efforts, business development, existing relationships, and PR outreach, they can influence decision makers to turn the process in their favor. This can create unpredictable trajectories for technology growth.

Seventh, collecting use cases does not mean you have the best solution visions. AI creates new business models. Use cases tend to represent the current realities and are often based on automating the existing processes. But the AI revolution is about changing the business models.

Eighth, and most importantly, we cannot ignore the presence of an adversary on a global scale. Everything that gets done requires critical thinking to evaluate what the adversary will do.

Hence, what we call collaboration under these conditions tends to be greatly biased, and teams lack reflexivity to challenge their own assumptions.

The truly commendable efforts by Herman and his colleagues led to the creation of a large reserve of ideas and use cases.

Herman would not last in the government beyond January of 2019. After giving the government a decent start, he went to work for the private sector.

 ## STRATEGIC PLANS

As thinking about AI matured a bit more than what it was in 2016, by 2018 agencies began developing their AI strategic plans. Most of the plans were not really strategic plans, but they represented the high-level will or aspirations. For example, the Department of Defense 2018 Plan (DoD 2018) outlines the following five strategies:

DELIVERING AI-ENABLED CAPABILITIES THAT ADDRESS KEY MISSIONS

Under this aspiration DoD committed to push several initiatives in which AI will be implemented "rapidly, iteratively, and responsibly." High-level areas of impact were identified as improving situational awareness and decision-making, increasing the safety of operating equipment, implementing predictive maintenance and supply, and streamlining business processes. This aspiration was based on automating tedious cognitive and physical tasks to free up talent deployment for more strategic deployment.

SCALING AI'S IMPACT ACROSS DOD

DoD was aspiring to establish a common foundation over which AI can be scaled across the agency via decentralized development and experimentation.

In the plan DoD views the innovative character of the American forces as a major capability and recognizes that the spirit of experimentation will lead to innovations. These innovations will be discovered by users who can then scale and deploy it for their use. Hence, the role of DoD should be to provide a platform for decentralized development and discovery. The DoD used the term "democratize access to AI." This, DoD claimed, will lead to scaling and adoption.

CULTIVATING A LEADING AI WORKFORCE

This included changing the culture of the organization as well as retraining the workforce to learn new skills. It also implies recruiting top AI talent.

Engaging with commercial, academic, and international allies and partners. This implies establishing deep alliances and partnerships with various parties who form the ecosystem of AI. This includes private sector, academia, and interagency cooperation.

LEADING IN MILITARY ETHICS AND AI SAFETY

This is about ethics, governance, and safety of AI. It includes focus areas such as explainable AI, testing, evaluation, certification, use styles, and validation.

The above aspirations, which are called strategies by DoD, require some analysis. There could be some unrelated or misleading assumptions embedded in the aspirations. The assumptions could be based on a non-AI-centric foundation, or they could be based on terms that are often developed by marketing research or consulting firms that sound good but don't carry any deeper meaning.

For example, while the capability of providing forward-edge solutions with reusability and access to users can be a viable option in non-ML technologies and RPA, an ML system developed to solve a problem for one area is most likely not usable for another area. The reason is that the underlying data distributions and the data used to develop the first solution represented its own problem domain. When the problem domain changes, there will be need to develop the solution again. The new solution implies not only using new problem domain-specific data but may also employ different models and algorithms. This means that something developed in one area may not be usable in another area. Similarly, even when a solution is developed to solve a particular problem, when the underlying data of that problem changes, a new solution would need to be developed. This could include discovering additional data, finding more relevant or additional features, or identifying that the underlying distributions have changed. This means that there are no scalability or user selection-based adaptation to new problem domains.

Similarly, if the term "democratization" implies decentralized experimentation, then it begs the question of how this will be integrated, coordinated, and brought back together to connect the parts in a whole, where the whole is greater than the parts. Enterprises can perpetually experiment, but if there is no way to connect the parts back to the whole, the part will only create extra cost in the long run. The history of legacy IT shows that centralized solutioning tends to work better. For example, the enterprise resource planning systems, the shared services models, and the customer relationship management models are all based on centralized planning and not decentralized sparks of innovation.

Then, the aspiration about hiring top talent is somewhat fictional. The best AI talent is picked by Big Tech and top financial firms. To hire that talent, government will have to compete with off-the-charts offers.

Then many other questions remain unanswered. For example, who will establish the allocation of resources and on what basis? How will priorities be determined?

Most importantly, who will determine that DoD is adhering to the strategy? How will the success be measured and determined? How will the five strategies translate into executable projects?

The above strategy of DoD led to the creation of JAIC, which was described as follows in the plan:

> We established a Joint Artificial Intelligence Center (JAIC) to accelerate the delivery of AI-enabled capabilities, scale the Department-wide impact of AI, and synchronize DoD AI activities to expand Joint Force advantages. Specifically, the JAIC will: Rapidly deliver AI-enabled capabilities to address key missions, strengthening current military advantages and enhancing future AI research and development efforts with mission needs, operational outcomes, user feedback, and data; Establish a common foundation for scaling AI's impact across DoD, leading strategic data acquisition and introducing unified data stores, reusable tools, frameworks and standards, and cloud and edge services; Facilitate AI planning, policy, governance, ethics, safety, cybersecurity, and multilateral coordination; Attract and cultivate a world-class AI team to supply trusted subject matter expertise on AI capability delivery and to create new accelerated learning experiences in AI across DoD at all levels of professional education and training. (DoD 2018, p. 9)

However, by April of 2021, JAIC was facing budget cuts, but that was seen as an opportunity to bring in even more AI, faster. FCW reported:

> Lt. Gen. Michael Groen, the JAIC's director, said budget constraints in current and potentially future fiscal years will only increase the department's need for enterprise-level artificial intelligence capabilities.

> "In an era of tightening budgets and a focus on squeezing out things that are legacy or not important in the budget, the productivity gains and the efficiency gains that AI can bring to the department, especially through the business process transformation, actually becomes an economic necessity," Groen told reporters April 9.

> "In a squeeze play between modernizing our warfare that moves at machine speed and tighter budgets, AI is doubly necessary," he said. (Williams 2021/Government Executive Media Group)

But the reality, as we point out throughout this book, was observed by Jacqueline Tame, JAIC's acting operating director. She said:

> *This is not a panacea, and that's a hard thing for a lot of people to swallow. You can't just sprinkle AI on all these legacy systems and expect them to work and talk together, especially when an adversary is actively trying to hack or jam your communications. That's not how it works. There's a mental model shift that has to happen across the department. The first step [is] not particularly sexy. . . ..The first step is helping to educate the department and our partners and all of our stakeholders. (Jr 2021/Breaking Media, Inc.)*

This was the most realistic assessment of the situation we had seen from anywhere. In May of 2021, Tame left and became a strategic advisor to DoD and took an advisory role in various companies.

Right before the year 2021 ended, DoD announced that it would be hiring a chief artificial intelligence officer (CAIO). The problem the new CAIO will face is not only he or she may have to do a lot of backtracking and ripping out existing technology but also in a technology universe dominated by CIOs and CDOs, the CAIO will have to define a new territory and face several political issues. It is likely that the collective immune system of agencies that is designed to stop change will work against such efforts.

Many AI-related RFPs were sent out by various organizations—including HHS, HUD, DSA, and DOC. Some RFPs did not reflect what was needed, others were less about AI and more about legacy IT, and yet others did not go anywhere since the strategic priorities were changed.

THE CIO AND AMERICAN AI

In our discussion with a now-retired technology leader who has decades of executive experience, we learned about some of the main challenges for implementing machine learning projects in agencies. What we discovered was deeply disturbing.

The retired executive shared with us his frustration about the government. Not only the agencies have now become politically charged and ideologically governed, but the way they approach strategy and conflict resolution has come to a new low. The meetings among executives can become heated quickly, and personal agendas are prioritized over national interests.

This is not only from the fact that the country is experiencing an ideological war and political instability but also because the existing infrastructures of several government agencies are not ready for AI. Some agencies are more advanced than others and want to move ahead faster. Others are still struggling to do basic things that should have been completed in 1995 or 2005. Significant efforts are spent on fixing existing problems, and that keeps people occupied. The spaghetti of systems has made it impossible to develop a modernization perspective. You can't throw out the entire information technology base, the executive explained. You have to work with what you have. When you are spending significant time and effort to fix your current problems, who has the time and resources to focus on innovation? No one is thinking big because no one can afford to think big, he mentioned. Add to that the pressure from the top is increasing to show progress in AI. So what will people do? They will just make up projects to show progress.

Some of the early projects by JAIC included fixing the Army accounting system—which was done via robotic process automation (RPA) and some machine learning (Barnett 2020). The result was to match transactions. That was modernization and adoption. The Defense Innovation Unit was fixing accounting errors with RPA.

We noticed that many agency modernization RFPs were sent out that simply did not cover the AI part appropriately. A majority of the focus was on just getting the old tech working. There was nothing modern about them in relative terms. So much so that even the modernization paths were not structured to develop the next generation of technology. It was as if the only thing these RFPs were focusing on was the immediate next move with no recognition about the following moves, the strategy of the game, or the adversary. They were rearchitecting the past—not building the future. And this reality of the state of technology is important to consider when making plans for the future. Your data comes from these systems. You cannot build advanced AI if your underlying systems fail to provide you with the data efficiently.

As the internal political and other battles intensified, the pressure to do something increased on all agencies. Caught between the burst of AI-related legislations and executive orders, the agencies were forced to show progress. This drove them to come up with at least some semblance of strategy. Many agencies published strategies and plans for AI-based transformation. In some agencies, at least some basic level of strategic structure started taking shape.

It was recognized that CIOs needed some level of training and skill development to handle the modern challenges. They needed to be the architects of the transformation. They were expected to develop the American AI to confront China.

The CIO Council, an initiative to educate and enhance the skills of CIOs, published a handbook to uplift the skills. The goal of the book was explained as follows:

> As a business executive, the Chief Information Officer (CIO) challenges executive leadership to think strategically about digital disruptions that are forcing business models to change and technology's role in mission delivery. As a technology leader, the CIO enables and rapidly scales the agency's digital business ecosystem while concurrently ensuring digital security. The CIO drives transformation, manages innovation, develops talent, enables the use of data, and takes advantage of evolving technologies. (CIO Council n.d/The Chief Information Officers Council/Public Domain)

Despite having a powerful and transformational vision, nearly 40 percent of the content of the book was about legal and regulatory matters that CIOs have to comply with, and the rest was about the old technology. There was no reference to artificial intelligence at all and just one brief reference to machine learning.

The opening line in the excerpt quoted from the handbook identified CIOs as "business executives," yet no effort was made to train these business executives on how to deploy a comprehensive process to develop the AI transformation strategy for their agencies.

Legislative initiatives and the OSTP-led mandates do not accomplish results unless they are grounded in on-the-ground realities. They do not consider the underlying realities. They do not remove the real organization and perception barriers.

 ## STRATEGY DEVELOPMENT IN AGENCIES

The strategy development process for a business, for an agency, or for a country requires applying well-developed methods and processes. It requires integrated planning and studying the complex nature of how business, economic, social, competitive, and political environments develop. But it also requires an in-depth understanding of operational, organizational, and financial constraints. It makes a strategist rise above the tactical aspects of day-to-day processes and analyze the forest while simultaneously diving into the operational details and then rising back above the trees. This rising up and down continues as the strategist identifies the pathways that lead to the mission success. This becomes even harder when the competitive environment contains a significant competitive threat. A little slip, and you can lose your competitive edge.

Coming up with the most obvious aspirations—develop skill, cooperate with industry, and develop solutions—is not a strategy. It is not only immature but also a highly naive way to think about strategy.

We stand with the federal employees who are trying to keep a balance between their daily struggles and at times unrealistic push from the top to embrace AI. AI is not a magic wand. It is not a discrete or linear process where you can simply throw enough resources and the technology system will be created. It is a revolution of its own, and it works with its own rules.

 ## THE DLA STORY

Collin J. Williams, a Defense Logistics Agency (DLA) historian, shared the story of SAMMS: Standard Automated Materials Management System. It was launched by DLA to integrate logistics functions spread over multiple supply chains that DLA managed. The work on the system started in 1964 when an HQ-based team started writing the code. The program ran into problems when an appropriate operating system was not identified. After several course adjustments and bouncing back from failures, DLA eventually launched the system in 1971—four years past the expected start date. But as soon as it was implemented, DLA experienced revolutionary productivity gains. Williams writes:

> DLA leaders informed the GAO of recent program changes and installed SAMMS only a few months later at the Defense Construction Supply Center in Columbus, Ohio. Performance improved immediately. Before the year ended, the system reduced back orders from 153,000 to 64,000, increased material availability from 78.9% to 89.8% and increased the on-time fill rate from 61.8% to 71.5%. It did so with 354 fewer people.

Other parts of the agency realized similar improvements in 1973 when DLA installed SAMMS at the Defense General Supply Center in Richmond, Virginia; Defense Electronics Supply Center in Dayton, Ohio; and Defense Industrial Supply Center in Philadelphia, Pennsylvania. (Williams 2020/Defense Logistics Agency)

DLA later connected SAMMS to the Defense Integrated Data System and Standard Automated Materiel Management Telecommunication System. While SAMMS was later retired, it provides a great example of technological transformation means and how it creates measurable results.

In the 1990s and 2000s, DLA went through further modernizations. In 2017, from a study done by DLA, an AI-related modernization opportunity was identified.

Later in 2019, as DLA was trying to develop a plan for transforming with AI, Manny Vengua, Weapon Systems Sustainment R&D program manager of the agency, identified four major constraints for implementing AI/ML:

- Data: ensure easily accessible, reliable, and consolidated data;
- Infrastructure: rapidly changing DoD IT, including consolidation of CIO and DoD cloud migration, challenge the implementation of AI computing resources and software approvals in new environments;
- Training: AI/ML requires advanced skills (programming languages, platforms, and mathematics); industry competition for AI/ML talent is also a concern;
- Governance: managing, documenting, and deploying AI/ML capabilities along with legal and ethical controls.

The moral of the story is simple. With good leadership and when people are given proper training and freedom to execute, they get things done. What they accomplish should be measurable and result in actual value. It should also be based on facts. Most importantly, the constraints should be properly understood and removed. As DLA indicated its constraints to implement AI, it will be able to develop realistic assumptions and plans. Even though the constraints are overwhelming and spread over the entire AI supply chain— composed of data, skills to develop models, infrastructure, and governance controls—we consider these challenges to be good news. The reason it is good news is because it is not some pie-in-the-sky delusion strategy or a lofty statement. It is real. With a history of making great accomplishments, as the above story shows, DLA will be able to lead in AI. But that is because the agency is operating with a sense of reality.

REFERENCES

Barnett, Jackson. 2020. "JAIC Looks to Fix Errors in Army's Financial Accounting Systems." [Online]. Available at: https://www.fedscoop.com/amry-ai-financial-management-system-diu-jaic/.

CIO Council. n.d. "Chief Information Officers Council Handbook." [Online]. Available at: https://www.cio.gov/cio-handbook/.

Department of Defense. 2018. "Summary of the 2018 Department of Defense Artificial Intelligence Strategy." [Online]. Available at: https://media.defense.gov/2019/Feb/12/2002088963/-1/-1/1/SUMMARY-OF-DOD-AI-STRATEGY.PDF.

Freedberg Jr., Sydney. 2021. "Culture, Not Tech, Is Obstacle to JADC2: JAIC." [Online]. Available at: https://breakingdefense.com/2021/02/culture-not-tech-is-obstacle-to-jadc2-jaic/.

Herman, Justin. 2017. "Emerging Tech and Open Data for a More Open and Accountable Government." [Online]. Available at: https://www.gsa.gov/blog/2017/08/24/emerging-tech-and-open-data-for-a-more-open-and-accountable-government.

Williams, Colin Jay. 2020. "Former IT System Integrated Logistics Functions, Improved DLA's Project Management." [Online]. Available at: https://www.dla.mil/AboutDLA/News/NewsArticleView/Article/2327074/former-it-system-integrated-logistics-functions-improved-dlas-project-management/.

Williams, Lauren. 2021. "JAIC Feels Pressure to Go Faster as Tight Budgets Loom." [Online]. Available at: https://fcw.com/it-modernization/2021/04/jaic-feels-pressure-to-go-faster-as-tight-budgets-loom/258184/.

10

A Chaotic Private Sector

H E NEEDED TO MEET the sales quota. A senior sales executive shared his story about selling AI. This story, he mentioned, was repeated at multiple positions he has held in various organizations. He had led sales in three top AI firms. "Selling ERP was easy. Selling Salesforce is easy. There is a clear business need-and-solution relationship. But when it comes to machine learning, what are you really selling?" He shared his battle story. "Day after day, we would walk into client boardrooms and tried explaining AI to them. We created true excitement. Everyone loved the glamorous part of it—the chatbots and all. They agreed that it is a large-scale disruptive technology. But when we asked them to apply it in a more strategic manner, they wouldn't go for it. With ERP, it was possible to make an enterprise sale, but not with AI. The alternative was to sell them baby steps, but that wasn't meaningful deal size for us or a big ROI for them. We were not able to sell large deals."

The above situation is typical for many AI platform companies. What are you really selling? AI is being sold like a panacea for all ailments but without specifying how it cures any. With no corresponding enterprise transformation visions with AI, the only path left for these firms was to sell insignificant use cases.

The absence of any direction from the government created a vacuum in the private sector. The gap existed on both supply and demand sides.

In another story, when nothing else worked, the board of a Boston-based AI platform company specifically asked the sales team to sell $50,000 deals. They were told by the board to forget about mega-sized deals and instead focus on "logo collection"—a term referring to the number of clients vs. the size of the deals. The board argued that investors respond to logos more than to the average deal sizes or quality of revenues.

As another sales executive explained,

> "It was not that we were not selling, it was just that we were selling peanut-sized deals. Everyone just wanted to experiment. There was no commitment to transform. There were no grand visions. Consulting firms became our partners, and they were also selling services—mostly old-style IT services. It seemed as if they just wanted to maximize their number of billable hours while bundling our software for nothing. We had sales, but they meant nothing. Most importantly they did not help our clients at all. No real value was added."

Right around the time when the government was seeking RFI responses in 2016, many AI start-ups were being formed. One of these start-ups was based in San Francisco. This firm was started by a math professor from a top university, and the executive team was composed of leading machine learning experts. The company developed powerful techniques in neural networks. When approached by a bank to solve a critical problem, the team analyzed the problem and was able to solve it using deep learning. Despite having a great grasp on algorithms and having a powerful success story from a use case, the firm started to experience problems with scaling up. The invested capital started bleeding quickly. The firm was unable to keep pace with the demands of the investors, who needed to see fast client buildup. The problem came down to how to sell machine learning projects. The firm tried to use the experience it had gained from the financial services client, but some potential clients could not relate to the problem while others did not have the data to train the algorithm. Some target clients did not understand the problem solved by the firm. Others were not ready to even experiment, while others did not understand the value proposition. And those who did understand the problem did not possess the data that the first firm did. Eventually the firm got sold to a regular IT tech firm.

A Texas-based AI platform company also had no luck in trying to secure big wins. The firm received significant funding from strategic investors. But it too faced the same challenges as other firms did. What were they really selling to the market? Was it a financial services platform? Was it health care? Was it just an AI platform that can be used to develop machine learning applications more easily?

To muddy the waters even further, many business intelligence (BI) firms erased the B from their BI and replaced it with an A and positioned themselves as AI firms. The AI in those platforms was like caffeine in decaffeinated coffee— but it was nonetheless marketed as AI. Firms that called themselves low code suddenly reemerged as AI firms.

When the supply side gets muddied, the transaction cost of technology adoption increases. There was no clarity about what AI did and what it meant. Anyone could have called themselves AI. In the DC area, government contractors began calling themselves AI firms, but only a few, like NCI, truly developed their capabilities. This part of reinvention was absent across the board.

THE SUPPLY SIDE PROBLEMS OF AI

American AI faced several supply side issues. Specifically there were five main problems:

1. Dominant design of an AI platform;
2. Confusion about machine learning;
3. RPA confusion;
4. Legacy IT issues;
5. Use cases.

The concept of transaction cost is important to understand. In simple terms it can be understood as the risk related to transactions to which transacting parties are exposed. When the perceived risk is higher, the counterparties to the transaction incur greater costs to verify the legitimacy of the transaction, of what is exchanged, and of the counterparty itself. This increases the overall cost related to the transaction. Markets with higher standardization and credible institutions reduce transaction costs and hence tend to function more efficiently than those where trading parties have to treat each transaction separately and invest time and effort to verify and validate the legitimacy, measure the value, and assess the credibility of the counterparties.

Just as transaction costs can be viewed in markets, they can be applied to study the technology adoption trends in society and businesses. Corporate executives have a responsibility to their shareholders. They also must protect their own careers and jobs. Acquiring and adopting new technologies carries a risk. If no one has defined for them what it means to adopt AI, what the new processes and business models are, who are the real AI players, and how to embrace the new technology, they will remain hesitant and wary of adopting new technologies. When they do adopt them, they will do it slowly and experimentally. As new models emerge and the perceived risk of adoption declines, the adoption will become more enthusiastic. It happened with ERP. When a dominant design of enterprise resource planning emerged—for example, from SAP—adoption became universal.

AI is a complex technology, and it requires a different mindset to develop it than regular IT solutions. It needs a different raw material, a different skill set, and a different process to develop. It redefines current processes and enables the creation of new processes that do not exist today. It requires immense creativity.

When both legitimate and illegitimate suppliers rush into the field claiming to do AI, when the definition of AI is muddied, when reports are issued that a large number of AI projects are failing, and when every time AI is brought up a cadre of ethicists, virtue signalers, futurists, and governance enthusiasts rise up to attach AI with a plethora of social, political, institutional, and economic issues, it becomes detrimental to quickly adopt the technology. The repeated messaging about AI's evil neither truly addresses AI's real ethical or governance issues nor does it provide a good social feeling to embrace the revolution. All it does is to create fear and panic about AI. It simply taps into the preexisting Hollywood-defined and celebrity-promoted fearmongering about AI and creates an unnecessary distraction. All of that increases the transaction cost associated with AI.

We had talked about the demand side of AI in agencies. In Chapter 9 we discussed how agencies are experiencing challenges with developing the AI strategic and execution map. One would think that the situation was different on the business side, but unfortunately, other than in few companies, the demand side in the private sector is just as bad.

 ## SENSEMAKING ABOUT AI

It was late in the evening, but the meeting continued. No one knew that within a few weeks the world would come to a halt and in-person meetings would become either a thing of the past or would be undertaken with masks and ample supply of hand sanitizers. The executive team of a large financial firm was pondering over their AI strategy, and passions were running high. Apparently, the CEO had discovered that his competitor had made AI one of their top priorities, and now the CEO wanted to build his firm's capabilities in AI. One of the authors (hereafter the consultant in this chapter) of this book was helping them with the strategy. "We need AI as soon as possible" a senior executive directed her team. "Why don't you just ask the programmers to write the AI code instead of writing regular code? Just teach them the AI language or whatever it is," she demanded. The consultant explained that AI systems are developed differently, and they require data to train the system. Somehow, it turned out to be quite a difficult concept to understand for the executive and her team.

They knew how to develop the regular IT systems and just couldn't get their heads around what it means to train the system. Along the same lines, one of the most senior auditors in a US ally country who is also technology savvy continued to ask one of the authors of this book why can't he just ask companies to provide the code of their machine learning systems so his audit teams can audit the AI systems. In their defense, in regular IT, you collect requirements, engineer the solution, and then give it to the programmers to develop. Programmers write the code and testers test the program. There is no design risk in terms of that: as long as the program can be designed (architected or engineered), it can be developed. In other words, while bad code or bad architecting can create problems, there is no uncertainty that a regular or legacy IT program will not work if done correctly. And they had all grown up with the regular or legacy IT.

In fact, there is little in common between AI development and IT applications development. AI takes shape from the data whereas regular IT is deployed for data. AI development is also not deterministic. In other words, until you actually start training the algorithm, you don't know whether the algorithm will learn at the desired performance level or not.

Back to the financial services firm story. By the end of the evening, the consultant realized that his explanations were not helping. They failed to show the executive team that their entire concept of AI was faulty. The executives insisted that all they needed was good programming staff and that they have "excellent programmers who have years of experience in developing IT applications" and "if they can do other systems, I [we] don't understand why they can't develop AI." They constantly requested a follow-up meeting, and the team met the following week.

After the meeting, the consultant realized he needed a different narrative to explain the AI process to the executives, and that was when he developed the concept of the AI supply chain.

THE AI SUPPLY CHAIN

When the consultant returned the following week, he began explaining the idea of the AI supply chain to the management team. He drew the following diagram on a whiteboard.

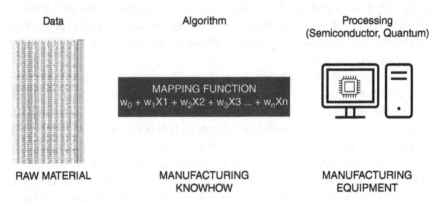

The artificial intelligence supply chain is composed of three capability areas: data, algorithms, and processing power. It is helpful to view artificial intelligence in terms of a supply chain. As previously mentioned in the book, AI systems arise out of data. It is helpful to compare AI with a manufacturing process, which results from raw materials, production equipment, and know-how/processes. If you are manufacturing widgets, you need the raw materials that go into making the widgets, you need the best manufacturing process and know-how, and you need the manufacturing equipment. The manufacturing concept requires further explanation. Unlike the manufacturing undertaken on an assembly line, the AI manufacturing can be viewed as customized manufacturing where each product being manufactured would require its own raw materials, equipment, and the assembly process and know-how.

Since machine learning systems come from data, data can be viewed as a raw material in the supply chain. Therefore, having the raw materials, in the right quantity and quality, in the right shape and form, and in the right packaging is important. In data's case that means having plenty of data that is organized, usable, reliable, timely, and relevant to solve a given problem. Note that the way AI works, a stated problem can lead to requiring a certain type of data or alternatively, data can lead to the identification of a problem. Hence, knowledge grows from various ways, at times self-generating without any theoretical support. Sometimes a solution emerges for which a problem has not even been formulated.

Data scientists organize and process data, develop models, train the algorithms, and study the performance of various algorithms to solve a given problem. Human skill is required to make the supply chain flow smoothly in all three areas. This can be viewed as the manufacturing process of AI systems.

Finally, the processing power over which the manufacturing of AI systems takes place—analogous to the manufacturing equipment—is composed of the processors (semiconductors) and can be viewed as the industrial equipment required to manufacture systems.

If you don't have the data raw material, you will not be able to manufacture the product. If you don't have the equipment and the manufacturing know-how to put the product together, you will not be able to make the product. It is not about the programming. Programming is one small part of developing an AI system. The real skill of developing AI systems is about being able to conceptualize an idea, preprocess data, train the algorithm efficiently, and deploy the system.

This view of AI in terms of a supply chain can help determine the performance potential of a nation. A country that has more usable data (in terms of magnitude, types, structures) possesses more raw material. A nation that possesses the talent and access to algorithms can create more AI faster. A country that has the semiconductor advantage can create bigger, better, and more advanced AI systems faster.

The story of American AI can be told in terms of the supply chain and when told that way, it gets even more interesting. America failed to manage its AI supply chain just as the country was unsuccessful in managing other supply chains. The world was changing, but America not only refused to change, its leaders doubled down and insisted on keeping the status quo.

 ## THE ERA OF DATA MANAGEMENT

One of the greatest errors happened in failing to identify data as the raw material and making efforts to cultivate, nurture, grow, and expand this essential raw material. To an outsider, it would seem that America was flourishing with data. After all the entire 2010s seemed to be about data management and big data. To an insider, it was clear that the early 2010s data management movement was not designed for AI.

Data is intangible and can be used by anyone to make things that you don't expect. In other words, you don't know what AI system can arise from data.

In the second decade of the twenty-first century a movement took hold in America. This movement came from the field of data management. It is important to understand the difference between data management and data science. Data management is where data professionals organize and govern data in an enterprise. These professionals study the data used or needed by a firm and then identify ways to govern data so that it can be used in various applications by the firm. Governing data typically includes understanding where data resides in a firm, identifying who owns, control, and contributes to that data, and how it is used by various applications and humans. This is not data science. Data management professionals are not necessarily AI or data science people. But due to the terminology that uses data in the description, many people confuse data management with data science.

The second decade of the twenty-first century saw the rise of data management. Companies rushed to hire chief data officers. CDOs and the CDO staff usually came from the business side and was augmented by people with some background in technology. These were not AI teams.

The idea was to help corporate America make use of years of data, reduce systems proliferation, make decision-making more efficient, and give firms greater visibility of their data. But as soon as CDOs landed with their lofty vision, organizational retaliation began. For one, no one was clear whether this was a business function or a technology function. In many cases data management departments received the wrath of both—often trying to find their place in the corporate world. After many trials and errors, these departments discovered that the best way to justify their existence was to turn the whole data management programs into collaborative endeavors and pass the ownership to business leaders. That created many roles, known as data stewards and data owners, for the managers on the business side. If you were a management accountant for a firm, you became the data steward for the accounting data. If you were in HR, you owned the HR data. These functional managers were expected to participate in the data management programs and perform work in addition to their regular jobs. Many hated it. But CDO offices prevailed, and companies began significant data management work. Many professional organizations, such as DAMA, were created to help codify the data management knowledge. The hype cycle of analytics, business informatics, and other such applied areas received significant attention. CEOs and CFOs bragged about their data management programs, although few could explain what the data management department was doing.

While data management functions received some discontent from the business functions, nowhere was this more prevalent than from the CIO offices. The IT and data management rapidly turned into one of the most prominent corporate rivalries and with an intensity that was putting the famous operations vs. sales rivalry to shame. First, the CDO offices were exposing many of the inefficiencies of the IT departments. IT shops grew out of the chaos left by layers of legacy technologies, mergers and acquisitions, and failed projects. Like the dead and injured left on the battleground after a medieval war, the remnants of this chaos were visible in the digital footprint of companies. Work was done on desktop spreadsheets, and the same data elements were repeated dozens of times in a firm. It was easy for the CDO office to point a finger at the CIO and link every corporate problem with the underperforming or troubled IT departments. If sales were not materializing, it must be because of a firm's failure to use analytics effectively. If costs were too high, it must be because IT failed to deploy a corporate-wide ERP. With the CDO in power, the CIO officer stood exposed. But the war didn't end there. Judging CIO vulnerability, many CDOs attempted to roll CIO organizations under the CDO office. In a few cases, such insurgencies succeeded, and CDOs became the owners of both data and technology, while in the other cases the CDO vs. CIO conflict continued. The data management function acquired maturity around 2014—perhaps the golden year for the data management function.

"They really did not understand the data management field," remarked a former CDO of a large financial institution. The data management projects were often combined with major IT undertakings such as large-scale data repositories and centralized data lakes. Many such projects failed to achieve results.

Nearly all major data management conferences focused on change management as selling data management in the corporate environment was not an easy undertaking. The biggest complaint was that the executive leadership teams of companies generally do not understand the contribution and role of data management organizations.

It is true that data management organizations played a role in introducing the need for analytics, but what is also true is that the data management field did not develop with the needs of AI or the data science revolution in mind. AI and if anything, data management, created a new corporate layer. The lack of standards in data management introduced a plethora of practices, and organizations approached data governance differently. If the AI revolution benefited from the data management layer, it was likely not by design.

Data management organizations were not tasked with the objective of identifying data that can be used as a raw material to develop new AI applications. Their job was data governance in accordance with the general needs of a firm or a government agency. Fulfillment of this goal requires setting priorities, being selective, and managing data that lives in the regular use patterns of companies—and not for developing new intelligent applications.

This is critical to understand. America was not preparing its data for the AI revolution. For the entire 2010s the focus of the data management remained on "relevant" data, where relevance was defined by what was in the immediate periphery of the corporate strategy and what can be executed by the technology departments. But when you think about data as a raw material, any data can acquire the state of "relevance." For example, weather data, shopping data, and psychological data seem to be very different. A firm interested in learning more about its customers may not use the weather data. But it is possible that weather can drive significant buying behaviors and patterns. This is where the idea of unmined "raw material" comes into play. You just don't know what data can become relevant for the strategy. This implies that you need to not only store and organize as much data as possible but also conduct a series of experiments to determine interesting links between data.

While Big Tech recognized the need for all data, most firms focused on a small segment of relevant in-use data. This was a strategic blunder on both fronts—government and companies. The White House report, if done with foresight, would have advised companies and agencies to not only focus on the immediate data they have but also to look for ways to add and organize data for AI.

 ## THINK WITH SENSORS

Data is everywhere, but you will never know about the data because you don't have the sensors needed to bring in the data. Just as eyes, ears, tongue, nose, and hands play a key role in capturing the data for human consumption, the AI supply chain needs data. It is simple to understand that eyes (the sensors) are needed to bring in the visual information, and the efficiency of how much information is brought in depends on the quality and performance of an eye. A human eye at peak performance can capture significant data—but someone who is color-blind or has eyesight problems can have a decreased performance of their eyes. On the other hand, the eyes of an eagle can capture more data than a human eye. Similarly, a dog's or a bear's sense of smell (nose) and a whale's listening (ears) are better performing sensors than human nose or ears. This gives us at least five measures of installing sensors:

1. How many sensors are installed?
2. How do they perform? (quality of data)
3. How many different types of sensors are installed?
4. How much data they can capture?
5. How quickly or efficiently they can capture the data?

Thus, to compete effectively in the AI supply chain, the data raw material specialization is critical, and to get that one needs to have sensors.

What happens when data is brought in is a different problem. Just because a sensor can bring data into an entity does not mean that entity can capture the data. A sensor's capability is limited to enabling an entity to bring the data in. It is the bridge through which an entity interacts with the external world. In our case, we can consider the AI supply chain of a nation as a living, breathing entity.

Long before the AI supply chain became the most critical supply chain in the world, corporate America failed to recognize the critical need to acquire and sustain a leadership position in this area.

 ## RPA IS THE AI IN AMERICA

At a dinner meeting at a restaurant in Atlanta, the VP of AI of one of the largest commercial banks shared his story.

> "We were implementing RPA and had set up a center of excellence (COE) where several people were working. Once the CEO walked past the COE room, stopped, turned back, and came in. We were shocked. He asked us what we were doing, and we explained to him that we were developing robots to do human work. He seemed fascinated with that and asked to see something in action. We showed him a chatbot that responded to a customer inquiry and interacted with a customer to answer some basic questions. Overwhelmed with excitement he invited the VP of AI to do a demo at the upcoming board meeting and then brought the board members to the COE. Once board members visited the COE and saw the demo, not only we received major funding to bring in additional RPA, but our program also expanded to develop more bots."

We (the co-authors) asked him if they are working on machine learning projects also; he said they couldn't think of many use cases so they will wait on that.

While there is nothing wrong with RPA, the problem was that while Chinese firms were embracing machine learning, American industry was trapped in the RPA world. RPA was shown as the AI that firms needed—so much so that it became analogous to AI.

While there was an abundant supply of a new and transformational technology, the demand side of AI was obscured and underdeveloped. The research on the possibilities of AI in business was in short supply.

Despite such confusion, there was no shortage of capital flowing into the industry.

A group of entrepreneurs from the UK created an interesting technology. It could read data and identify input tags on screen and insert data to update forms. This was a very basic digital robot. There was no learning involved in its operation. It was set up to do something, and it performed the operation. They named their firm Blue Prism. The firm's technology was perhaps less innovative than the powerful marketing the entrepreneurs used to describe their technology: robotic. Little did they know that one day RPA would become the symbol of automation in America.

As the AI wave rose, RPA was able to position itself as the AI technology—so much so that for many American businesses and agencies, their AI strategy became synonymous with their RPA strategy. Never before had a technology taken advantage of a rising wave like that. Never before had such a misnomer triggered this level of adoption. To a large extent, RPA became the face of the AI revolution in America.

While at a social level, the Chinese experience of artificial intelligence happened with the game of go, America had no such parallel. America experienced a completely different path to sensemaking about AI.

Besides RPA, America was receiving other marketing communications about AI and based on which a social and business meaning was being formed. A series of television ads, news articles, magazine articles, and other mass media introduced America to cognitive automation. Microsoft placed an ad where the term "AI" was repeated several times by Rapper Common. Ads began showing robots and intelligent machines. The social psychology of America was not responding to an intelligent machine that learned to defeat the grandmasters in a game that was considered a national pride but instead it was being shaped by marketing. So while the Chinese concept of AI turned out to be deep learning, the technology used to train the algorithm to play and win the game of go, America faced a gigantic vacuum to give meaning to what AI means. To some extent, this vacuum was filled by RPA.

Blue Prism's, and other RPA firms', bold and dynamic marketing and use of the term "RPA" was strategically aligned with the AI wave. Many foreign RPA start-ups and firms established US operations and captured a significant market share in the early stages of market shaping. Blue Prism announced many large-scale clients. Many other major RPA firms—for example, UiPath, Automation Anywhere, and WorkFusion—expanded the market and gained significant market share.

THE FUTURISTS AND VIRTUE SIGNALING

The rise of artificial intelligence had taken a lethal turn. In an experiment gone bad, machines developed consciousness and began taking over the world. As their first action, they launched nuclear weapons to destroy humankind. From the ashes of what was left of humanity rose a rebellion and resistance movement that attempted to take the world back from the robots. Sci-Fi plots such as these were part of the American social consciousness long before the modern AI revolution. It is safe to say that American understanding of intelligent machines was very much shaped by the fear of the machines viewing humans as adversaries and trying to take over the world. While this sci-fi scenario made hundreds of millions for Hollywood producers and directors, more recently it was used by futurists and virtue signalers to take a stake in the AI future.

The futurism and virtue signaling became just as much an issue in the corporate world as in the government. It was as if guilt by association was being established for AI. Futurists come in two forms: Futurists who focus on the future of work and the ones who paint a picture of what the world of the future would look like. AI governance and ethics became favorite topics and departments. In many companies AI governance people were recruited—mostly with HR experience—as if AI deployed to automate accounts payable or accounts receivable was going to become some kind of a racist, chauvinistic, and bigoted robot. The governance marketing was so strong that when companies talked about their AI programs they felt obligated to discuss their governance and ethics program. Money was being spent on spokespeople whose job would be to reduce the fear of Americans about AI. This was the money that should have been spent on building data capabilities. The fearmongering continued, and guilt by association gripped the corporate world. All that while the real culprits of governance and ethics problems in AI—Big Tech—developed without such concerns. In some cases when their ethics and governance boards did not conform to how Big Tech wanted to define the ethics and governance, the boards were dismantled with total impunity.

For everyone else, AI remained a combination of RPA and governance hodgepodge, a formidable, fearful force of potential evil that required significant ethics and governance. All that while China rapidly acquired the sophisticated deep learning capability and moved at the speed of relevance.

CHAPTER ELEVEN

Of Capital and Measurements

W HILE CONVERSING WITH A truly accomplished venture capitalist from New York, we brought up the idea of AI as a national force. In other words, we wanted to explore the potential of AI being viewed as a national asset and hence AI firms being branded as national brands. To us it made perfect sense. In a world where data is being considered a national asset and it is understood that adversaries can use our data to build and deploy capabilities counter to our interests, AI should be viewed in nationalistic terms. To our surprise, the VC had an extremely adverse reaction to our proposal. He said that Silicon Valley does not work that way.

You must dial back the nationalistic thematic, which is hugely unpopular with institutional investors who are apolitical—he advised us. He said that calling anything "American AI" is a huge turnoff to investors in the current hostile political environment. Companies, AI or not, must be positioned as non-US centric, and there should be no fear of the Chinese infiltrating our supply chains and country. Business and political considerations must not be mixed. He said that he has seen patriotic cyber companies spun out of the federal contractors' universe and their sense of duty and mission made them terrible businessmen. He told us that we carry a beltway bias that we must isolate and temper to grow out our vision. He then told us that Silicon Valley's success is based on hoping the government and regulation goes away and how they can help people be free of tyranny—PayPal, Apple, Uber, Crypto, the list goes on.

While we did understand that what had inspired America in the past were the vision of globalization, of collected betterment, and of shared prosperity—we just could not fathom that all of that is even possible in the new geopolitical environment. The recent Russian invasion of Ukraine and the American (and Western) response show that the world stands divided between global powers. We recognized that the "global" narrative had been fed to America for years. But can this narrative carry the American AI to emerge as a force to reckon with? We were not so sure.

THE PRESIDENTIAL SPAC

In an unprecedented action, Twitter and Facebook permanently removed President Trump's social media accounts. The world stood in shock, perplexed, and wondered how a company can have that much power. President Trump, who communicated with his followers using social media, was now completely cut off from the world. This was the president who perfected a new way to reach out to masses and to make people feel as part of the daily decision-making and drama. To deprive him of that stage was quite a harsh move.

A year later, however, President Trump put together a plan for his own social media. He would not be dependent on the existing social media and would go on to create an alternative avenue to communicate with his followers. This led to a Special Purpose Acquisition Company (SPAC) known as Digital World Acquisition Corp (DWAC) invest in Donald Trump–linked social media assets. Right after the investment, SPAC's amazing performance (800%+) indicated market confidence in the deal. This also showed the dawn of the new reality in America that money is no longer apolitical. However, instead of deploying that political platforming to develop a nationalism-focused America standing against global rivals, it was being deployed to fight the domestic battles. Social media was now becoming politically charged with traditional Big Tech taking the liberal platform (only where it suited their interests) and the emergence of new media firms to represent the opposing, typically ultraconservative views. This was not only happening in America but also in other Western countries. Jair Bolsonaro, Brazil's president, was also ousted by Facebook and Twitter for spreading false stories about Covid. He first moved to an alternative media firm run by a Trump ally and got 500,000 followers rapidly. Later he embraced Telegram, a Dubai-based firm.

America, along with many other Western countries, had now entered a new phase of nationalistic capital and patriotic profits. We felt that the world was no longer "global" but instead "zoned" into regions of influence of the two great powers. Could this arguably be the sole response possible to a powerful adversary who is no longer following the "strategic patience" paradigm (China)?

We communicated with our VC friend and informed him about our position. When such geopolitical-led economics develop, then money has no choice. Policy holds. National interests are prioritized. The lofty or grandiose planet-changing visions of Silicon Valley will be slaughtered in the altars of DC. Like Caesar's assassination at the Curia of Pompey, what's to stop the political elites of today's Rome to dismantle the power of the tech legends and to ensure that American might and power—in all aspects—are retrenched and concentrated in what's "American"? In other words, the beltway bias will prevail as both technology and companies will be developed and deployed to function on this side of the new Iron Curtain. The so-called tyranny of the government will be seen as the necessary evil and the only way to survive in this new world—with supercharged nationalism and patriotism as the new normal and social realities—and that is where both capital and Silicon Valley will have to comply. The only way to make America great again or to build back better will be "America first." And for that we will have to learn to think inside the box.

 ## THE CAPITAL INVESTMENT IN THE PRIVATE SECTOR

In a meeting with a top-tier consulting firm, one of the co-authors of this book was interested in finding out about the robotic process automation (RPA) players. The meeting took place in a steak restaurant in NYC. Several people from the consulting firm showed up, and the discussion quickly turned to what is the best RPA solution. One of the partners shared a story. He said that his firm has a huge development office in India where they develop and deploy RPA solutions for companies. He said he visited that development center, and in a meeting with over 100 technical employees he posed the question about which is the best RPA solution. The partner said that he was surprised that nearly 90% of employees said that they found Blue Prism to be the most technically advanced and comprehensive solution compared to its competitors. Other reports from several market research firms confirmed that assessment. But despite such a vote of approval, he said, he respects the choice and inclination of his clients and that he would not suggest a solution. He then explained that while a solution can be comprehensive, it may not cater to the needs of the organization, be overly complex, or too hard to implement. And despite such a vote of confidence, Blue Prism could not sustain its position.

Blue Prism was an early success in the AI/RPA world—but its success was short-lived. In late 2021, the firm got sold to SS&C Technologies for $1.65 billion after SS&C won a competitive bid fight against Vista. Compare that to UiPath, a competitor of Blue Prism, which reached valuation of nearly $30 billion. UiPath and Automation Anywhere were the recipients of the mega investment when they received hundreds of millions of dollars in investment.

MEGA INVESTMENT

Venture capital used to be about managing investment risk. Start-ups tend to be risky. Entrepreneurs must tread through thousands of factors to build their firms. For that reason, the VC industry was designed to approach investment in terms of real options. The investment process started with a tiny investment into the firm, and as the firm achieved its milestones, it received more money. The investment will depend on the accomplishments according to a preestablished criterion—and hence a series of investments. This provided a mechanism of managing risk while ensuring that the firm can develop and perfect its survival instincts.

But when it comes to AI, a new model seems to have emerged. The VC industry now seems to be split between two types of investors—the legacy-style investors and the mega investors. The legacy investors continue to invest in firms to build designer companies to be sold to Big Tech, and their investment model is consistent with the staged investment. Their portfolio strategy and risk management have the characteristics of the traditional venture investment model. The mega investment model—which was introduced by a small number of firms—is driven by investing huge sums of money in a firm at an early stage. Where in the olden days a firm would have gotten $10 million, in mega investment structures it would receive $100 to mindboggling $500 million from private investors. Championed by investors such as Masayoshi Son of Softbank, this model seems to be very different than the traditional VC model.

MEGA INVESTMENT IS MADE IN LARGE BLOCKS

The mega investors try to manage risk by making investment in extremely large investment blocks. This model is based on an assumption that if a technological feasibility and a dominant design have been established, then the real reason firms fail is because they fail to develop the market or find clients. The failure in business development is often compounded by the fact that management has to spend considerable time to raise money. Many of such risks can be managed by flushing the company with tons of cash and allowing the company to focus on business development. This way both the management teams and the investors can focus on building the operational capabilities of the firm. The firm is never undercapitalized. This is analogous to creating a "too big to fail" scenario in the venture capital industry. By pouring hundreds of millions in an entity, the venture capitalists can pretty much buy their way to success. Even if revenues materialize at a slower pace than expected, the firm creates a strong brand and becomes the dominant player in the industry. Since in the mega investment model, a firm can leapfrog to the next level without fighting street battles against rival firms, it becomes exit-ready faster and can create a bigger bang for the market.

This is what happened with many AI firms.

MEGA INVESTMENT IMPACT ON INNOVATION

The beauty of the old venture model is that it follows that natural course of evolution where a firm must fight for survival, and the one with the best adaptation emerges victorious. By putting a firm on a fast pace to success, the model implies that the fighting spirit may not develop in a company, and its business model and management team acquire market power too quickly. The firm does not develop the survival instincts. Rapid growth makes firms complacent, and rapid ascension creates operational and governance gaps.

Many would consider leapfrogging the competition with a large influx of money unfair, but unfair could be fine if it creates and produces national value. However, our analysis shows that in this case the process reduces America's competitiveness. By flushing down unlimited pools of funds, the firms that emerge victorious and market leaders may not advance the best solutions. They were made successful by the influx of capital and via financial engineering and not through scientific, engineering, and technical excellence. That would be like feeding steroids to an animal or a human to grow muscles quickly but not acquire the discipline of athleticism. The dominant design of the technology that emerges would be less efficient than the one that could have emerged had the competition been fairer and more natural.

When that happens, a firm will gain market share primarily because it can afford top talent in business development and create more sales activity. Consequently, its product becomes the face of the market, and its brand acquires the central position to a point where its product is viewed as the market standard. But what is market standard is not necessarily what lies on the technology frontier standard or what can be developed. What carries these companies forward is their brand power and not their technological superiority. They float, but they don't fly. And eventually they fall.

In the long run, this means that America will have produced firms that will carry very little real technological superiority, whose natural instincts to compete would not have been developed, and their distinguished feature would have been their brand.

We have seen that happening in the past with many firms. Intel is a great example of a firm that once had both—technological superiority and a strong brand. Later, as Intel lost its competitive edge, its strong brand carried the firm—but eventually the firm realized that marketing-based floating is not flying, and it is not sustainable.

That is exactly why the OSTP and then the Congress-led investment plan does not guarantee that America will achieve returns. That model works when you have significant competitive latitude, not when you are running out of runway. At this time, America must do everything possible to increase investment precision by extracting and applying greater information from the marketplace. We believe this directed model of investment is what is needed.

THE INVESTMENT PLAN

Investment in AI is happening in three parts of the AI supply chain. As shown in Chapter 10, the AI supply chain is composed of three broad areas of data, skills to model, and processing. Here we develop each component from an investment perspective.

DATA

Investing in data would involve not only sensors and servers (data centers) but also in developing data management practices suitable for AI. This would include several variables against which data will be managed. Such data sets will be identified but also designated for potential use. This can create significant jobs, and educational programs would need to be developed to build those capabilities.

SKILLS DEVELOPMENT

Data science skills development will not achieve results in the way it is being done currently. The AI field is intentionally kept closed to masses. People are not sure how to enter the field. Many think they are in AI because they do RPA or other rules-based logical systems. Machine learning is still quite complicated to learn. The training regimen is fairly complicated, and professors who teach machine learning come from a background of teaching advanced classes to graduate students. Machine learning is also not taught on specific software platforms—which have now helped to simplify building models. Many subspecialty areas—for instance, data preprocessing—can be developed. The educational system is designed to keep AI knowledge in the hands of the few. There is significant condescension and elitism where a closed club exists that prohibits access at a national level. Top universities get a disproportionate level of attention, funds, and publishing preference. They also get access to the OSTP- and NSF-type organizations. This creates a huge imbalance. In fact, these universities, despite their top talent, may end up contributing less to the nation than other schools because many elitist professors have deep commercial interests. Deep commercial interests mean that they would influence the direction of funding to flow toward those projects that will help them build companies that they can sell to Big Tech. This type of investment will end up producing more functions and features for existing products. Additionally, many of the big-name professors from top universities work at Chinese firms and may continue to have those deep connections. Just recently, a university professor (not from the AI field) was arrested for not properly disclosing his relationship with China. That, among many other reasons, makes us recommend that America must invest heavily in second- and third-tier universities—and not just in top-tier schools.

SEMICONDUCTORS

In 2018 both co-authors of this book met in Intel's manufacturing plant in Arizona. They were looking at the manufacturing operation and identifying supply chain improvement opportunities for Intel. Despite being a global leader and possessing incredibly talented people and powerful technology, Intel was facing operational, leadership, and innovation issues—problems that eventually led to Intel replacing its chief executive. *Financial Times* covered the story and noted that the problems had led to Intel's competitive decline (Bradshaw et al. 2021).

This was an area in which America once had significant market share and lead. The semiconductor market has three global leaders—Taiwan Semiconductor Manufacturing Corp (TSMC), Samsung, and Intel. *Wall Street Journal* reported that while the capital investment of the three firms between 2012 and 2016 was not materially different, TSMC and Samsung stock returned significantly more than Intel (Jie et al. 2021). Factors such as the research and development process, investment prioritization, the operational model, the processes, market development, financial focus, and market understanding all contribute to a firm's performance. At this time, the eyes of the US, China, and European Union are laser-focused on the chip industry. Unlike in areas such as data and AI skills, where China has been able to close the gap and even pass the US capability, the competition in the semiconductor market is wide open. China has made chip production and semiconductor independence its top national priority. To eliminate its reliance upon the leading suppliers in Taiwan, South Korea, and the United States, China is trying to develop its domestic industry. The threat of a China-Taiwan war is also increasing risk for the semiconductor supply chain. TSMC has agreed to invest in the United States and will be building a plant in Arizona. Samsung has agreed to build a plant in Texas, and Intel has announced building two new plants. Collectively, about $50 billion capital will be flowing into chip manufacturing in the US just between these three players. With these plants in operation, America will have a major advantage—however; the top-of-the-line semiconductors will still be made in Taiwan. TSMC has also announced its plans to invest $44 billion to increase its manufacturing capacity. South Korean firms Samsung, Hyundai, SK Group, and LG have hired lobbying groups in America to lobby Washington to allow them to supply semiconductors and other technologies to the US blacklisted Chinese firms (Jung-a 2022).

The Russian invasion of Ukraine has further constrained the chip supply as Ukraine supplies 50 percent of the world's neon gas which is critical for chip manufacturing (*Financial Times* 2022). The American semiconductor production strategy will be essential for America's future.

 WITH AN EYE ON THE WORLD

Jamey Butcher, CEO of Chemonics, recalled his trip to Shenzhen in 2019, as chairman of the board of directors of Unleash. Unleash helps entrepreneurs develop financing, scaling, business planning, and other such tasks. Part of the activities were sponsored by Ping An, a large Chinese company. During the visit, Jamey was given a tour of the Ping An Finance Center, claimed to be one of the tallest buildings in Asia. In there, he was shown the power of artificial intelligence being used in China. "From this screen we can monitor the beaches and see if people who are going to the beach have obtained the necessary permits. We can even see if someone parked their car wrong. From here we can monitor the entire culinary staff working in the kitchens. If someone is not wearing the hairnet or is slacking, the AI tells us. Here is an AI-based orchestra," someone explained to him. Butcher, whose background is not in AI, was amazed at the application of AI in China. Despite his astonishment he could not help asking the person showing him around, "How do citizens feel about this kind of scrutiny?" and the guide seemed shocked that this question was asked to him.

Based on Butcher's experience, we realized that Chinese deployment of AI has become a self-emerging phenomenon. Since AI systems are not for data but instead from data, AI applications attract more data that in turn creates more AI or perfects the existing AI. In other words, as more data comes in, it opens the possibility of designing additional systems and of improving the existing systems. As the Chinese AI deployment becomes prevalent, every system will capture more data, and that will result in more AI.

Our discussion with Butcher was designed to understand the link between AI and supply chains. Chemonics manages humanitarian supply chains all over the world, and Butcher has significant experience managing those. The humanitarian supply chains are formed to support humanitarian and developmental aid to developing countries, to natural disaster areas, in refugee crisis due to wars, and to other similar humanitarian initiatives. Humanitarian aid is not new—but underlying this powerful and critical supply chain strategy are the new dynamics related to AI. We found the idea of humanitarian supply chains linked to AI fascinating and began listening to Butcher's explanation.

He explained to us that the American model of aid has been to directly help the needy communities, to provide support, and to help support global communities to embrace the powerful ideas of free press, democratic elections, and freedom. There are three goals, and our strategy is driven by one or more of them: national security, economic support, and values. This model of aid delivery became the American way to help communities all over the world, and it brought aid to millions. But when China spread its wings and began its global push, they dealt directly with the governments. There they would evaluate the infrastructure and other similar needs of a country and then launch megasized projects to help build those economies. In those projects they will bring in their own people and finance the projects from their own balance sheet. In some cases, the Chinese labor force will just stay in those countries, and hence that would provide a natural extension of the Chinese culture and business. But this is not all. What we are observing, Butcher said, is that as the Chinese bring the physical infrastructure projects such as railroad, roads, bridges, and dams, they also demand that the receiving country embraces their 5G and telecom technology. Since countries have no choice but to accept it, they adopt Chinese telecom technologies. These technologies in turn become a powerful source of data for the Chinese. With that they can study demand patterns and apply algorithms to develop other business opportunities.

As Butcher talked, we recognized the immensely powerful strategic moves attached to the global expansion of Chinese technology. In today's world even humanitarian aid can have technological repercussions. How countries provide aid and build bridges can give access to powerful sources of data that can be exploited as one would extract minerals from a mine.

"The holy grail is to get the demand data." Butcher continued, "Imagine walking into a country and giving them billions of dollars of much-needed infrastructure projects and then having the ability to capture all that data. Who do you think will be able to directly sell to those billions of customers? Who will be able to build and respond to demand?"

This was an eye-opener for us. The sophistication of this model was impressive. America needs a similar or better model to stay competitive in the global markets. That model may include financing such international projects with US government guarantees, increasing foreign assistance, and providing a gateway for the private sector to get involved.

Butcher then explained to us that the American model of aid, which often comes tied with various social objectives—including democracy, open society, capitalism, human rights, climate change, gender rights, and economic security—seems quite complicated to undertake. Certain governments would consider that as a strategy to drive regime change. We were fascinated to hear the link between the development assistance and AI. This meant that the Chinese AI strategy was being designed for a global market.

 CAPITAL INVESTMENT IN AI

We are concerned that the American investment style, model, and approach have become short-term profit-seeking centered. The key institutions—especially research labs and top universities—cannot be trusted to invest in areas that will create long-term national value. Even if research labs can be trusted to allocate the funds, they do not have an allocation mechanism and model to allocate funds in the business and competitive environment that captures today's unique challenges. Our recent history shows that we have not been able to realize significant return on research investment in the last few years. The investment model is in need of change. America needs a new beginning. A new phase of R&D in America has started.

 REFERENCES

Bradshaw, Tim, Water, Richards, and Aliaj, Ortenca. 2021. "Intel Replaces Bob Swan as Chief Executive after Series of Setbacks." *Financial Times.* January 13, 2021.

Financial Times. 2022. "Russia's Invasion of Ukraine Adds to Pressure on Chip Supply Chain." March 3, 2022.

Jung-a, Song. 2022. "South Korean Chip Companies Step Up US Lobbying Efforts." *Financial Times.* January 2, 2022.

12

At the Speed of Relevance

I F THERE IS ONE thing that the history of research and development teaches us, it is that an R&D system cannot be independent of the economic, social, political, and technological environments it operates in. In the United States alone, the country has developed through at least four R&D systems (Mowery and Rosenberg 1989). The first was the pre-World War II system where research and development were undertaken by large manufacturing firms that invested in labs. The federal government's participation in that system was minimal. Post–World War II a different system emerged, which was led by the federal government. The federal government not only financed research and acquired the output but also facilitated the creation of research centers and supported institutions and universities. The third R&D system evolved during the 1980s, which called for significant collaboration between academia, industry, and the government and where international research collaboration increased. The fourth R&D system developed during the Internet revolution and involved opening up R&D to individuals and small firms. Through open source and crowdsourcing, R&D in many areas became democratized. Each one of these systems was marked with its own environmental factors and was in response to the economic, social, political, and technological environments of its time.

Ignoring the environmental factors of the R&D and the related techno-logical transformation leads to inefficiencies in R&D. For example, Britain's inability to deploy an R&D system that was organized from an industrial research perspective is often identified as a reason for low research outcomes during the first half of the twentieth century (Mowery and Rosenberg 1989, 99). This leads us to the second important factor: research outcomes matter. R&D outcomes are also dependent on the times during which they happen. The need of the hour determines what would be considered important and a good return on R&D. The outcomes, therefore, should set the measurement scale by which the performance of R&D will be determined.

The process of R&D must also consider the value chain of research in an industry. For example, the research value chain in health care extends far back into preclinical on one hand and population management on the other hand.

Then there are issues of research related to the approach to research, and that opens discussions about the style of research—for example, originality of research vs. imitation or copying.

Lastly, the nature of competition greatly affects research priorities. The structure of competition itself can be triggered by geopolitical forces or by the nature of competition within a sector, across industries, and globally.

Thus, prioritizing and planning R&D implies determining the nature of the R&D that is consistent with the above factors and is very much dictated by the forces defining your times. Applying an R&D system that is inconsistent with your times or incompatible with the surrounding environmental factors will lead to substandard outcomes and inefficiencies. Approaching R&D as fanning money out to drive innovation without understanding all the environmental factors is a recipe for disaster.

In the past there have been periods where prevailing R&D systems deployed in America were incompatible with the environmental factors (economic, social, political, and technological) and they led to unproductive outcomes (Rosenberg 1994). R&D productivity returned only when adjust-ments were made to align the R&D system with the environment in which it was operating. One example is when in the 1980s Japanese innovation and focus on speed and quality forced America to reconsider the regimen of fed-erally led R&D, which lacked significant industry participation. Only when America changed the R&D system did the performance of American firms start increasing.

The main question and the need of the hour is to determine what R&D system would be most suitable to compete in the AI revolution. We contend that the environmental factors, competitive rivalry, scientific process, value chain, and the style of research have all changed to a new state of equilibrium. What lags, however, is the prevailing R&D system, which has now become chaotic and is a hodgepodge of various previous R&D systems deployed in the United States. While it reflects the multigenerational features of R&D systems, it is completely incompatible with the environment of the day. And that is having a hugely negative impact on America's productive potential.

 ## WHY THE CRITICAL TONE?

In this book we took a critical view of the American AI policy and implementation. We could have taken a softer, less critical, and more mellow approach. But we feel that would not have been in the best interest of America. There are critical flaws with the current strategy. Many of those are related to the people who are held responsible to make AI successful in America. Others are due to inefficient processes. And yet others due to the unique features of AI. What is consistent, however, is a strange cognitive dissonance where in report after report we are recognizing the failure of American AI, and yet we are continuing to go down the same path that has already cost us our leadership position.

Our journey in the book started by pointing out the ugly truth: America is falling behind in AI, and by some standards the situation appears hopeless. At least that is what Chaillan said when he resigned. Since similar vibes are coming from other sources as well, including the National Security Commission on Artificial Intelligence, they must not be ignored. Some would choose to reject those voices. Others may accept the situation but ignore it. And others may prefer to live in denial. However, we decided to directly confront the problem. We recognize that our approach may feel negative or cynical to some people, but we prefer to be safe than sorry. The nature of competition is such that we cannot ignore these developments.

We also talked to two executives who shared their perspectives about the challenge we face as a nation. Tom Maher, a supply chain professional and senior executive at Dell, with 30 years of experience, shared his concern about China's rapid adoption of AI compared to America's anemic embracing. But he was clear that decoupling makes sense not just because of the geopolitical issues but because it will increase supply chain resiliency. "It makes business sense, and it will happen anyway," Maher said. "What will really make a difference, and what has helped China propel, is whether we have the data sets or not." Another executive, Robert Bruck, who was formerly at Intel and now is helping develop supply chain strategy at Applied Materials, talked about the

R&D systems in terms of collaboration platforms. He mentioned that many years ago Intel ignored building adoptive coalitions, and that turned out to be a "huge mistake." That is something that Samsung and TSMC did not do. They both shared information with international partners, and that helped them overcome operational and development problems. Intel has recognized that as a problem and is fixing that. Both executives point to the fact that research and development cannot be divorced from the industrialization and supply chain needs of a firm or a country.

Throughout the book we took a pragmatic approach and analyzed the situation without providing the underlying theory behind the arguments we were making. Here we would like to provide some theoretical basis for our concerns.

UNDERLYING THEORY

We begin by explaining the reason behind our heightened state of concern. Technology adoption is not a straightforward process. As Rosenberg, an economic historian, explains, technologies do not develop in a linear manner (Rosenberg 1994). Information is embedded in new technologies. The process by which information is embedded is of value to determine the development path a technology will take. The trajectory of an innovation is determined by many factors, and technological change is a complex process. However, the key question, Rosenberg argues, is to determine how much information can be extracted from existing bodies of theoretical knowledge. The theoretical knowledge domains are spread over scientific and technological areas, as well as economic, social, political, and technological systems. There are information interdependencies, and that affects the technological change and the direction it takes. Rosenberg argues that such information embedding makes the technological change path dependent, and the initial conditions as well as the prevalent conditions at every step in the evolution of the technological change will nudge the movement and the direction of the change. The catch is that there is a cost associated with finding that information and exploring the information dependencies. Foresight is not free.

Rosenberg clarifies that: (1) new technologies at birth are in primitive form; (2) their development depends on other factors—including complementary technologies; (3) major technological innovations introduce entirely new systems; and (4) technological feasibility alone does not determine its success—what does determine success is identifying human needs in new ways and contexts that have not been done before and in accordance with the new technology.

Based on the above discussion, we argue that the cost-benefit analysis of getting information that can help determine both the direction of the trajectory of technological change and its current state is important. In other words, the direction in which a technological change moves and the future states it can acquire can have economic consequences such that each path-dependent state can represent a certain outcome. Each of those outcomes can be approached from a risk perspective, and cost can be assigned to the risk itself. Extracting more information can be justified if the initial analysis shows that risk and the associated cost can be reduced.

The above also shows why we are so concerned that the initial conditions—what we have termed the anchoring bias—created by the OSTP will continue to determine the direction of the path that the technological change has taken in the United States. The farther we move on this path, the harder it becomes to fix the course.

Technological change does not transpire in isolation. The structure of the economy affects it. This includes the incentive systems, the institutions, and property rights (North 1981, 1990). These factors affect transaction costs, which determine the performance of the markets. Extrapolating the concept and applying it to determine which path-dependent states can reduce the transaction costs, increase adoption, and allow a technology to diffuse faster at a socioeconomic level can help identify the compatibility of the existing socioeconomic structure with the progress outcome expected from the technological change.

Extracting information, therefore, can be a worthy exercise, if it can help determine the path or the trajectory a technological change can take and most importantly if such an information can be useful to influence or nudge the trajectory to better outcomes.

None of the above is compatible with the "fanning out the money and opening research centers" approach taken by the federal government in the current AI technological revolution. The peculiar and uniquely revolutionary dynamics of AI are not being considered. The investment in AI is happening in accordance with the legacy models and systems of R&D. The "build it, and they will come" style of investment ignores the dozens of social, political, economic, and technological constraints pointed out in the book.

But the absence of economic compatibility is not the only problem with how both federal and private R&D investments are being made in AI. The AI revolution has become a transformation for the elitists and a source of fear, concern, and anguish for the rest. Lacking the egalitarian identification of the revolution, it is destined to fail. It is increasing the wealth and power concentration to a point where it is necessarily forcing the masses to accept it without questioning it. In some ways, it is worse. It is creating a system of epistemic oppression where people do not even know the difference between what is hurting their interests and what is helping them. Hence, it should not be surprising that the social and ideological conflict in America is at an all-time high.

Throughout this book we have shown the examples of negligence, of nepotism, and of blatant disregard for facts. We have shown how the OSTP office has not been able to move the needle on the American AI strategy. What is being measured as performance are the activities and not the results. How many dollars are being invested, how many institutions are being opened, how many conferences are being organized, and how many agencies have started AI projects are all measures of activities. They do not exhibit whether the technology is making improvements in productivity and improving the American economy. They also do not show how such performance factors compare to those of the great-power adversary or a competitor such as China. Not only the national AI strategy is fully detached from traditional economic measures, but it does also not consider the unique nature of the AI revolution, which has made many of the traditional economic measures irrelevant. The nature of the competition is at least two generations past than how it is being measured and reported in America. And most importantly, it does not show how American lives are becoming better.

The point is that we need a strategy that truly captures all of the above factors and a real scorecard that makes measurement relevant to the national goals and priorities. In the following discussion we make several recommendations on how to reset the AI launch in America.

RECOMMENDATION 1: MAKE A DISTINCTION BETWEEN NATIONAL AI STRATEGY AND R&D PLAN

As we have pointed out in the book, national strategy should not be confused with the R&D plan. The R&D plan is part of the national strategy but not the other way around. The OSTP and all the other related offices and committees must stop calling their plans national AI strategy because they are not. National strategies do not result from closed-door brainstorming sessions by a few scientists or 46 RFI responses. They also cannot be triggered by a plethora of legislation being directed to jump-start AI in America. These knee-jerk reactions neither create positive results nor are they strategies. Strategy development process is a complicated process that requires applying a rigorous process and understanding both environmental factors and the complex interdependencies that form the basis of the competition. It is important to employ a rigorous planning process to develop the strategy.

In one of our conversations with a senior executive at GSA, we brought up the need for rigorous planning, and she asked an extremely relevant and powerful question. She said, Does this type of rigorous planning that you are suggesting turns into a central planning model [Soviet Union and China style]? The author explained that at an extreme it could, although what is needed is not to go to the extreme but to develop a sensible policy based on facts. The idea is not to control every economic action in the economy but to provide institutional guidance so capital is not wasted and the technological revolution develops under favorable conditions. She agreed with that approach.

RECOMMENDATION 2: DEVELOP A REAL NATIONAL STRATEGY

The American Institute of Artificial Intelligence has done significant pragmatic AI industrialization work for the past six years. The authors recommend that government should conduct and engage in a national strategy development process outside of the OSTP. This process, undertaken as a committee, should include the following members:

- American Institute of Artificial Intelligence: 2 members;
- Top strategy firms: (McKinsey, BCG, Deloitte, Accenture): 2 members each, senior level;
- CEOs or heads of strategy of firms from non-tech sectors (manufacturing, consumer, pharmaceutical, financial, others);
- Supply chain experts (2 experts);
- Economists (4 experts, 2 from economic history with focus on technological revolutions and 2 from applied economics with mathematical models of AI competition);
- Technology experts (2 technology experts, 1 from the AI field);
- Military experts (4 military experts from various branches, could be retired generals);
- Professors and researchers from political science (policy) and sociology.

Note that our committee does not include significant number of members from government agencies (other than military), ethicists or futurists, or AI experts. All of the above members must disclose their financial or other conflicts (companies they have invested in, equity they hold, or funding they have received). This committee should be tasked to develop a national strategy and be funded by the government. The committee may bring in other experts, agency heads, and others on an as-needed basis. The committee is tasked to develop a strategic plan and not just soft policy statements. A strategic plan has specific goals and objectives, is measurable in terms of progress, and has clear timelines. It has a strong execution dimension, and it considers the interdependencies and factor in as many relevant elements as practical. We expect this will be a one-year project.

The plan should be able to provide a mechanism for determining how to allocate research grant for maximizing favorable national outcomes. Favorable national outcomes are not just economic, they are also social and political. Factors such as AI governance and ethics are also considered for achieving favorable national outcomes and not as meaningless boilerplate statements. Ethics and governance are implemented and architected an implementable in the strategic plan.

The plan should also analyze the gaps between where current policy is and where it needs to be. The plan is not a recommendation—but instead a path that needs to be followed to achieve certain results.

The plan will also include a path to evangelize and communicate the strategy, of change management at national level, of getting various stakeholders onboard, and of socializing the plan. This will include a way to talk about the AI at a national level, on how inspire the nation, and how to mobilize the country behind the technology.

Legislation alone cannot accomplish a transformation. You can't legislate your way through a technological revolution. Strings of unsynchronized legislations do not lead to a coordinated national performance. If anything, it confuses people. With dozens of directives and hundreds of instructions, legislations are policy responses and not policy initiators. The plan will highlight the need for various legislative interventions, if necessary.

The focus of the plan will stay on industrialization, the long-term performance of the US economy, and national interests. An "America first" paradigm will drive the plan—and in this case America first does not mean isolationism, it simply means that the interests of the American people will be the sole determinant of strategy, and not factors such as special interest or lobbies. It also means developing an America-centered supply chain.

The plan must possess industrialization maps, including determining the needs of sectors, of developments across sectors, of supply chains, and of foreseeable applications. Efficiencies and the structure of the economy should be considered.

The plan should include a comprehensive analysis of the supply chain changes happening from the geopolitical drivers. In other words, a national AI strategy must corroborate with the geopolitical situation unfolding with China. This means rebuilding American supply chains with AI and building AI with supply chains in mind.

A $1000 monthly AI fund is not what America is all about. The plan must find a way not to turn America into an Elysium city. It is illogical to assume that automation based on data will create massive joblessness. If anything, it should be the opposite. All the new data will point and identify new types of problems that need to be solved. This means humankind will be solving many more problems that affect survival. The goal should be to engage the population, to retrain them, to reskill them, and to inspire them to be part of the revolution. People should not be forgotten and left behind when technological revolutions happen. The focus of retraining should not be on producing data scientists from a handful of schools or retraining federal acquisitions teams or launching competitions. A person who is from central Illinois or rural Georgia should be part of the transformation just as much as someone from Silicon Valley or Boston or New York.

The plan must take into account the political rhetoric and the ideological conflicts in America and include a way to minimize the negative energy and develop greater harmony and unity in the nation.

Finally, and most importantly, the plan will become the basis for both the decoupling strategy to reinvent American supply chains and for rebuilding the American infrastructure.

What America needs is an integrated plan that captures all of the above. Only that plan can be called a national strategy for AI.

 ## SUMMARY OF THE BOOK

We started by pointing out that the nature of relationships between various drivers of the economy, society, technology, and politics have changed. Now, we argued, all of those factors must be understood in light of the most powerful revolution in the history of human civilization: artificial intelligence. We also argued that almost all of the current problems and their solutions are directly

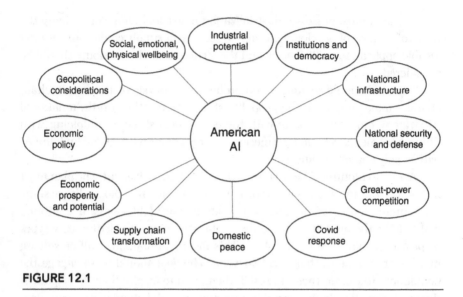

FIGURE 12.1

related to AI (Figure 12.1). The ability to identify our problems and discover solutions are now very much dependent on AI.

Hence, AI is not just a technological revolution, it is a comprehensive transformation of the economy, political systems, society, institutions, science, and technologies. A change of that scale should not be managed by half-hearted, politically expedient, or pretentious initiatives. When one considers the competitive environment of the world, the responsibility to get this right becomes even more important. In no uncertain terms, we called it the existential competitive threat to the United States.

Despite the importance to get this right, we have seen a series of actions that have destroyed value, and as a consequence America is losing its competitive advantage. America is sliding, and the AI leadership position is slipping. However, even though this change is happening and even accelerating, there is no awareness to identify the root causes of that decline. There is no appetite to confront the truth. There is no worry about the consequences of such a dramatic shift in competitive power. In fact, the situation is worse. The same exact factors that led to the current decline of America are being now reinforced via legislation and presidential directives. Instead of reflecting on what went wrong, America is doubling down on the exact path that led the country to its current situation. This will only increase the speed of decline. The same actors who were responsible for the decline have seen their powers multiply and their responsibilities increase. There is no accountability, and despite report after report pointing out the decline, the American leadership is following the same course.

We believe the OSTP-led policymaking has created and accelerated the loss of America's leadership position. It is not that OSTP is not doing what it is supposed to do, but it has greatly expanded in areas in which it has no expertise. This includes developing and presenting a so-called national strategy. Not only it is creating a massive confusion, but it has also resulted in a plan which is misleading. An R&D plan is not a national strategy. The constituents and collaborators of the OSTP are not trained to develop strategy. The OSTP has not deployed a formal process that is used to develop strategies of nations, businesses, or military. Most importantly, both branches of the government, executive and legislative, are relying on AI technologists to develop the AI policy. Technologists can advise on the technical aspects of the technology and perhaps on R&D priorities. But they are not trained to develop national strategies. Neither are the ethicists, governance experts, and futurists, the other party that the government is relying upon. What is missing is a practical industrialization plan—a plan that China has successfully deployed.

Surrounded by professors and technologists who are part of a complex and biased network of commercial relationships, the OSTP has architected plans that either cater to the interests of a few universities or Big Tech. To cover the blatant policy failure and biased policymaking, a cadre of ethicists and futurists have been invoked to create an unnecessary distraction. AI's social perception has been framed as the killer robots. This automatically creates a negative perception, which keeps the AI field in the hands of the few. Those who stand at the frontline of the governance and ethics mishaps and disasters can barely keep their ethics boards intact and for the most part pay only lip service to ethics. But the average Joe and Jane on the street are being told that AI is dangerous and there is a need for responsible AI. There is absolutely a need for responsible AI, but since when did we start launching new technological revolutions (or professions) based on their negative aspects? Did we launch auto industry with a focus on drunk driving or the Internet with a concern about sexual exploitation or the cell phone with apprehension about texting and driving or the audit field with the concern about corrupt auditors? It is understood that "responsible" and "ethics" must be a part of anything a society undertakes. But when it comes to AI, it has somehow become a necessary addition to the field as if it were okay to be unethical in other areas but not in AI. All that despite the fact that most ethical violations in AI are happening in firms who appear to be above the law.

In response to the loss to China, America has now initiated several strategic moves on the geopolitical front. These are aimed at retarding or slowing down the Chinese progress or increasing the transaction cost for Chinese businesses. This is directly from the Cold War playbook, and it can be effective to some degree. The other playbook deployed is from America's Japanese experience from the 1980s. While all of those strategies have their place, unless there is a real winning strategy on the domestic front, it is likely that the American situation will not improve.

We are concerned and urge the government to change its course. We ask the government to pay attention to the interdependent environmental factors that are contributing to the decline. Technological revolutions need care, love, and nurturing. They need a positive environment to develop. They need constant monitoring and a sincere leadership. Aspirations should be balanced with pragmatic realities.

America must change its path. We started the book with the powerful concept of "speed of relevance." That is where we need to be. To win the AI race, America must move forward at the speed of relevance.

REFERENCES

Mowery, David C., and Rosenberg, Nathan. 1989. *Technology and the Pursuit of Economic Growth*. Cambridge University Press.

North, Douglass. 1990. *Institutions, Institutional Change, and Economic Performance*. Cambridge University Press.

North, Douglass. 1981. *Structure and Change in Economic History*. New York: W. W. Norton & CO.

Rosenberg, Nathan. 1994. *Exploring the Black Box: Technology, Economics, and History*. Cambridge University Press.

Index

Page numbers followed by *f* refer to figures.